YOUTH, CRIME, AND JUSTICE SERIES

General Editors: Franklin E. Zimring and David S. Tanenhaus

Homeroom Security: School Discipline in an Age of Fear
Aaron Kupchik

Kids, Cops, and Confessions: Inside the Interrogation Room
Barry C. Feld

Choosing the Future for American Juvenile Justice
Edited by Franklin E. Zimring and David S. Tanenhaus

Juvenile Justice in Global Perspective
Edited by Franklin E. Zimring, Máximo Langer, and David S. Tanenhaus

The Evolution of the Juvenile Court: Race, Politics, and Criminalizing of Juvenile Justice
Barry C. Feld

Ages of Anxiety: Historical and Transnational Perspectives on Juvenile Justice
Edited by William S. Bush and David S. Tanenhaus

Ages of Anxiety

*Historical and Transnational Perspectives
on Juvenile Justice*

Edited by

William S. Bush and David S. Tanenhaus

NEW YORK UNIVERSITY PRESS

New York

NEW YORK UNIVERSITY PRESS
New York
www.nyupress.org

References to Internet websites (URLs) were accurate at the time of writing. Neither the author nor New York University Press is responsible for URLs that may have expired or changed since the manuscript was prepared.

Library of Congress Cataloging-in-Publication Data
Names: Bush, William S., 1967– editor. | Tanenhaus, David Spinoza, editor.
Title: Ages of anxiety : historical and transnational perspectives on juvenile justice / edited by William S. Bush and David S. Tanenhaus.
Description: New York : New York University Press, 2018. | Series: Youth, crime, and justice series | Includes bibliographical references and index.
Identifiers: LCCN 2017055036 | ISBN 9781479833214 (cl : alk. paper)
Subjects: LCSH: Juvenile justice, Administration of. | Juvenile justice, Administration of—History. | Juvenile delinquency—History. | Juvenile delinquents.
Classification: LCC K5575 .A945 2018 | DDC 364.36—dc23
LC record available at https://lccn.loc.gov/2017055036

New York University Press books are printed on acid-free paper, and their binding materials are chosen for strength and durability. We strive to use environmentally responsible suppliers and materials to the greatest extent possible in publishing our books.

Manufactured in the United States of America

10 9 8 7 6 5 4 3 2 1

Also available as an ebook

To the memory of Norman Dorsen (1930–2017)

CONTENTS

Conclusion: Whose Children? A Comparative Anatomy of
Moral Panics
William S. Bush and David S. Tanenhaus

SERIES EDITORS' FOREWORD

FRANKLIN E. ZIMRING AND DAVID S. TANENHAUS

This volume is an important contribution to the series of studies in juvenile justice that we launched in 2012, and its publication is also an appropriate occasion to consider the rationale and uses of the edited collections in the series. Most of the scholarly materials available for analysis of juvenile justice in the generation after the Supreme Court's decision *In Re Gault* were parochial in three respects. Their focus was on judicial procedures rather than the broad substantive aims of a juvenile court. There was no emphasis on the history of legal efforts to deal with youth outside of law enforcement. And the experience of youth and juvenile justice that informed policy discussion was confined to the United States. Further, very few disciplines contributed to the conversation about youth crime in the United States. Lawyers and criminologists primarily talked to each other and to themselves.

Our aim with this series of books was to expand the temporal, the spatial, and the disciplinary perspectives available to students of youth policy and the juvenile court. The first volume in the series, *Choosing the Future of American Juvenile Justice*, was an explicitly interdisciplinary analysis of legal policy choices for youth in the United States. The second volume, *Juvenile Justice in Global Perspective*, expanded the parameters of comparative juvenile justice by reporting on India, China, Latin America, South Africa, and eastern Europe.

Ages of Anxiety further expands the disciplinary focus of the series to include social histories that analyze youth crime as a special concern in a wide variety of twentieth-century settings. The case studies are widely distributed around the twentieth-century world—from Ankara to Zanzibar—and the methodology is that of narrative social history. The stories told in this volume are rich and detailed. The potential lessons from these histories are of great value, but finding the parallels and legal policy implications from the case studies is in substantial part a task for the readers of the volume rather than the responsibility of the historians who have told the stories.

THE DIVISION OF LABOR

We think that it is appropriate not to expect historians to be law professors. The previous volume in this series, *Juvenile Justice in Global Perspective*, was an exercise in comparative law that was produced by lawyers and law professors. It was high-quality legal analysis, and many of its policy conclusions were relatively easy to find. But the chapters in that volume did not provide any rich or detailed social histories.

The chapters in this volume are much better social history than the national portraits found in the global perspectives volume, but the policy implications available from these stories are the job of legal policy analysts who read the social history, not of the social historians who have told the stories. And we expect that different legal analysts will draw different lessons, sometimes even conflicting lessons, from the historical materials assembled in this book. Social histories provide the legal reformer with raw material—a do-it-yourself kit to assemble appropriate legal reforms. The level of effort required to best use the case studies in *Ages of Anxiety* is not small, but the lessons for legal reforms are of great value. And the editors include a helpful theoretical model in their introduction to assist readers in this translation process.

Introduction

WILLIAM S. BUSH AND DAVID S. TANENHAUS

Over the course of the twentieth century, the development of two differ-ent court systems to address the same behaviors by adolescents became a nearly universal feature of modern governance.[1] Depending on age and circumstance, an adolescent charged with a law violation could be processed and sanctioned by either a juvenile or an adult court. Franklin Zimring and Máximo Langer have started an important conversation about why this is so, and the theoretical implications of this global his-tory for understanding and sustaining the mission of juvenile justice in the twenty-first century.[2] This volume adds a historical dimension to this urgent conversation about youth, crime, and justice. This includes the value of learning from those who struggled with these issues in past contexts in order to understand the hard choices that they made on a daily basis. By focusing on magistrates, social workers, probation and police officers, and youth themselves, this volume highlights the role of human beings as meaningful and consequential historical actors.

This work also emphasizes transnationalism as an overarching but often ignored theme in the history of youth governance. Since the 1980s, historians have developed this concept in exploring the circulation of populations, goods, ideas, policies, and cultures across national bound-aries. This "transnational turn" has encouraged scholars of international history to draw upon sources from multiple national origins, and to ex-plore relations between both state and nonstate actors across national borders.[3] Providing "a perspective rather than a clear-cut method," transnationalism prompts scholars to widen the contextual lens for a given study to include not only local and national but also global and border-crossing contexts.[4]

Until recently, transnationalism rarely informed scholarly histories of juvenile delinquency and juvenile justice. This is beginning to change.

For example, *Juvenile Delinquency and the Limits of Western Influence, 1850–2000*, a collection of essays, focuses on the transnational flow of information, ideas, and policies between the global East and West. Its contributions collectively challenge the presumption that Western theories and policies regarding juvenile delinquency exerted a determinative influence in other parts of the world.[5] More focused on formal juvenile justice systems, the edited volume *Juvenile Justice in Global Perspective* demonstrates that the historical development of separate systems for juveniles comprised a common feature around the world, and also explores the tensions with adult criminal systems.[6] *Ages of Anxiety* builds upon these books by surveying the emergence of an international policy discourse around juvenile delinquency and juvenile justice in the early twentieth century, and by linking local case studies with the ongoing transnational circulation of ideas, policies, and populations.

In highlighting the importance of transnational history, this volume makes visible key features that have always been present in the history of juvenile delinquency and juvenile justice. For over a century, local and national concerns about juvenile delinquency often have emerged in response to the appearance of "diasporic" migrant populations in urban centers.[7] The most prominent example is the birthplace of the modern juvenile court, Chicago, where more than three-fourths of its 1.7 million residents were either foreign-born or born to foreign parents at the time of the court's inauguration in 1899.[8] Along with a host of other social services, the juvenile court served predominantly first- and second-generation immigrants from southern and eastern Europe. Sociologists at the University of Chicago developed theoretical models of generational and cultural conflict by studying the "foreign" youth who passed through the juvenile court and related agencies.[9] It is no stretch to say that the American juvenile court was a product of transnational migration.

Where those early social scientific studies took acculturation and "Americanization" as their starting points, the case studies presented in this volume explore the responses of colonial, developing, and modern governmental regimes to juvenile delinquency. A particular area of emphasis here are the middle decades of the twentieth century, which are often neglected in the literature about juvenile justice. It was during this period that international bodies, led by the League of Nations and later the United Nations, established norms for the governance of children and youth that became the benchmarks for evaluating local and national policies and practices. The emergence of the Internet and wireless media have made it possible for commentators to draw instantly on these norms when assessing cases of youth crime that have gained notoriety.

A recent example was the case of Dzhokhar Tsarnaev, the nineteen-year-old Chechen immigrant who, along with his older brother, carried out the Boston Marathon bombing in April 2013. A seemingly "Americanized" immigrant youth, Tsarnaev turned out to have been leading a double life: an American college student and laid-back "stoner," according to his friends, but also an increasingly observant Muslim shaped by his brother's transatlantic travels to eastern Europe along with virtual excursions to radical websites and social media feeds.[10] Tsarnaev's criminal trial took place in Boston amid debates about whether his age should mitigate a possible death sentence, with reference to the U.S. Supreme Court ruling in *Roper v. Simmons* (2005), which in turn had cited "international norms" as well as emerging "teenage brain" science implying reduced adolescent culpability for criminal acts.[11] Some observers suggested that Tsarnaev's case resembled that of Lee Malvo, the seventeen-year-old Washington, DC, sniper, who was spared the death penalty on the premise that an adult accomplice had influenced him.[12]

Such high-profile cases demonstrate how adolescent crime can expose anxieties about family, social order, and national identity. These cases also highlight the significance of reformers' rhetorical choices, such as the current obsession with brain science. As Terry Maroney perceptively points out, "The brain is not what we are really talking about when we talk about the juvenile brain. We use the juvenile brain to talk about other things. Adolescent brain science has become a quick, culturally salient way to reference those qualities we think are special about juveniles, such as immaturity, impulsivity, and malleability."[13] In the United States, children's rights advocates now routinely use brain science as part of their concerted efforts to put "the juvenile back into juvenile justice."[14]

Collectively, the six case studies in this volume provide a transnational perspective on the historical processes of forging, circulating, and recycling ideas about how children are different from adults, and why those differences should matter for the administration of justice. In this regard, *Ages of Anxiety* demonstrates the usefulness of social histories of children and youth for policy analysis and decision making in the United States and elsewhere in the twenty-first century. Social histories of children and youth are more abundant than the limited studies of juvenile courts and more broadly conceived than narrowly focused institutional histories.

Such social histories include evidence with which to test a theoretical model for understanding how public anxiety can either reinforce or undermine the rationale for a separate juvenile justice system. Table 1 provides a two-by-two scheme that identifies four strands of anxiety about delinquency and crime.

Table 1

1. Youth Specific and Endogenous	2. Youth Specific and Exogenous
3. Crime Specific and Endogenous	4. Crime Specific and Exogenous

We can use these strands to analyze past policy making. For example, we need to know whether contemporaries worried about crime because they were concerned about kids (i.e., youth specific) or whether they worried about crime in general (i.e., crime specific). If their concerns were youth specific rather than crime specific, this emphasis should reinforce a separate juvenile justice system. From this perspective, it does not matter whether they used the juvenile court as an instrument of benevolence or social control. The key point is that they responded in a "youth specific" manner. But if their concerns were crime specific, rather than youth specific, this approach should support only one court to try all offenders. Similarly, it matters whether historical actors considered troublemakers endogenous (i.e., "our kids") or exogenous (i.e., "their kids"). The problem of endogenous children should reinforce the juvenile court, whereas fears of exogenous children should weaken it.

The combination of concerns may also make a difference. According to this model, social anxiety about "youth specific" crime by "endogenous" children should be a recipe for strengthening the dual system. In contrast, "crime specific" concerns about "exogenous" children should undermine it, since the issue involved the criminal actions of other people's children. Other combinations, such as "youth specific" concerns about "exogenous" children or "crime specific" concerns about "endogenous" children, suggest that a strand may simultaneously pull in opposite directions. Fortunately, social histories of children and youth, including the case studies in this volume, provide evidence with which to test this predictive model.

The past, like the present, is a complicated landscape to comprehend. Historians of childhood and youth have shown how modern societies use categories of social identity, such as ethnicity, class, race, gender, age, religion, region, and nationality, to identify and classify who belongs to "in-groups" and "out-groups." And with respect to youth crime, assessments of "respectability" often cut across these categories. Our predictive model is not a substitute for painstaking and nuanced social-historical investigations into past practices. Instead, it provides an interpretive framework for applying this body of research to developing child-friendly justice.[15]

Part I first examines how reformers used the idea of modernization to build and legitimize juvenile justice systems in Europe and Mexico. The opening chapter, by David Niget, focuses on the role of Belgian reformers and the International Association of Children's Judges in developing and disseminating proposals for juvenile courts based on the "American" or Chicago model. This approach emphasized the importance of judges as experts who presided over courts that provided treatment to children instead of punishment for criminals. Subsequent reformers, as Niget demonstrates, reconfigured this youth-specific model of juvenile justice to fit into a world shattered and reshaped by two world wars and the Cold War.

The second chapter, by Shari Orisich, examines the transformation of the juvenile court in Mexico City from the 1930s to the 1960s. By analyzing the *estudio social* (social studies, or reports) compiled by caseworkers, she shows how these life histories helped establish professional authority and control over state institutions, the streets, and adolescents. Moreover, as her chapter reveals, these caseworkers were part of the transnational circulation of scientific ideas about delinquency and youth governance. These caseworkers literally inscribed modern "youth specific" theories and practices onto the everyday administration of juvenile justice. Yet, as her chapter points out, their clients had their own ideas about how to live their lives.

Part I concludes with Corrie Decker's chapter about the limits of modernizing juvenile justice in an empire over which the sun never set. Decker examines why British colonial administrators in the Zanzibar Islands of East Africa, unlike their counterparts in Kenya and South Africa, did not think juvenile delinquency was a major problem that required them to build new institutions such as a juvenile reformatory for exogenous children. Accordingly, they resisted calls from the Colonial Office, beginning in the 1930s, and later from the United Nations in the 1950s, to follow either British or international blueprints for the administration of juvenile justice. As Decker reveals, juvenile delinquency was in reality a major problem but one that local chiefs (*masheha*) and Islamic legal representatives (*mudirs*) generally handled. They resolved these cases before colonial administrators even knew about them. The indigenous peoples during the colonial era (1890–1963) in effect retained authority and control over their juvenile law violators. This case study reminds us that the history of juvenile justice is the product of what did and did not happen in particular places at specific times, and not necessarily the result of legislative or judicial actions.

The colonial context or framework also suggests a way of thinking about tensions between specific communities and larger governmental bodies, such as local minority communities and external, majoritarian-dominated city, regional, and state authorities. And the idea of endogenous versus exogenous children highlights the importance of race, ethnicity, class, and other categories of identity. This approach includes studying how and why certain populations became "our kids" over time, and why others did not. These categories, of course, could coexist in tension and contradiction, depending on the historical context.

Part II presents three histories of policing and punishing youth crime, beginning with Tamara Myers's chapter about the so-called Montreal Miracle of the 1940s. Her chapter analyzes how the Montreal Police Department reacted to a perceived juvenile crime wave that began during World War II. The police response to this "youth specific" crisis included developing delinquency prevention programs, which redefined the role of police officers as role models who should mentor children and adolescents in the city's playgrounds, on the streets, and in the schools. Her chapter reveals the enduring tension between preventing juvenile crime and increasing state supervision over endogenous and exogenous youth, and how these policies contributed to new ideas about liberal citizenship.

Building on this theme of expanded state supervision as part of modern liberalism, Guillaume Périssol situates the history of *liberté surveillée* (supervised freedom or probation) within Alexis de Tocqueville's theory about the power and cultural effects of democratization on social relations. Périssol uses this framework to compare the histories of juvenile probation in Paris and Boston during the 1950s. Since the creation of the world's first juvenile court in Chicago in 1899, probation had been the cornerstone of the American model of juvenile justice that emphasized keeping children out of secure confinement so they could grow up in their own homes and communities. Périssol demonstrates the continuing importance of probation for both the court systems and the youths being supervised.[16] He argues that the continued use of probation in this period had a net widening effect that brought new cases of rebellious, middle-class teenagers into the court system. Although supervised freedom spared many youths from incarceration, this use of "soft power" expanded the number of endogenous adolescents caught in the justice system in both Boston and Paris.

Part II concludes with a haunting chapter, by Nazan Çiçek, about Turkish rejection of a separate justice system for juvenile offenders. Until 1979, Turkey processed and sanctioned child law offenders as adults, or in a "crime specific" manner. When Turkey finally passed its first juvenile court law, it limited the jurisdiction of these new courts to the cases of children younger than fifteen years old. Çiçek draws on this history to analyze the media coverage and prosecution in a State Security Court of four adolescents (ages thirteen to seventeen) for the gang rape, torture, and murder of a twenty-year-old kindergarten teacher and rape, knifing, and attempted murder of her mother. The history of resistance to western European conceptions of juvenile justice, she shows, complicated Turkey's long campaign for admission into the European Union. It also demonstrates what happens when policymakers draw on "crime specific" fears to punish "exogenous" children. In this instance, Turkish authorities handled these adolescents as if they were terrorists.

Turkish commentators countered that their government had treated these "monsters" more leniently than the United States would have. They argued that Americans would have executed them or at least sentenced them to die in prison. During the 1990s, almost every American state had passed laws to make it easier to prosecute and punish juveniles as adults. The authors of a 1996 U.S. government report, for example, emphasized how "crime specific" fears led to the passage of so many "get tough" laws.[17] As they explained, "It is clear from conversations with juvenile justice planners, prosecutors, judges, legislators, and corrections administrators across the country that public fear—more precisely, the fear of being killed by a young person—was the driving force behind recent changes to stem the tide of violent crime by juveniles." They added, "Frequently, legislatures responded to that fear with proposals to get even, punish, or hold juveniles accountable. Quite often the responses were couched in rhetoric such as 'If they can kill like an adult, they can be treated just like an adult' or 'If you do the crime, you do the time.'"[18]

The Turkish use of the term "monster" to describe juvenile offenders was similar to how some American social scientists, prominent lawmakers, and many media outlets in the 1990s described juveniles as "super-predators."[19] This rhetoric went far beyond distinctions between "our kids" and "their kids." Instead, the term "predator" and the adjectives "godless," "fatherless," and "remorseless" implied that these children were not children and barely members of the same species.[20] For instance, a 1994 editorial in the *Arkansas Democrat-Gazette* pointed out that "locking up kids with adults is not a palatable prospect" but that "some of these defendants are 'kids' only chronologically. The time has passed when novels like *Lord of the Flies* can shock by displaying the human species' capacity for wanton brutality at an early age. Just look in Little Rock's jails, or worse, on its streets for examples."[21]

Even as juvenile crime rates dropped precipitously and continuously during the 1990s, some commentators, such as John J. DiIulio, a professor of politics and public affairs at Princeton University, and James Alan Fox, a professor of criminal justice at Northeastern University, contended that the crime drop might "merely be a lull before the next storm of juvenile violence."[22] According to their prognostications, "the next generation of 'super-predators' would be even worse" and the 1990s would look "like the good old days."[23] As it turned out, their predictions about a coming bloodbath in the twenty-first century were wrong and wrongheaded.[24] Unfortunately, many of the "get tough" policies enacted by states and the federal government remain in place.[25]

Accordingly, policymakers who wish to avoid repeating such mistakes should remember why "youth specific" justice systems were created in the first place, and why they spread across the globe during the twentieth century. Lawmakers must also be aware of the perils of drawing distinctions between "our kids" and "their kids," especially since the history of doing so has been regrettable. "Crime specific" concerns need not trigger amnesia. Historical sensitivity and awareness can be antidotes.

The concluding chapter to this volume uses our theoretical model to provide a comparative anatomy of moral panics about juvenile delinquency and crime. Beginning in the 1970s, sociologists used this concept initially to study societal overreactions to "shallow-end phenomena such as soft drug use, sexual deviance, and juvenile offending rather than to murder, rape, or robbery."[26] Similarly, historians have employed this concept to analyze social anxieties from libertine youth in mid-seventeenth-century Holland to a myriad of concerns about teenagers in modern America.[27] Building on this research and our case studies, we analyze to what extent such moral panics about juvenile delinquency focused on children as undifferentiated criminals or as young persons, whether perceptions of the protagonists as "endogenous" versus "exogenous" affected the official response, and whether international norms made a difference. This historically informed perspective suggests why some moral panics about youth deviancy led directly or indirectly to positive reform, instead of serving merely as a recipe for repressive policies. And, as the recent Turkish and U.S. examples suggest, how and why rhetoric that denies the humanity of youthful offenders erodes public confidence in both the juvenile and criminal justice systems and undermines international norms.

NOTES

1 Franklin Zimring, Máximo Langer, and David S. Tanenhaus, eds., *Juvenile Justice in Global Perspective* (New York: New York University Press, 2014), 1–5.

2 Franklin E. Zimring and Máximo Langer, "One Theme or Many? The Search for a Deep Structure in Global Juvenile Justice," in *Juvenile Justice in Global Perspective*, 383–411.

3 See Thomas Bender, ed., *Rethinking American History in a Global Age* (Berkeley: University of California Press, 2002), particularly Akira Iriye, "Internationalizing International History," 47–62; "AHR Conversation: On Transnational History," *American Historical Review* 111, no. 5 (December 2006): 1442–1464.

4 Bernhard Struck, Kate Ferris, and Jacques Revel, "Introduction: Space and Scale in Transnational History," *International History Review* 33, no. 4 (2011): 573–584, at 579.

5 Heather Ellis, "Introduction: Constructing Juvenile Delinquency in a Global Context," in *Juvenile Delinquency and the Limits of Western Influence, 1850–2000,* ed. Heather Ellis (New York: Palgrave Macmillan, 2014), 1–18.

6 Zimring, Langer, and Tanenhaus, *Juvenile Justice in Global Perspective.*

7 For a concise overview, see Kevin Kenny, *Diaspora: A Very Short Introduction* (New York: Oxford University Press, 2013); see also Robin D. G. Kelley, "How the West Was One: The African Diaspora and the Re-Mapping of U.S. History," in Bender, *Rethinking American History in a Global Age,* 123–147. For a more recent example of this phenomenon, see Miroslava Chávez-Garcia, "Latina/o Youth Gangs in Spain in Global Perspective," in Ellis, *Juvenile Delinquency and the Limits of Western Influence,* 93–118.

8 Michael Willrich, *City of Courts: Socializing Justice in Progressive Era Chicago* (New York: Cambridge University Press, 2003), xxx.

9 For an overview, see Martin Bulmer, *The Chicago School of Sociology: Institutionalization, Diversity, and the Rise of Sociological Research* (Chicago: University of Chicago Press, 1986), esp. 45–63; for exemplars, see William I. Thomas and Florian Znaniecki, *The Polish Peasant in Europe and America* (Urbana: University of Illinois Press, 1996 [1918–20]); and Clifford R. Shaw, *The Jack-Roller: A Delinquent Boy's Own Story* (Chicago: University of Chicago Press, 1930).

10 "Boy at Home in U.S., Swayed by One Who Wasn't," *New York Times,* April 19, 2013; Janet Reitman, "Jahar's World," *Rolling Stone,* July 17, 2013.

11 Dana Goldstein, "The Teenage Brain of the Boston Bomber," *The Marshall Project,* May 15, 2015 (www.themarshallproject.org).

12 See, e.g., Laurence Steinberg, "Dzhokhar Tsarnaev, Adolescent or Adult?," *Boston Globe,* March 30, 2015.

13 Terry A. Maroney, "The Once and Future Juvenile Brain," in *Choosing the Future for American Juvenile Justice,* ed. Franklin E. Zimring and David S. Tanenhaus (New York: New York University Press, 2014), 203.

14 Ibid., 197.

15 For an introduction to "child-friendly" justice, see Ton Lieefard, "Child-Friendly Justice: Protection and Participation of Children in the Justice System," 88 *Temple Law Review* (2016): 905–927.

16 On the centrality of probation, see Steven L. Schlossman, *Transforming Juvenile Justice: Reform Ideas and Institutional Realities, 1825–1920* (DeKalb: Northern Illinois University Press, 2005).

17 Patricia Torbet, Richard Gable, Hunter Hurst IV, Imogene Montgomery, Linda Szymanski, and Douglas Thomas, *States Responses to Serious and Violent Juvenile Crime* (Washington, DC: Office of Juvenile Justice and Delinquency Prevention, 1996).

18 Ibid., 53.

19 For an introduction to the literature on the role of the news media in shaping racialized perceptions of youth crime during the 1980s and 1990s, see Perry L. Moriearty, "Framing Justice: Media, Bias, and Legal Decisionmaking," 69 *Maryland Law Review* 4 (2010): 850–909. In *Punished: Policing the Lives of Black and Latino Boys* (New York: New York University Press, 2011), Victor M. Rios examines this history from the perspective of Black and Latino youth who were continuously treated as criminals.

20 William J. Bennett, John J. DiIulio, and John P. Waters, *Body Count: Moral Poverty . . . and How to Win America's War against Crime and Drugs* (New York: Simon and Schuster, 1996).

21 "Grading the Session: A Fine Start toward a Safer State," *Arkansas Democrat-Gazette*, August 29, 1994, 4B.

22 Shay Bilchik, *Juvenile Justice Reform Initiatives in the States: 1994–1996* (Washington, DC: Office of Juvenile Justice and Delinquency Prevention, Office of Justice Programs, United States Department of Justice, 1998), 6–7.

23 Ibid. Also see James Alan Fox, *Trends in Juvenile Justice: A Report to the United States Attorney General on Current and Future Rates of Juvenile Offending* (Washington, DC: U.S. Bureau of Justice Statistics, 1996).

24 Franklin E. Zimring, "American Youth Violence: A Cautionary Tale," in *Choosing the Future for American Juvenile Justice*, ed. Franklin E. Zimring and David S. Tanenhaus (New York: New York University Press, 2014), 7–36.

25 Franklin E. Zimring and David S. Tanenhaus, "On Strategy and Tactics for Contemporary Reforms," in *Choosing the Future for American Juvenile Justice*, 216–233.

26 David Garland, "On the Concept of a Moral Panic," *Crime Media Culture* 4 (2008): 20.

27 Benjamin B. Roberts and Leendert F. Gorenendijk, "Moral Panic and Holland's Libertine Youth of the 1650s and 1660s," *Journal of Family History* 30 (2005): 327–346; Steven Mintz, *Huck's Raft: A History of American Childhood* (Cambridge: Harvard University Press, 2004).

PART I

Juvenile Delinquency and Modernization Projects

1

From Criminal Justice to the Social Clinic

The Role of Magistrates in the Circulation of Transnational Models in the Twentieth Century

DAVID NIGET

The invention of the juvenile court in the early 20th century gave rise to a transnational movement in which Belgium was a major player. Reconciling legal orthodoxy and the socialization of criminal law practices, the country was a bastion of "social defense," a penal doctrine that aimed to reconcile child protection and the protection of society through a preventive approach combining penal and social techniques. Belgium was also a prominent actor in the process of medicalizing juvenile delinquency. In a country where moral tradition meets scientific thinking, a system of medical and pedagogical guidance was set up to rehabilitate young offenders to make them useful, autonomous citizens. Belgium's juvenile justice system was the synthesis of a postpenal approach with a medical one.

From the late 19th century, Belgium played an important role on the international scene, contributing to the international movement that introduced the juvenile court as a legal and institutional model. The first International Association of Child Welfare (1921) had its headquarters in Brussels. This association played a key role in the Child Welfare Committee of the League of Nations (LON) created in 1924, following the adoption of the first Declaration of the Rights of the Child. It gave rise to the first International Association of Children's Judges (IACJ, 1930), also based in Brussels.

But the international scene was a field of concurrences. Aside from the normative approach adopted by Belgian jurists, new actors in the field, such as the Save the Children International Union (SCIU), established in the aftermath of the First World War, advocated humanitarian intervention, which was deemed preferable by the British Foreign Office. Several conceptions of child welfare thus appeared in a context of increasing child welfare policies as a means of political pacification in Europe.

More broadly, we can discuss the tension that plagued the field of child advocacy throughout the 20th century between risk management imperatives aimed at protecting vulnerable children and the individual rights of minors who acquire citizenship status in the name of political emancipation.

Belgian child savers and the International Association of Children's Judges influenced the evolution of models and proposals that were disseminated internationally. We shall explore the main issues that were debated on the international scene following this "transnationalization" of child welfare policies, through the construction of a cause presented as universal even though it was the fruit of highly specific, historical contingencies.[1]

From Philanthropy to Public Policies: The "Transnationalization" of Child Welfare

The end of the 19th century saw the emergence of a vast international movement supporting the introduction of specialized justice for minors. The international cosmopolitan philanthropy of charity and national aspirations found common ground.[2] Individual countries at the time were seeking to introduce public policies to deal with poverty, of which juvenile delinquency was an alarming manifestation.

A popular means of bringing about social reform during this period was the congress. As an international meeting, albeit on a private basis, the congress became the modern means of political communication, allying expertise with lobbying for reform. The transnational space carved out here was not only a broad stage for communication occupied by a network of diverse actors; the transnational concept became a source of knowledge and expertise in itself, enabling the circulation of know-how. Furthermore, the transnational structure even served as an argument for reform: by encouraging national legislators to cast off potential conservatisms, the foreign example was held up as a reason to "modernize" legislation and public action.[3] This movement also gained currency in an age that we nowadays describe as the "first globalization," which reached its height between 1880 and 1914. The "social question" at the time became a popular subject of transnational exchanges in the name of a shared sense of the limitations of liberal laissez-faire, alongside the socialist political "threat" that was alarming the elites. In this context, the dialectics between the "Old" and the "New" world paid off: social innovations crossed the Atlantic, associated with all the trappings of expertise and modernity.[4]

Through these congresses, the new reformers formulated their aspirations and so defined an ideal type of juvenile justice, based on the "American model."[5] A symbol of social innovation, juvenile courts, the first of which opened in Chicago in 1899, subsequently became the universal reference.[6] The American and European reformers adopted its principles. Edouard Julhiet, a French engineer who traveled abroad, gave an enthusiastic talk on the subject at the Musée social in Paris upon his return from the United States.[7] In Belgium, after several aborted reforms following Jules Lejeune's proposals of 1889, which were inspired by French legislation on the destitution of paternal authority, the more family-oriented American innovation was presented at the congress for child protection in Liège in 1905 by the philanthropist Madame Juliette Carton de Wiart, following a visit to the United States.[8] As the wife of the minister for justice appointed in 1911, she played a decisive role in passing new legislation in Belgium, despite reticence in legal circles.[9]

The penitentiary congress held in Washington in 1910 endorsed the reform movement and proposed more precise definitions of institutional standards, making the children's judge central to the reformed system:

> The magistrates responsible for hearing the cases of juvenile delinquents, including the examining magistrates for such cases, should be selected above all based on their aptitude to understand and sympathize with minors, and they should also have some specific knowledge of social and psychological sciences.

The acceptance of the measure attests to its perceived significance: the resolution was adopted unanimously by the fourth section of the Penitentiary Commission.[10] A similar impulse emerged in Paris in 1911, at the first Congrés des tribunaux pour enfants (Juvenile Court

Congress). There, as in Washington, the conferees agreed that the juvenile judge should be specialized, sit alone in the manner of a benevolent father, and "may only take measures to protect, defend and assist the child."[11]

The age of criminal responsibility then became the subject of debates and strategies among "child savers." Raised from 16 to 18 years in France by law in 1906, it remained at 16 years in Belgium with regard to offences, and was increased to 18 in the event of incorrigibility. Many countries have maintained the age of 16 as the border between childhood and adulthood.[12] The effort to establish a fixed boundary aimed above all at presenting the child as a vulnerable figure, far removed from the image of the corrupted youth promoted in the first mass media from the mid-19th century onwards. Astonishingly, the notion of adolescence, which was fundamental to the establishment of the American juvenile courts, remained far less conspicuous in Europe.

Although the suggestion that adolescence was "the penultimate stage before the eradication of juvenile delinquency" was met with great enthusiasm, the American representative at the Paris congress was met with hostility by a section of the French lawyers.[13] Albert Rivière, honorary secretary of the Société générale des prisons, condemned the scheme as "neglectful of all the most elementary principles of our public law and criminal law," arguing that it ignored the guarantee of rights to a defense and would give too much power to the social worker, who in the case of secular France took the form of a monk or a nun.[14] The debate extended to the contradictions between protection and rights, which were not as yet the rights of children, whose interests were subsumed within those of the community, but the rights of the family and more specifically the rights of the father, from whom this intrusive law would sap the "natural" authority. In this respect, it is interesting to note that the model of a dedicated juvenile court in the United States, specifically in Chicago, was actually opposed by the Democratic Party, owing to its discretionary nature. As explained by David Tanenhaus, in the legal battle that in 1913 nearly saw the court closed down, Judge Julian Mack defended his institution by invoking the "revolution" at work in America, Europe, and Australia.[15] The institution's legitimacy hinged on its proliferation around the world. Thus, through a circular legitimization process the new institutional models and mechanisms for managing social problems fueled the international transfer of ideas, which in turn reinforced their position within their own national borders.

In spite of a certain reticence and with the specific nuances of each national context, a hard core of countries crystallized in support of the reform of juvenile courts: the United States, the United Kingdom, Canada, Belgium, France, Switzerland, and the Netherlands. The circulation of key figures and philanthropic sociability introduced a "contagion of reform," to borrow the expression from contemporary observers.[16] A shared *doxa* was created, albeit within a flexible framework. Indeed, despite the invocation of "models" and real legislative convergences (the 1908 laws in the United Kingdom and Canada, and the 1912 laws in France and Belgium), national variants of this reformatory ideal remained specific to each legal system, reflecting the local professional concurrences and national political tensions.[17] French, Swiss, and Belgian reformers at the first International Congress for Child Welfare in Brussels in 1913 envisaged the establishment of an international organization that could generalize a certain number of norms in a transnational spirit of cooperation. Although a permanent international commission was indeed set up to organize child welfare congresses after the First World War, the arrival of the Second World War brought an end to any vague attempts at creating a permanent institutional body in Brussels.[18]

In this system, the role of the children's judge was crucial. From the outset, he was the spokesperson of a new cause, the defense of the child who was a victim or in danger. We then see the appearance of media-friendly proselytizers: Judge Ben Lindsey in the United States and Judge Henri Rollet in France, soon followed by Judge Paul Wets in Belgium.[19] Childhood then became a higher moral cause, requiring a certain number of social reforms and justifying the mobilization of society as a whole. In so doing, children's judges sought to promote a new "moral economy" of childhood, emphasizing the fact that the "social value" of childhood was reaching zero in economic terms but was morally incommensurable, as highlighted by Viviana Zelizer.[20] This cause of the child did not, however, result in any rights being granted to the children themselves. Indeed, as guarantors of public order, children's judges sought to reconcile children's and society's welfare, through the doctrine of "social defense" initiated in Belgium.[21] Beyond being a security measure in direct response to the political instability of democratic regimes faced with the rise in workers' militancy, this doctrine bore witness more broadly to the paradigm shift from a liberal vision of the law that delivered sentences in proportion to the seriousness of the offence, to a preventive or social vision, focusing on the individual's treatment and their socialization, rather than the crimes they had committed. In this perspective, the child embodied a strategic vector making it possible to implement crime prevention policies that guarantee social order.[22]

Importantly, the children's judge was also a reassuring, consensual incarnation of social reform, who was only inviting a slight shift in liberal laissez-faire. Indeed, although justice for minors was an invitation to address the "social question" through the fate of the child, it was still only through the highly restrictive filter of criminal justice and charity policies. By maintaining the conditionality of state assistance and the related social services, placed under the leadership of a judicial mechanism whose rationale remained penal, it was possible to dress the wounds of the most urgent social ills without actually acknowledging the right to receive assistance.[23]

The Rearrangement of Associative Networks: Child Welfare at the League of Nations

The First World War altered the configuration of international exchanges. Philanthropic systems of alliances were replaced by international concurrences around child welfare policies, which became increasingly strategic. Although the child was placed at the heart of the wartime culture, it was difficult for defenders of children to promote the figure of the "universal child" during the war, when the issue of "race" was being ramped up in nationalist propaganda.[24] Nevertheless, a strong consensus became established after the war around child welfare, both out of a demographic necessity faced with the human disaster and as an omen of European political and moral restoration. Compared with the barbarity of war, the figure of the child symbolized a new international, pacific order, in accordance with the democratization of political practices and promotion of welfare among populations. Childhood became a transnational issue in a profoundly destabilized world, the focus of numerous humanitarian policies that were being developed at the time, including the Commission for Relief in Belgium, an American organization promoted by Herbert Hoover to save Belgian children who had become victims of the continental blockade.[25] However, this consensual vision should not overshadow the ideological (national, ethnic, religious and political) issues underlying this investment in children, in particular the fear of the spread of Bolshevism, which drove the actions of the American Relief Administration in Central Europe.[26]

The agenda of the pre–First World War "child savers," united in 1921 in the International Association of Child Welfare (IACW), was thus greatly altered by the emergence of a more urgent question: how to deal with the child victims of the war, who were orphaned, undernourished, ill-housed, and displaced. The humanitarian question was then taken up by an organization in competition with the child welfare network formed before the war, the Save the Children International Union. Created in 1920, the SCIU originated from the British organization Save the Children Fund, and was connected with the Geneva-based International Red Cross Committee.[27] The SCIU undertook active money-raising campaigns, notably to combat the famine in Russia in 1920, demonstrating a masterly use of modern means of communication (such as images, films, and charity galas), and created its own operational structure for food aid distribution in the field. Emphasis here was placed more on children than adolescents, as the youngest ones ideally epitomize innocent victims.[28] This strategy differed from that of the promoters of justice for minors who, on the contrary, sought to gradually extend the benefit of *welfare* policies to all minors, up to the age of 18 or even 21.

Thus the SCIU's humanitarian objectives diverged significantly from the plans for international regulation sought by the IACW. A major congress was organized in Brussels in 1921 by the IACW, detailing all the legislative proposals that nations should consider to sustainably improve the lot of children, from the "moral preservation of childhood" to "abnormal childhood," and from health and childcare to the question of war orphans. Belgium once again took up the torch for a cause that it had initiated before the war, while at the same time emphasizing its wartime experience, during which children constituted a strong, symbolic element. "Belgium has hosted numerous congresses focusing on the improvement of the lot of children," Minister for Justice Emile Vandervelde pointed out, opening the congress. "Now that the global

disaster has ended, it is our duty to set up an international meeting. . . .
The efforts made by the Belgian people to save children and improve
the race have placed this country among the leading ranks of progressive nations. This position makes it quite uniquely placed to organize
the International Bureau of Child Protection [Office International de la
protection de l'enfance]."[29] Once again, we see here the determination to
host a permanent international institution for child welfare, at the same
time as Switzerland was vying for a dominant position in the field.

But behind the SCIU, the British government sought to reduce the
role of this new transnational sphere of child welfare, believing that associations should be confined to an advisory role and selective intervention. In this respect, it was satisfied with the SCIU's humanitarian role.
Conversely, the IACW attempted to influence traditional diplomacy in
an effort to bring about international child welfare legislation. This explains why the Belgian government sought to become identified with
this transnational policy, presenting itself as an intermediary country
supported by France. In 1922, the IACW responded to the issue of displaced children by establishing an international convention for the repatriation of minors between neighboring countries.[30]

Hence the critical question of the relations between the IACW and
the newly established League of Nations was posed, resulting in the 1923
meeting in Geneva of the association's principal representatives, including Henri Carton de Wiart for Belgium and Henri Rollet for France. The
discussions were turbulent, with great fears of seeing the association ab-
sorbed by the LON's authorities. A strong argument was that Germany,
as the defeated nation, did not belong to the LON, while simultaneously
the internationalist child savers were seeking to promote new, international norms there.[31]

In this confrontational context between the IACW and the SCIU, the
LON created the Child Welfare Committee in 1924, a body composed
of government representatives alongside "assessors" from international
child welfare associations, including the two competing networks.[32] In
spite of this attempt at reconciliation within a neutral institution, both
associations maintained their rivalry and continued to encroach on each
other's respective prerogatives. Thus, faced with the IACW's expertise in
juvenile delinquency—a topic revived by the postwar social instability—
the SCIU, whose humanitarian argument was waning as wartime con-

cerns faded into the past, attempted to move into the legal sphere. To this end, the SCIU's founder and ardent lobbyer Eglantyne Jebb drew up in 1923 the first Declaration of Children's Rights.[33]

The declaration, adopted in 1924, is marked both by its simplicity, which makes it a universal, nonrestrictive tool for the spreading of its ideas, and by its general and therefore extensive nature, addressing the issues of justice and education, the right to healthcare, and the right to harmonious development. Its ambitions were immense, but at a time when international institutions were just taking shape, its legal powers were very limited. It did not promote new rights and was initially more concerned with moral considerations than any determination to modify public policies. The 19th-century legal laboratory constituted by child welfare congresses gave way to humanitarian considerations. The vision of childhood that it promoted looked more like a martyrology of vulnerable children rather than a promotion of the child citizen.[34]

In this competitive context, the idea arose for an International Association of Children's Judges in 1928, at the 2nd International Congress for Child Welfare, organized by the IACW in Paris. During this congress, the diversity of models for the judicial management of delinquent children was highlighted, and in particular the differences between the French, Italian, and German systems, which had not opted for specialized children's judges, and the Belgian, Dutch, Polish, and American systems, which advocated the establishment of completely autonomous, specialist juvenile courts. Thus the congress's rapporteur, Henri Donnedieu de Vabres, who was a professor of criminal law in the Faculty of Law, Paris, proposed "technical training" for all magistrates involved with minors, whatever the extent of their court's specialization.[35] In his view, ignorance of social issues, children's health and hygiene, housing issues, and urban development impaired the quality of the work of magistrates who focused solely on the law.

For certain champions of the movement, such as Henri Rollet, a Parisian judge, and Paul Wets, a judge in Brussels, childhood was above all a cause. The latter set out his vision of the judge's function in 1928: he should "be sustained both by a deep-seated faith in the beauty of his function, by a genuine love of children and youth, and by a boundless devotion, devoid of any skepticism or pessimism. . . . The qualities required of a new magistrate are not necessarily those expected of an eminent lawyer. In these functions, the heart should be assigned at least as much importance as reason."[36] Magistrates from all nations, meeting in Paris in 1928, were caught up in a "shared ideal, so high and so pure" that they were unable to tolerate even the idea of a "barrier between men and races. . . . The protection of unfortunate children knows no borders."[37]

Thus the association's dual function was apparent from the outset: promoting a cause and laying down the foundations for expertise in matters concerning children. The project became reality in 1930 when the IACJ held its first meeting in Brussels, in the presence of children's judges from a number of countries: Brazil, Czechoslovakia, France, Germany, Great Britain, Hungary, Italy, Japan, Poland, Portugal, Spain, Switzerland, the United States (Chicago and New Jersey), and Yugoslavia. The association presented itself, unlike the LON bodies, as a neophilanthropic entity of an entirely private nature, based on individuals' voluntary participation: "The IACJ has to be a place of cordiality and fraternity between the men of goodwill who are children's judges from all countries," explained Wets.[38]

Nevertheless, it assigned itself two mandates that reveal its ambitions within transnational bodies:

—The knowledge, diffusion and harmonization of national models of justice for minors, centered round the juvenile court. The idea highlighted is that the causes of juvenile delinquency are now transnational after the experience of the war and that, consequently, the solutions introduced to combat this scourge should also be transnational;
—The question of conventions for the repatriation of foreign children in each national space.

This issue made it possible to situate the association's action in the context of international law, of which the LON was the custodian.[39]

This new association brought important new developments to the model of juvenile justice. At the first congress in 1930, Count Carton de Wiart, a leading figure of the reform movement, drew attention to the influence of the positivist school of criminology and the individualization of sentences, emphasizing the moral dimension of child welfare over its "scientific" dimension. Pierre de Nemeth, a Hungarian magistrate, outlined the "teleological" dimension of the activity of the judge, who had to act not with regard to past events, but in accordance with the objective to be reached: the reform of the juvenile delinquent, guaranteed by social workers who should acquire a professional status. On the one hand, therefore, we see a departure from a criminal rationale to the advocacy of "treatment" in a quasi-therapeutic rehabilitation process. There was also a departure from the charitable activity characteristic of the prewar years in favor of systematic, rational social action. The problem of juvenile delinquency was viewed from a perspective of risk management and governmentality, that is, an assessment of future dangers in the light of past actions, and orientation of the behavior of young people in difficulty in accordance with the social norms of the time and the political values promoted by liberal democracies: autonomy and responsibility.[40]

Thus, while the questions of new social policy models were circulating within these newly formed international organizations of the LON and the International Labour Organization, based both on knowledge and far more preventive social protection systems, the IACJ recommendations concerning the juvenile justice model was tending toward expertise that had become indispensable: social work and psychological sciences.[41] According to Pierre de Nemeth, "the charitable judge has become the medico-pedagogical judge, familiar with the social terrain in which he has to operate."[42] According to Wets, "There is no guilty child . . . only society is responsible. There are no delinquent children, but there are unfortunate occasions and eventualities. Furthermore 80% of the children who appear before us are abnormal."[43] The congress participants thus visited the child guidance clinic in Moll, a veritable international model in the interwar years, a psycho-pedagogical laboratory at the exclusive service of justice for minors in Belgium.[44] We can see here the definition of a new paradigm structuring the field of justice for minors: that of "maladjustment," combining the social and psychological causes of deviance.

If the initial model of paternalistic justice was revised in favor of the scientific expertise of social work, the role of the juvenile magistrate remained primordial, that of moral arbiter in these troubled times of economic crisis and diplomatic tensions, as Wets pointed out in the IACJ's 1935 congress: "Faced with the anxiety generated by the international political and economic situation, the child . . . is the final rampart of our

civilizations in turmoil."[45] Two new ideas emerged from the debates. On the one hand, faced with the economic slump of the 1930s, the sociological explanation of juvenile deviance acquired a legitimacy that it had never truly achieved during the era of triumphant liberalism. On the other hand, we clearly see the issues here contributing to "diplomacy by the child" in its incipience.[46] The child had become the instrument for the construction of democratic, liberal stability, in the face of threats that had come to light since the First World War. The need arose to train a useful worker and a good citizen, as the aims of the 1930 congress indicated: "We have to help them find work, because providing them with work maintains their sense of social worth and establishes the basis of their moral and material independence, in order to glean the fruit of the social effort directed at their education."[47]

Alongside the creation of the IACJ, the LON Commission for Child Welfare, through the work of a subcommittee consisting notably of Isidore Maus (Belgium), J. I. Wall (United Kingdom), Mrs. Woytowicz Grabinska (Poland), and Henri Rollet (France) before his death, examined the mechanisms for taking care of "depraved children in moral danger" throughout the world, until the establishment in 1937 of a certain number of principles of best practice.[48] With Rollet and Grabinska, the IACJ was well represented in this body, which was also supported by Maus. The principles laid down by the LON in 1937 correspond effectively to the IACJ's prescriptions, as stated at its congresses in 1930 and 1935: specialization of the court, specialization of magistrates, social inquiry, and medico-pedagogical observation and individual educational measures aimed at enabling young people to "become useful member[s] of society."[49] Belgium remained a model in this landscape. As Grabinska, the committee's reporter, stated, "Among the pioneers of the liberal [i.e., reform] movement, Belgium in particular has been and remains the model for more than one country with its method that manages to combine the need to combat juvenile criminality and modern notions of special education and social prevention."[50]

From Child Welfare to Children's Rights: Juvenile Justice and the United Nations

After the Second World War, the developing United Nations sphere assigned a major place to children, with the creation of the United Nations Children's Fund (UNICEF) in 1946 through the reconstruction fund. The question of juvenile delinquency soon became a focus of the UN's attention. In 1948 the Secretariat General decided to launch a work program on the judicial treatment of delinquent youth, in an approach aimed at protecting the family, a fundamental institution of Western democratic societies.[51] The UN also began sending experts to visit governments, including Poland, India, the Philippines, and others, to address practically the problem of juvenile delinquency. Some magistrates from the IACJ took part in these missions.[52] This move inspired enthusiasm among certain actors and public opinion,[53] as well as fear in associations, which for a long time had been engaged in the cause of children, and which accused international institutions of hijacking the issue, thus limiting their capacity for initiative.[54] In this new institutional landscape, the competition between child aid associations became more complex. The IACW (which still included many magistrates who were also members of the IACJ) and the SCIU merged in 1945 to form the International Union for Child Welfare (IUCW), whose first honorary president was Count Carton de Wiart, a historic figure in the Belgian youth protection movement. The associations therefore unified their networks, funds, and communication tools, such as the journal *Revue internationale de l'enfant*. Above all, the IUCW acquired a "consultative status" on the UN Economic and Social Council, enabling it to express its opinion on subjects falling within its competence, a status that the association of judges also obtained in 1952. Even if this consultative status gave it only minimal powers in the UN bodies, its acquisition and preservation were considered crucial for the survival of the association of magistrates.[55] In this respect, the association took part in the Congress for Crime Prevention and the Treatment of Delinquents in 1955, 1960, and 1965, and meetings on the same subject in 1965 and 1967.[56]

Despite a notable broadening of the field of public policies aimed at children and the family in the context of the welfare state, the question of juvenile delinquency remained central during Europe's reconstruction. The IUCW organized a major congress "of experts" in Geneva in 1947, addressing "War and Juvenile Delinquency," in which the principal representatives of the IACJ took part.[57] The attendees emphasized the "role of juvenile courts" in the fight against "the increase in juvenile delinquency and antisocial social behavior of minors." Wartime conditions contributed to an interpretation of the causes of juvenile delinquency in terms of trauma and more general psychological problems that had to be treated through preventive action:

> Wartime juvenile delinquency is generally the result of a climate created by exceptional circumstances or factors (mobilization; foreign occupation; totalitarian ideologies; disorganization of family life; the collapse of moral values that are accepted in normal times) . . . [but is also] due to emotional causes whose effects will be long-term.[58]

Thus, a return to political, economic, and social order was advocated, along with the introduction of public mental health policies in the field of justice for minors, in order to "broadly take into account the relationship between mental debility and juvenile delinquency."[59] Nevertheless, this increasingly therapeutic intervention could not take place to the detriment of the law.

In this singular political context, between the emergence from World War II and the entry into the Cold War, where the role of "totalitarian ideologies" was condemned as the cause of juvenile delinquency, its remediation had to go hand in hand with civil rights. The vice-president of the IACJ, Judge Knuttel of the Netherlands, stressed this point at the inauguration of the first postwar congress, held in Liège in 1950: "The work of children's judges is to educate children to turn them into truly free citizens."[60] Recognizing that "any judicial intervention is a breach of the citizen's freedom and should be limited as far as possible," he proposed the following way forward: "We see that severe, punitive jurisdiction of young criminals . . . has turned into a social service for the maladjusted child, exercised by a democratic judge."[61] An alliance was advocated between the judge's authority and the voluntary collaboration of families encouraged by the social worker, through the technique of *casework*. According to Knuttel, these "American" psychosocial research methods based on individual case histories established "relations of an entirely democratic nature" with the families.[62] Magistrates therefore had to reconsider respect for privacy and the fundamental rights of minors and their families while preserving their authority, which aptly summarizes the Dutch magistrate's opinion: "The task of the truly modern children's judge is to find the middle ground, which surpasses the antithesis of authority and democracy."[63] This tension between expertise and rights structured the postwar field of justice for minors. Children's judges attempted to position themselves carefully at the intersection of the two rationalities, as protectors of vulnerable children and the interests of the state, but also as guarantors of the freedom of families and minors.

In terms of expertise, the IACJ pursued the reflection initiated in the 1930s in the postwar years on judicial, medical, and social hybridization. Psychology was acknowledged here as a new means of addressing the problem. At the congress in 1950, emphasis was placed on the personality of the minor, the family psychology, and the "affective disorders" of which delinquency may be the manifestation. Adolescence, a concept widely ignored by European reformers in the early 20th century, was then given specific attention. A certain number of expert analyses nurtured this reflection among magistrates, who considered adolescence as an age of psychological vulnerability and conflicting norms.[64] The World Health Organization was also preparing an important report on the "mental health" of young delinquents, highlighting the need for early detection, therapeutic treatment, and professional orientation toward young people, who were then considered to be "maladjusted." The report declared, "We know nothing precisely in the field of juvenile delinquency [which] is not an aspect of social maladjustment." In addition, "The prevention . . . of delinquency has to consist in a vast crusade for mental health in general, for the mental health of children."[65] As a result, explained Knuttel, "[t]he children's judge has to be a specialist judge who has studied psychology and education."[66] The instrument of this prevention policy should be the child guidance clinic, which Belgium had pioneered starting in 1913. To this end, the IACJ magistrates meeting at the 1950 congress in Liège and in 1954 and 1958 in Brussels attentively visited the Belgian institutions for boys at Moll and for girls at Saint Servais.

The magistrates were entirely objective regarding the tension that can exist between expertise and rights, as Judge Knuttel pointed out when he was president of the association in 1954: "The more our decisions are scientifically based, the more they become 'personalized,' and the greater the danger of them being misunderstood."[67] Thus the judge must precisely strike a balance between general crime prevention, social protection, and citizens' rights: "The rights and interests of children, parents and society are asking to be assessed. This assessment of opposing and often incompatible rights is the true function of the judiciary."[68] This view that social defense that aimed to protect the child and defend society were only two facets of the same approach did not last long. The criminal field no longer appeared as the testing ground for protection policies. Also, the predicted evolution of justice for minors in the 1950s resided in the extension of its prerogatives toward civil justice, whose intervention is less punitive and is concerned with the notion of the "interest of the child" in relation to his or her family environment. North America, which by this time had seen some of its juvenile courts transformed into "family relations courts," was once again serving as a model, as it did in the early 20th century.[69] The resolutions of the 1954 congress thus stated that "the traditional view of the magistrate should be altered such that his intervention should no longer be restricted solely to settling conflicting rights, but should also be of a highly social nature and essentially inspired by the interest of the child."[70] Thus, it appeared necessary for judicial "interventions, wherever possible, to avoid breaking the ties that bind the child to his or her family, but on the contrary, these links should be used to strengthen the family." Parents "should no longer be considered as unworthy or guilty parents, but as people who may themselves be in difficulty and who should be helped."[71]

Hence, the philosophy of children's judges found renewal in the field of civil justice, in ruling on custody rights and educational assistance to parents. The extension of children's judges' prerogatives to civil matters became the IACJ's main demand, then influencing a second wave of legislative reform affecting countries initiating protective juvenile justice systems, as occurred in France in 1958 and Belgium in 1965, to name but two. Children's judges were then advocates of a "new social defense," abandoning determinist, or even eugenicist, theories in favor of a democratic humanism, and appealing to social and human sciences. At the time, following the example of Jean Chazal, a Parisian judge and new figurehead of the movement, they described themselves as "the walking wing of the judiciary."[72]

Beyond family rights, the very citizenship of the child was called into question in the 1950s and 1960s, a citizenship considered not just as a guarantee of individual rights but also a means of rehabilitation in itself[73] and ultimately a guarantee of social cohesion worldwide. The debates and resolutions of the congress of the IACJ, which in 1958 became the International Association of Youth Magistrates, stressed this notion of citizenship. Initially considered as a limitation on judicial intervention, in the name of individual rights (congresses of 1954 and 1958), the argument for children's rights became an element in the judicial remediation process: at the 1966 congress, emphasis was placed on how judicial decisions should as far as possible meet with the "support" of the minors themselves, as a necessary part of the "rehabilitation" process. Also stressed was "the importance of the judge-minor and judge-family dialogues."[74] In addition, judicial intervention had to be measured rather than simply substituting welfare measures. As Gaston Fedou, president of the Juvenile Court in Paris, explained when concluding the congress, "Judicial power has to be brought to bear only in cases where there is a conflict between the respective rights of the individual, the family and society; it has no intention of letting itself be invaded by welfare."[75]

The congress in Geneva in 1970 focused on "the role of the children's judge in the community" and established an "evolution towards a new judicial humanism" that placed citizenship at the heart of the project of justice for minors.[76] At this stage, it involved discussing the consequences of the 1959 Declaration on the Rights of the Child on positive law. The category of the minor had to be broadened extensively, with the age of criminal responsibility aligned with that of civil responsibility and in any case tending toward an increase in the age limit. It was explained that "it is important that whilst retaining his judicial status, the judge should be able to turn himself into a social educator . . . without straying into paternalism."[77] The congress adopted resolutions emphasizing "reinsertion" into the "community" each time the situation permitted, for minors were now considered as "having rights rather than only being subjected to laws."

Thus, in the postwar years, advocacy on the part of IACJ magistrates gave rise to contradictory reasoning and projects. Young people were sometimes seen as vulnerable individuals requiring authoritarian protection; on occasion, they were viewed as "maladjusted" and handicapped, to be taken in hand medically and subjectified by means of psychological techniques. At other times they were considered as citizens in the making, with rights to be guaranteed and a need to be educated in democratic culture by appealing to their sense of responsibility.

Conclusion

Through the 20th century evolution of the juvenile court model, which distanced itself from the criminal, charitable system and moved toward a medico-social system of expertise, we witness how public policies to manage social risks and governmentality gained ground. The harnessing of policies aimed at children clearly demonstrates this emerging orientation toward preventive mechanisms in which "the conduct of conducts"—behavior management—prevailed over repression.[78] On the international scale, child welfare took on an ideological quality, with the rising influence of the human rights paradigm. In a changing world, courted by authoritarian regimes that also made much of the figure of the child and youth, child welfare aimed to epitomize democratic values.[79] This explains why the new transnational institutions invested in these policies, from the LON to the UN, in the name of building transnational, democratic citizenship. Beneath the veil of a universalist discourse presenting the child as an apolitical icon, we discover in reality a history of child welfare that is greatly marked by Western democracies, which promote a "model" that is intimately bound up with their political identities.[80]

The figure of the children's judge, the embodiment of juvenile justice, also demonstrates these paradigm shifts. The judge's role changed from a charismatic into an expert function, incorporating knowledge from medical and psychiatric sciences, as well as the rapidly developing human and social sciences, while striking a balance between these new forms of authority and respect for individuals' rights. The IACJ bore witness to the increasing transnational circulation of knowledge and practices and, beyond this, their hybridization within the Western geopolitical space.

The changes in the 1950s and 1960s, with the extension of children's judges' mandate to civil justice, clearly denoted a determination to respect the fundamental rights of the child, just as the United States witnessed a "due process revolution."[81] These years are remembered as being a "golden age" of justice for minors, which was legalized through a shift toward civil law and the embrace of "children's rights," supported by expertise that assigned it an undeniable authority. But this synthesis is fragile, as it is based on contradictory rationalities. The psychological sciences, as an initial form of expertise, were limited by social criticism and the sociological contributions of symbolic interactionism in the 1960 and 1970s. Furthermore, by emphasizing the rights of minors, the justice system opened a debate on the obligations of minors, and the notion of citizenship soon gave way to a neoliberal discourse on the responsibility of minors, encouraging a return to the criminal treatment of juvenile delinquents.[82] Finally, by reestablishing respect for legal guarantees, lawyers opened the way to abandoning specialized justice for minors, which was soon considered as exceptional justice whose differences had to be effaced. These debates have not been closed and we must now show how the specific functions of justice for minors, through the transnational history of the institution, are based on pedagogical, social, and political conceptions rather than on pure legal reasoning.[83]

NOTES

1 For "transnationalization," see Yves Denéchère and David Niget, *Droits des enfants au XXe siècle. Pour une histoire transnationale* (Rennes: Presses universitaires de Rennes, 2015); Heather Ellis, *Juvenile Delinquency and the Limits of Western Influence, 1850–2000* (London: Palgrave Macmillan, 2014).

2 Marie-Sylvie Dupont-Bouchat, "Du tourisme pénitentiaire à 'l'Internationale des philanthropes'. La création d'un réseau pour la protection de l'enfance à travers les congrès internationaux (1840–1914)," *Paedagogica Historica* 38, nos. 2–3 (2002): 533–563.

3 Dominique Marshall, "Dimensions transnationales et locales de l'histoire des droits des enfants. La Société des Nations et les cultures politiques canadiennes, 1910–1960," in *Genèses* 71, no. 2 (2008): 47–63.

4 Daniel T. Rodgers, *Atlantic Crossings: Social Politics in a Progressive Age* (Cambridge: Harvard University Press, 1998).

5 Marie-Sylvie Dupont-Bouchat, "Le mouvement international en faveur de la protection de l'enfance (1880–1914)", *Revue d'histoire de l'enfance "irrégulière"* 5 (2003): 207–235.

6 Margaret K. Rosenheim, Franklin E. Zimring, David S. Tanenhaus, and Bernardine Dohrn, *A Century of Juvenile Justice* (Chicago: University of Chicago Press, 2002).

7 Edouard Julhiet, "Les tribunaux pour enfants aux Etats-Unis," *Le Musée social. Mémoires et documents*, no. 3 (1906): 165–228; Edouard Julhiet, Henri Rollet, Marcel Kleine, and Maurice Gastambide, *Les tribunaux spéciaux pour enfants aux États-Unis, en France, en Angleterre, en Allemagne* (Paris: Administration de la revue L'Enfant, 1906). For the role of the Musée social in French reforms at the turn of the century, see Janet R. Horne, *A Social Laboratory for Modern France: The Musée Social and the Rise of the Welfare State* (Durham: Duke University Press, 2002).

8 Marie-Sylvie Dupont-Bouchat, "Femmes philanthropes. Les femmes dans la protection de l'enfance en Belgique (1890–1914)," *Sextant* 13–14 (2000): 96.

9 Ibid., 97.

10 *Actes du Congrès Pénitentiaire International de Washington, Octobre 1910*, vol. 1, Procès verbaux des séances (Groningen: Bureau de la Commission Pénitentiaire Internationale, 1912), 299 and 417.

11 Kleine, *Premier Congrès international des tribunaux pour enfants*, 61.

12 Ibid., 309.

13 Ibid., 61.

14 Ibid., 337–338.

15 David S. Tanenhaus, *Juvenile Justice in the Making* (New York: Oxford University Press, 2006), 98.

16 Joëlle Droux, "Une contagion programmée. La circulation internationale du modèle des tribunaux pour mineurs dans l'espace transatlantique (1900–1940)," in *Les sciences du gouvernement. Circulation(s), traduction(s), réception(s)*, ed. Martine Kaluszynski and Gilles Pollet (Paris: Economica, 2013).

17 David Niget, *La naissance du tribunal pour enfants. Une comparaison France-Québec* (Rennes: Presses universitaires de Rennes, 2009).

18 Marcel Kleine, *Premier Congrès international des tribunaux pour enfants: Paris, 29 juin-1er juillet 1911* (Paris: Impr. de A. Davy, 1912), 669, 686; Joëlle Droux, "L'internationalisation de la protection de l'enfance. Acteurs, concurrences et projets transnationaux (1900–1925)," *Critique internationale* 52, no. 3 (2011): 21–22.

19 For Lindsey, see D'Ann Campbell, "Judge Ben Lindsey and the Juvenile Court Movement, 1901–1904," in *Growing Up in America: Children in Historical Perspective*, ed. Joseph M. Hawes and N. Ray Hiner (Urbana: University of Illinois Press, 1985), 149–160.

20 Viviana A. Rotman Zelizer, *Pricing the Priceless Child: The Changing Social Value of Children* (New York: Basic Books, 1985).

21 Françoise Tulkens, *Généalogie de la défense sociale en Belgique (1880–1914)* (Brussels: Ed. Story-Scientia, 1988).

22 David Garland, *Punishment and Welfare: A History of Penal Strategies* (Brookfield, VT: Gower, 1985).

23 David Niget, "Du pénal au social. L'hybridation des politiques judiciaires et assistancielles de protection de la jeunesse dans la première moitié du XXe siècle," *Histoire et sociétés. Revue européenne d'histoire sociale* 25–26 (2008): 10–27.

24 Stéphane Audoin-Rouzeau, *La guerre des enfants: 1914–1918* (Paris: Armand Colin, 2004); Andrew Donson, *Youth in the Fatherless Land: War Pedagogy, Nationalism, and Authority in Germany, 1914–1918* (Cambridge: Harvard University Press, 2010); Manon Pignot, *Allons enfants de la patrie. Génération Grande Guerre* (Paris: Seuil, 2012). For the difficulty of promoting the "universal child," see Bruno Cabanes, *The Great War and the Origins of Humanitarianism* (London: Cambridge University Press, 2014), 272–282.

25 The assistance of the Commission for Relief in Belgium was not directed exclusively at children, but they were greatly highlighted in the campaign to collect donations in the United States. It also justified the American entry into the war in 1917, in the name of "civilization," of which the child is an innocent incarnation faced with the "barbarity" of the Germans. Ibid., 285.

26 Dominique Marshall, "The Construction of Children as an Object of International Relations: The Declaration of Children's Rights and the Child Welfare Committee of League of Nations, 1900–1924," *International Journal of Children's Rights* 7, no. 2 (1999): 103–147. The American Relief Administration was set up by Herbert Hoover based on the model of the Commission for Relief in Belgium. Sébastien Farré, *Colis de guerre. Secours alimentaire et organisations humanitaires* (Rennes: Presses universitaires de Rennes, 2014), chaps. 3–4.

27 Linda Mahood, *Feminism and Voluntary Action: Eglantyne Jebb and Save the Children, 1876–1928* (London: Palgrave Macmillan, 2009).

28 Cabanes, *Great War and the Origins of Humanitarianism*, 293.

29 Deuxième congrès international de la protection de l'enfance, Bruxelles, 1921, tome III, Compte rendu général des séances, Office de publicité, Brussels, 5.

30 Paul Kahn, "Séance du 23 janvier 1924. Rapport sur la session de l'Association internationale pour la protection de l'enfance à Genève en 1923," *Revue pénitentiaire et de droit pénal. Bulletin de la Société générale des prisons.* 48, no. 2 (February 1924): 80.

31 Ibid., 80, 84.

32 Joëlle Droux, "La tectonique des causes humanitaires. Concurrences et collaborations autour du Comité de protection de l'enfance de la Société des Nations (1880–1940)," *Relations internationales* 151, no. 3 (2012): 77–90.

33 Clare Mulley, *The Woman Who Saved the Children: A Biography of Eglantyne Jebb, Founder of Save the Children* (Oxford: Oneworld, 2009).

34 Cabanes, *Great War and the Origins of Humanitarianism*, 296–297.

35 *Congrès international de protection de l'enfance* (Paris: Impr. F. Deshayes, 1928), 680–681, 693.

36 Ibid., 715–716.

37 Association internationale des juges des enfants, Première assemblée générale de l'Association internationale des juges des enfants. Journées des 26, 27, 28 et 29 juillet 1930 (Brussels: Office de publicité, 1931), 1–2.

38 Paul Wets, Première assemblée générale de l'association internationale des juges des enfants, journées des 26, 27 et 28 juillet 1930 (Brussels: Œuvre nationale de l'enfance, 1931), 258–260.

39 Joëlle Droux, "Migrants, apatrides, denationalizes," *Revue d'histoire de l'enfance "irrégulière"* 14 (2012): online, www.rhei.revues.org.

40 David Niget, "L'enfance irrégulière et le gouvernement du risque," in *Pour une histoire du risque: Québec, France, Belgique*, ed. David Niget and Martin Petitclerc (Québec: Presses de l'Université du Québec; Rennes: Presses universitaires de Rennes, 2012), 297–316.

41 For the social policy models of the LON and the International Labour Organization, see Sandrine Kott, "Une 'communauté épistémique' du social? Experts de l'OIT et internationalisation des politiques sociales dans l'entre-deux-guerres," *Genèses* 71, no. 2 (2008): 26–46.

42 Henryka Veillard-Cybulska, *La protection judiciaire de la jeunesse dans le monde. Ses débuts* (Brussels: Association Internationale des Magistrats de la Jeunesse [AIMJ], 1966), 100.

43 Ibid., 185.

44 Margo De Koster and David Niget, "Scientific Expertise in Child Protection Policies and Juvenile Justice Practices in Twentieth-Century Belgium," in *Scientists' Expertise as Performance: Between State and Society, 1860–1960*, ed. Joris Vandendriessche, Evert Peeters, and Kaat Wils (London: Pickering and Chatto, 2015), 161–172.

45 Retranscription of his inaugural speech in L'association internationale des magistrats de la jeunesse (AIJE) et ses congrès (Brussels: AIJE, 1970), 13.

46 Yves Denéchère, "Diplomaties privées et autonomisation des ONG humanitaires dans l'espace de la cause des enfants," *Monde[s]* 7 (2014): 1–17.

47 L'association internationale des magistrats de la jeunesse (AIJE) et ses congrès (Brussels: AIJE, 1970), 15.

48 "Société des nations. Principes applicables aux tribunaux pour mineurs et organismes analogues, aux services auxiliaires et aux institutions destinées aux enfants," *Revue de Droit pénal et de criminologie* 17 (1937): 782–798.

49 Ibid., 789.

50 Wanda Woytowicz Grabinska, "Le problème de l'éducation des enfants dévoyés et délinquants," *Le Service social* 9–10 (September–October 1934): 129.

51 Speech by Mr. Louis Gros, spokesperson of the Department for Social Affairs at the UN, "Troisième congrès de l'Association internationale des juges des enfants (Liège, 17–20 juillet 1950)," *Protection de l'enfance*, Ministère de la Justice, Office de la protection de l'enfance, s.d., 44; Tara Zahra, *The Lost Children: Reconstructing Europe's Families after World War II* (Cambridge: Harvard University Press, 2011).

52 "Troisième congrès de l'Association internationale des juges des enfants (Liège, 17–20 juillet 1950)," *Protection de l'enfance*, Ministère de la Justice, Office de la protection de l'enfance, s.d., 44.

53 Dominique Marshall, "Peace, War, and the Popularity of Children's Rights in Public Opinion, 1919–1959. The League of Nations, the United Nations, and the Save the Children International Union," in *Children and War: A Historical Anthology*, ed. James Alan Marten (New York: New York University Press, 2002), 184–199.

54 This is true of the new International Union for Child Welfare (IUCW); UNESCO Archives, Registry, 1946–1956, "Child, UN appeal" dossier.

55 Archives of the Association des magistrats de la jeunesse et de la famille (no. de versement 2005–033), cote 66. Fonds CNAHES, Archives nationales de France, site de Pierrefitte-sur-Seine.

56 AMJF Archives (2005–033), cote 102.

57 "La guerre et la délinquance juvénile. Conférence d'experts réunie à Genève du 29 avril au 2 mai 1947 au Secrétariat de l'Union internationale de protection de l'enfance", *Revue internationale de l'enfant* 11, nos. 2–3 (1947).

58 Ibid., 57.

59 Ibid., 59.

60 "Troisième congrès de l'Association internationale des juges des enfants (Liège, 17–20 juillet 1950)", *Protection de l'enfance*, Ministère de la Justice, Office de la protection de l'enfance, s.d., 18.

61 Ibid., 24–25.

62 Ibid., 25. For casework, see Karen W. Tice, *Tales of Wayward Girls and Immoral Women: Case Records and the Professionalization of Social Work* (Urbana: University of Illinois Press, 1998).

63 Ibid., 26.

64 Jean Chazal, "L'examen médico-psychologique et social des mineurs délinquants," *Revue internationale de criminologie et de police technique* 6, no. 4 (October–December 1952): 290–301.

65 "Troisième congrès de l'Association internationale des juges des enfants (Liège, 17–20 juillet 1950)," *Protection de l'enfance*, Ministère de la Justice, Office de la protection de l'enfance, s.d., 48 and 50.

66 Ibid., 23.

67 Association internationale des juges des enfants, *Actes du 4ᵉ congrès, Bruxelles, 16–19 juillet 1954*, Imprimerie pénitentiaire, s.d., 56.

68 Ibid.

69 The 1954 congress contains a detailed report of the functioning of the Domestic Relations Court of the City of New York. Association internationale des juges des enfants, *Actes du 4ᵉ congrès, Bruxelles, 16–19 juillet 1954*, Imprimerie pénitentiaire, s.d., 96–107.

70 Ibid., 294.

71 Ibid., 295.

72 Chazal became the president of the association at the end of the 1954 congress. *L'association internationale des magistrats de la jeunesse (AIJE) et ses congrès* (Brussels: AIJE, 1970), 28–29.

73 Louise Bienvenue, "La 'rééducation totale' des délinquants à Boscoville (1941–1970). Un tournant dans l'histoire des régulations sociales au Québec," *Recherches sociographiques* 50, no. 3 (2009): 507–536; A. Wills, "Delinquency, Masculinity and Citizenship in England 1950–1970," *Past & Present* 187, no. 1 (2005): 157–185.

74 L'association internationale des magistrats de la jeunesse (AIJE) et ses congrès (Brussels: AIJE, 1970), 48.

75 Ibid., 50.

76 Ibid., 58.

77 Ibid.

78 Graham Burchell, Colin Gordon, and Peter Miller, *The Foucault Effect: Studies in Governmentality* (Chicago: University of Chicago Press, 1991).

79 On authoritarian regimes, see Nicholas Stargardt, *Witnesses of War: Children's Lives under the Nazis* (New York: Knopf, 2006); Antonio Gibelli, *Il popolo bambino. Infanzia e nazione dalla Grande Guerra a Salò* (Turin: Einaudi, 2010); Anne Gorsuch, *Youth in Revolutionary Russia: Enthusiasts, Bohemians, Delinquents* (Bloomington: Indiana University Press, 2001); Juliane Fürst, *Stalin's Last Generation: Soviet Post-war Youth and the Emergence of Mature Socialism* (Oxford: Oxford University Press, 2012).

80 Apart from the East-West conflict mentioned here, the question of young people's rights conflicting with the law, important in the North, remains a blind spot in the South for magistrates in the international association. This different conception of children's rights, at a time of globalization, bears witness to a fragmented citizenship. Cf. also Heather Ellis, "Introduction: Constructing Juvenile Delinquency in a Global Context," in *Juvenile Delinquency and the Limits of Western Influence, 1850–2000*, ed. Heather Ellis (Houndmills, Basingstoke: Palgrave Macmillan, 2014), 1–16.

81 David S. Tanenhaus, *The Constitutional Rights of Children: In re Gault and Juvenile Justice* (Lawrence: University Press of Kansas, 2011).

82 Francis Bailleau and Yves Cartuyvels, *The Criminalisation of Youth: Juvenile Justice in Europe, Turkey and Canada* (Brussels: VUB University Press, 2011).

83 Franklin E. Zimring and Máximo Langer, "One Theme or Many? The Search for a Deep Structure in Global Juvenile Justice," in *Juvenile Justice in Global Perspective*, ed. Franklin E. Zimring, Maximo Langer, and David S. Tanenhaus (New York: New York University Press, 2015), 383–411.

2

The Modernization of Authority

Juvenile Delinquents and Their Caseworkers
in Postrevolutionary Mexico City

SHARI ORISICH

The rapid growth of Mexico City's population between the 1930s and the 1970s, along with new forms of public entertainment, industrial expansion, and a burgeoning consumer culture, presented challenges to urban governance in the first decades after the Mexican Revolution. Rural to urban migration as well as a decline in infant mortality rates saw more children and adolescents in Mexico City than ever before.[1] Minors' use of urban space was especially disconcerting to police, local businesses, tourists, and the growing numbers of middle-class residents in the capital. Social scientists argued that parents who allowed youth to work as newspaper boys, street vendors, or in one of the hundreds of small workshops that dotted the city placed them at risk of exploitation, vice, and physical harm. If youth were not working in this informal sector, their use of city parks, sidewalks, and movie houses drew public outcries over the threat of gangs, public harassment, begging, purse-snatching, and the generalized fear of the decline of revolutionary family values built around productivity, sobriety, thrift, and discipline.[2] Many criminologists and sociologists considered parents' lack of supervision and, in other cases, their bad example of drunkenness or prostitution as the cause of children's criminal behavior. And while work in the informal economy—shining shoes, washing cars, laundering clothes—was seen as a necessary evil for the *clases humildes*, or the popular classes, it was also believed to contaminate the development of what scientists considered a "normal" childhood, a concept itself that emerged in contrast to juvenile delinquency. Media echoed the idea of "youth at-risk," calling working-class and poor youth a "plague" on public space designed to be modern, alluring, and safe for commerce and leisure.

This chapter examines one of the new federal institutions that forged Mexico's welfare state in the 1930s through the 1960s, the juvenile court, founded in 1926. The inauguration of the juvenile court was, in the eyes of Mexican criminologist Salvador Lima, "the most glorious spiritual achievement of the Mexican Revolution."[3] It represented the culmination of social reformers' aims for the protection and regeneration of Mexican youth and spoke to the centrality of youth in rebuilding the nation and the state in the first decades after Mexico's violent revolution. My approach to this institutional history looks at transformations in the juvenile court in this period by examining the role of state agents in the process of the consolidation of the postrevolutionary government. After their arrest, minors were sent to the juvenile court where batteries of tests were performed before they were assigned a caseworker. Social workers had access to the most intimate details of young people's lives—their work history, friendships, level of education, home life, and sexual history—via the process of interviewing both the minor and any relatives or neighbors who appeared in court or in their home investigations. Their final report, called the social study (*estudio social*), was the longest part of the minor's case file. It contained opinions of these state agents, their accumulated data from exams by doctors and psychologists on the minor's mental and physical health, and caseworker's final recommendations to the judge.

A historical analysis of these studies reveals the influence of transnational ideas about science, crime, and social reform in forging ideas about delinquency and groups deemed at risk, or "in danger of perversion," in the language of the Mexican courts. Understanding how risk was defined and determined also illustrates the working of postrevolutionary politics at both the institutional level and the level of everyday experience. Institutions like the juvenile court reflected the modern practices of inkblot tests, intelligence tests, and blood scans used across correctional systems in Europe and the United States. The authority to determine who was at-risk became part of the correctional discourse taken up by new experts in criminology, sociology, and medicine. The power to access homes, interview families, and build a knowledge base about children and adolescents "in danger of perversion" reveals the concomitant modernization of authority taking place in these new institutions and in the growing metropolis. The expanded police force to handle delinquency, the numerous studies conducted in the laboratories of the juvenile court, and the use of parole to monitor minors' work and education performance were all expressions of this new power relationship between citizens and the state.

The juvenile court was a showpiece of the postrevolutionary government's reformist impulse, yet little is known about the social workers who carried out this mission. Reading minors' case files "along the archival grain," as historian Ann Stoler describes, reveals the methods and logic shared by civil servants in creating modern knowledge about youth and crime.[4] Because scientific claims about criminality became authoritative explanations of transgressive behavior, this chapter also seeks to revisit the relationship between authority and experience that has been reignited in new scholarship by political theorists.[5] Studying juvenile delinquency provides a window into this struggle for authority in modern Mexico. For one, poor youth comprised the overwhelming majority of minors brought in to the juvenile court. They did not just challenge authority as represented by law enforcement or family, but delinquency raised the specter of social disorder, backwardness, and degeneracy. My analysis of juvenile court records considers the agency of minors as a legitimate force in the production of the correctional discourse, as much as in the work of social scientists and doctors in the court. What is revealed in the lacunae of these reports is a look into the politics of everyday life, yielding a new understanding of both the critical role social scientists played in building the modern, postrevolutionary state, and the reactions of youth to modernity.

Transnational and Local Foundations of the Juvenile Court

In 1920, a new judicial law (Ley Organica de los Tribunales del Fuero Comun) was passed that created a separate court for the protection of families and the rights of minors, but it functioned mainly as a civil and penal protection for wives, mothers, and minors under 18, and never broke very firmly with the adult criminal justice system. In the First Congress of the Mexican Child a year later, plans were approved for the creation of the juvenile court. In 1924, President Plutarco Elías

Calles founded the first Federal Council of Childhood Protection and two years later the governor of the federal district (*distrito federal,* or D. F., known as the area encompassing Mexico City) asked for a ruling to place the D. F. in charge of the establishment of the correctional system. Crucial to the formation of the juvenile court was not just the awareness of children as needing separate protection from adult offenders and different types of rehabilitation, but reformers argued that modern corrections required an understanding of infancy, childhood, and adolescence as distinct phases of human development. This warranted segregated facilities within the juvenile court and special approaches to rehabilitation based on age and gender.[6] In 1926, Roberto Solís Quiroga, professor of jurisprudence at Mexico's National Autonomous University (UNAM) and scholar of child pathology and psychology, and Salvador Lima, principal director of prisons in the federal district, coordinated to create the law that sought to establish a distinct juridical—but intentionally not penal—space for minors. The Centro Tribunal para Menores Infractores, or juvenile court, was inaugurated on December 10, 1926 and the first minors entered the court on January 10, 1927. The Mexican design and system operations were based on juvenile courts in Chicago (1899) and Philadelphia (1901), but Mexican reformers developed new specifications. The Mexican system would work to understand the complexities of delinquency arising from the new urban demographic. Specialized treatment practices were used to address mental deficiency, malnutrition, domestic dysfunction, and physical abuse, but, most importantly, the juvenile court was planned to operate as a "systems of corrections" rather than as an institution of punishment, with various correctional homes and schools attending to rehabilitation needs with different levels of surveillance and freedom of movement. Lastly, the idea of supervised freedom (*libertad vigilada*) would be introduced as a type of probation for minors who committed one or more infractions. *Libertad vigilada* would require the court to make home visits and periodic checkups to the minor's school and place of employment to ensure that "moral convalescence" was taking place.[7]

Historian Donna Guy observes how the birth of Pan Americanism in this same period reflected the region's shared interests in protecting youth from urban dangers, including neglect and abandonment, as a consequence of dual-income heads of household and the problem of absentee fathers. Inspired by talks from the First Mexican Congress on the Child (1921), the creation of the National Association for the Protection of Childhood (1924), and the Pan American Child Congresses of the early twentieth century, physicians, sociologists, educators, and criminologists saw the formation of normal childhood and adolescence as a key to progress. Their policies were written as a "guiding light for hemispheric reform."[8] By the 1930s, Mexico's juvenile court, informed by this field of new experts, created observation centers for psychological, intelligence, and blood tests, interviewing rooms, and cells to hold minors prior to their sentencing.

The juvenile court proved to be a work-in-progress that established and reaffirmed its place as a social institution of regeneration in the decades following its inauguration in 1926. The demand for social workers in Mexico City in the postrevolutionary period was tied to the proliferation of welfare agencies that required the intervention of state agents who needed to assess the private lives of those receiving state assistance.[9] Their professionalization was also connected to the existence and expansion of the juvenile court. In the popular press, for example, reporters made periodic calls for the necessity of social workers in Mexico City. Historian Jeroen J. H. Dekker's observation of "the history of risk [as] a story of expansion"[10] helps us to understand the role of new urban professionals and the birth of the idea of "at-risk" in Mexico City. The child sciences, which were themselves the product of the rationalization of childhood, became a path of discovery of the "magical" secrets of the life of the child, believing it was something that could and *should* be known.[11] Social workers were a bridge between the scientific and the social, utilizing their connections to criminologists and court physicians, and their privileged access to minors' homes and barrios, to develop the concept of "at-risk" youth. However, these ideas were not developed in isolation.

Training for social work was truly a transnational process, informed by scholars from sociology, education, jurisprudence, medicine, criminology, and psychology who came to Mexico to study and participate in conferences and conduct research. Numerous teachers from normal schools in the US came to Mexico in the 1930s to participate in the cultural mission of rural education, and these educators had taken short courses in social worker training in the US.[12] Mexican social workers also studied in the US, with scholars from both nations utilizing data and theories from European studies. Mexico's postrevolutionary institutions focused on the socialization of the working class and the poor and gave social workers who were operating within a transnational milieu the chance to apply their training to local and national projects.

Some of the first state agents of Mexico's welfare government worked at the centers of Infant Hygiene and Medicine, established in 1922 by Dr. Isidro Espinoza de los Reyes. He recruited a group of mostly female investigators to study and document the sanitation practices and social lives of women of the popular classes who were seeking state medical assistance for their children. Espinoza also worked with physician Aquilino Villanueva in creating the National Institute of Child Protective Services in 1929 and designated 10 "special inspectors of public assistance" to investigate the home and work life of those families that solicited help from welfare institutions. These inspectors would make home visits to families seeking state help, interview relatives and neighbors, and then make conclusions determining their level of need. According to sociologist María Luisa Flores González, these inspectors were typically drawn from a pool of women from *buenas familias* (good families) who were wealthy, sometimes widowed, and therefore had leisure time to devote to philanthropy. However, their lack of education, sometimes limited to the third or fourth year of schooling, notes Flores González, prompted administrators to recommend more rigorous training, and to look to places outside of Mexico that already had well-developed curricula as potential sites of education for Mexican professionals.[13] For instance, after several attempts to secure funding for Mexican social workers to study in the US, the director of the School of Domestic Training, Professor Julia Nava de Ruiz Sánchez, was finally awarded scholarships for her students to study in the US and return to Mexico armed with knowledge and training to build the profession at home.[14] This exchange fostered a broader network of binational collaboration and study through grants provided by the Mexican government and private Mexican companies like Sears and Roebuck of Mexico, Coca-Cola, Anderson Clayton, and 3M, which sent UNAM students in the 1950s to study in US universities.[15] The professionalization of social work in Mexico was also integrated into development programs such as the Alliance for Progress, built in 1961 under President John F. Kennedy. With international support from the Alliance, more schools of social work formed and others were retooled to train state agents to deal more directly with the social realities of poverty and crime and to develop interinstitutional projects to respond to these realities.[16] The influence of developmentalism in social work engendered what scholar Aida Valero Chavez refers to as the Movement of Reconceptualization of Social Work in 1967, centered at UNAM, where debates from both inside and outside the field assessed the necessity of the social worker in the postwar period, standards of preparation, use of scientific methods, and alternative approaches to understanding and solving social problems.[17] Contemporary Mexican sociologist Diego Ezekiel Pereyra has noted the confluence of ideas streaming from Auguste Comte, Max Weber, Émile Durkheim, and Georg Simmel, including the work of US sociologists like George Lundberg, Pauline Young, and Robert Park that were referenced in most student handbooks of the 1930s and 1940s.[18] What Pereyra's analysis illustrates is how methods of social work and training were transnational from the start and how academic presses, like the Journal of Mexican Sociology (*Revista Mexicana de Sociología*), shaped that exchange through its publications and by holding over 16 national conferences from 1951 to 1965 to advance the field.[19]

The inauguration of the juvenile court in 1926 also had an immediate measurable impact on the development of social work: in just two years after the tribunal was created, UNAM began to design specific courses for personnel and caseworkers who would staff the many clinics and offices of the court. This program was still considered "experimental" until delegates of the juvenile court demanded more unified training among caseworkers, leading to the direct implementation of a new three-year program of study in 1940 that established the social work career track through the Department of Jurisprudence and Social Science at the UNAM campus.[20] In 1954, UNAM adopted changes to the plan of study that reflected what Eli Evangelista observed were new methodological considerations. The expanded curriculum included enhanced coursework within the three-year plan in the areas of psychology, biology, anthropology, psychopathology, and mental hygiene, reflecting the growing influence of psychology in institutional and therapeutic settings.[21] Reflecting on the First National Congress of Social Research in 1950, Mexican sociologist Oscar Uribe Villegas recognized that sociology's roots in positivist thought—the "Comtian inspiration" of work by its earliest practitioners, Justo Sierra and

Gabino Barreda—shaped the discipline's early specialized, ethnographic research of the late 1920s, explained Uribe, who also forged the use of eugenic biotypes to scientifically classify and rationalize bodies to "measure" the norms of a social group."" Clinicians and social workers in the juvenile court utilized practices like precise body measurement and tracked potentially "dangerous" lines of inheritance to build more comprehensive life histories of minors, which would in turn inform the sentencing and program of rehabilitation.

Nowhere are the positivist and eugenicist influences in social work clearer than in the *Manual de Trabajo Social* (Social Work Manual) written by Dr. Alfredo M. Saavedra who was a founding member and lifetime president of the Mexican Eugenics Society formed in 1931. In her pioneering work on eugenics in Latin America, Nancy Leys Stepan notes how Saavedra had argued for "an extensive program of eugenically oriented sex education" that received a lot of national press but was never implemented.[23] His influence in social work was greater, and he successfully expanded the notion of social work beyond the job of public assistance services. Saavedra's manual was less of a practical guide to social work—although he included methods for interviewing and necessary lines of questioning—than a philosophical and intellectual handbook that laid out the biological, social, and minor technical aspects of the job. Referring to social work as a "noble art" and an "apostolic mission," he transferred the honor of religious charity to the caseworker who sought to understand poverty and crime while simultaneously promoting the modern status of the field.[24] Saavedra's work underscored the strong currents of eugenic thought in social work training in Mexico and conceptualized social problems in terms of weak inheritance related to alcoholism in parents or poverty; unstable home life, which could include absentee or abusive parents; and more generalized individual psychopathologies that would help caseworkers determine "at-risk" youth.

In her 1949 essay printed in the *Revista Mexicana de Sociología*, US sociologist Pauline V. Young, who studied under Professors Ernest Burgess and Robert Park at the University of Chicago in the 1920s and was a frequent contributor to Mexican sociological publications and conferences, claimed that the interview was the most penetrating tool in the discovery of the "real" origins of social problems. For Young, and the contemporaries Beatrice Webb and Emory S. Bogardus that she cited, the interview was one of the most important instruments in the case-worker's toolkit; it had the power to make the subject recall significant details of places, events, and social interactions where "attitudes, opinions, and prejudices were embraced, to document an accurate account of experiences that lie behind conflict and accommodation."[25] The personal interview promised to provide the personal point of view of the client, a picture of the cultural and social world in which the person lived, what stimuli shaped his or her personality and relationships, and the details of habits and events of the past that had determined his or her troubled present. Better than simple observation, interviewing developed "new spheres of knowledge" on sectors of the populace, such as juvenile delinquents, that were previously unknowable. And while history as a discipline "is interested in each unique event as it actually occurred in time and place," claimed sociologist Vivien Palmer, "sociology's aim is to abstract from these individual events the laws and principles of social interaction, irrespective of time and place."[26]

Reading "Along the Grain" of the *Estudio Social*

The interview that formed the basis for the social worker's study is, itself, a historical document that holds the traces of debates over subject testimony, the role of the observer, and the perceptions held by established experts in sociology, law, psychology, and criminology on the growing ranks of social workers, a majority of whom were women. The documents that came to be used in standardized question and answer methods for sociology were embedded with contemporaneous ideas about race and ethnicity, gender, and urban life that permeated the science of investigation for decades beyond their first use. With its roots in the prolific ethnographic studies coming out of the Chicago school of sociology between the 1890s and the Second World War, students of Burgess and Park employed these techniques in their interrelated projects and "wove a 'theoretical tapestry' in which patterns of social relations emerged and reinforced each other for more than four decades."[27]

Vivian Palmer, another graduate of the Chicago school, pioneered early methods of questioning for sociology in her foundational work, *Field Studies in Sociology: A Student's Manual* (1928), which were reproduced in sociology textbooks for years, and her own text was published throughout Latin America and used in classes for social work certification. In the first edition of her book published in 1928, she stressed the importance of making use of case analyses, the use of diaries, and the life history approach—the guided self-narration of a subject's story—as central to proper data collection. She argued that the "attitudes of individuals interviewed are the most distinctive contribution to the social research interview, as significant to the sociologist, not as individual expressions but as representative expressions of different groups of which the person is a member."[28]

According to social worker Lizbeth del Carmen Perez Irabien, working in the 1950s, the fundamental portion of the case file was the *estudio social*. Social workers, she argued, should interview the minor to try and exact not just a confession but the minor's own reasoning for bad behavior. Social workers should make the minor believe that the juvenile justice system has the capacity to reform them and that judges and other experts of the court are sincere in considering his or her well-being.[29] The technical aspects of social work in Saavedra's manual outlined the interview questions for caseworkers that included the birth and death of parents; their place of origin; sibling information to include work, sexual partners, and education of brothers and sisters; the home life of the minor; typical daily meals; number of light fixtures in the home; occupations held by father and mother; type of clothing worn; furniture material and number of pieces; available medicines; family income and savings; number of people living in the home; recreation or leisure activities; and so on.[30] Some of this information could be observed, while other personal information required the social worker to interview family members, neighbors, employers, and teachers, who were also considered important sites of contact for building the minor's case file.

In this way, the *estudio social* is a single narrative with many voices. The professional language encompassing varying scientific disciplines within the court, the verbatim interview of the minor, the caseworker's analysis, and dialects from family, friends, bosses, and neighbors is echoed in Mikhail Bakhtin's concept of *heteroglossia*, making this social study a rich and multidimensional source.[31] The social study of juvenile offenders—in what appear as recorded dialogue or sociological research notes—was not the end product of the social worker's investigation, but it was a discursive device that communicated who and what constituted delinquency in Mexico City, a discourse that reflected deeper class and cultural anxieties in a time of great social change.

In addition to obtaining knowledge about the immediate crisis that landed the client in the court, the interview had to cut far and wide across the life of the subject, with no query seeming too insignificant or intrusive for the accumulation of knowledge about the life of the minor. Regardless of the charge, minors were questioned about family background—birthplaces, dates, work histories of grandparents and parents—as well as personal hobbies and interests, places of employment, names of friends, religious affiliations, and frequency of masturbation and first sexual experience.[32] As a subtext, interviewers were also trained to observe the behavior of the minor during the interview process. Social workers made regular notes on the conduct of the interviewee during questioning, as some appeared "timid," "nervous," "mendacious," "lazy," "crafty," "sincere," and "guilty" in social workers' notes.[33] Young's article in the *Revista Mexicana Sociología* stated that

> [i]nterviewing was more than just the question and answer of the census taker . . . it is a *verbal laboratory study.* The primary interest is in the answers, but also the attitude and conduct of the subject are revealed, including his gestures, facial expressions, tone of voice—all are applicable in reaching our goal and purpose.[34]

As minors in the court revealed the corresponding details of his or her life, they simultaneously provided new knowledge about adolescent and childhood behavior, and submitted to the new representations of authority in modern Mexico, social workers. But not all young people would readily expose the intimate details of their personal lives, and the case files provide evidence of the ways in which they negotiated their position as delinquents in the system.

Writing Life Histories: The Interview and the Home Visit in Practice

The following cases reveal the methods of the interview and home visit, and also highlight the significant role of the social worker in creating categories of "at-risk youth." The studies also reflect how their views of home environment or heredity built up notions of class difference around this new social knowledge and shaped the futures of young people who entered the court.

When David A. entered the juvenile court on September 11, 1943, it was not his first time being held in the Center for Observation of the tribunal, awaiting the formal interview by a court-appointed social worker, but this visit perhaps had him feeling more anxious than before. The caseworker for his current violation, Esther Juárez, would learn through her own research of court records about David's prior arrests for vagrancy that after his release from the tribunal 12 months ago, David had failed to return home and instead did odd jobs for food and money: performing household chores for neighbors, working as a *voceador* for a newspaper vendor, and selling straw baskets that a street peddler taught him to weave by hand.[35] But these jobs had only allowed him to continue to live "without order" and as "a libertine," in the social worker's eyes. He was, in her description, "morally and materially abandoned," lacked self-discipline, and his current infraction, engaging in a "sex act" with another boy in Chapultepec Park, was, for Juárez, proof of his lack of self-control and proper guidance. When further questioned about his sexual history, 15-year-old David would reveal to Juárez his first sexual experience occurred one year ago in the very same juvenile court where he was now being questioned. There he was raped by several other boys who were also awaiting interrogation and sentencing in one of the dirty, overcrowded cells; David's cries of help to the security guards standing nearby were heard, but he claimed that they denied his pleas, saying that it was "not their job to take care of him." From this moment on, according to the social worker, David had become a homosexual and continued to develop this "vice" with other vagrant boys both in and outside the tribunal. Armed with Esther Juárez's report, the panel of three judges resolved that David required more schooling and recommended that he should learn "a useful and honest trade" in one of the youth workshops of the Escuela de Orientación para Varones, a correctional facility for boys that traditionally harbored the worst juvenile offenders. Having "confessed" to homosexual "habits" during his interview, the judges also suggested that David receive some specialized, though undisclosed, medical treatment that would help to "disappear his homosexual instincts."[36]

In the case of nine-year-old Jesús R., the social worker assisting judge and famed criminologist Dr. Roberto Solís Quiroga claimed the twin corruptions of the street and hereditarian alcoholism worked against Jesús by fostering an "abnormal" childhood. His mother wrote to the Tribunal on June 20, 1937 soliciting their help to detain her "incorrigible" son whom she claimed never obeyed authorities at home, was expelled for being a *guerrista* (agitator) at school, routinely sacked the house for items he could sell on the street for money, and ran around with other *malviventes* (bad kids) from the neighborhood.[37] The home visit took the social worker to his aunt and mother's apartment on Ecuador Street in the Colonia Obrero, a neighborhood that was described as "proletarian," "deficient," and "lacking in basic sanitation and transportation services." Not only was the proximity of cantinas and gambling venues a corruptive influence on the minor, argued the caseworker, but even the materials in his home's construction—wood and secondhand scrap—were considered "pernicious influences" contributing to Jesús's degeneration. His father had suffered from pulmonary disease and passed away five years prior to this arrest, though the social worker contended that his frequent alcohol consumption was likely the basis for his demise. Jesús's mother and aunt worked every day, including Sunday, in the neighboring barrio as domestic workers, but their "proper" example did not influence Jesús as much as his friends "El Pantera" and "El Máximo," members of the local *pandilla* (gang) who pressured him to steal from his aunt's home and from other residents on the outskirts of the Zócalo. His only job was an eight-day stint at a local pulquería (bar), and the social worker indicated that in his nine years Jesús had not yet learned any formal vocational training, only "bad" knowledge from *chicos viciosos*. Despite his clean record, judges of the juvenile court, after referencing his social study in their resolution, found him "in danger of perversion," and sentenced him to three months in the more lenient Children's Section of the Escuela de Orientación para Varones, which the section's administrator would later conclude was a disastrous decision. In the halls of the correctional school, employees observed how Jesús became even more of an agitator by inciting other minors to go on strike (*huelga*) in the reformatory's workshop, and by "fomenting bad habits like these among the other *alumnos* [students]." With these reports, judges approved Jesús's transfer to a stricter correctional facility for older boys (the same site that housed David A.) where he was sentenced to instruction in an undetermined "efficient vocation."[38]

From the interviews with David and Jesús we see how social workers drew from a confluence of often contradictory theories and research on biological determinism, environmental pathology, and psychological and sexual development to produce these new criminal biographies of youth. For minors like David, neo-Lamarckian notions of "bad" genes from his alcoholic father armed the social worker with an accepted explanation for his proclivity to crime and social disruption, and for Jesús his innate undisciplined behavior, combined with the trauma he experienced in the tribunal, conceived the "libertine" life that landed him in the court a second time. Looking at these minors through the lens of the social worker articulates the connections that the state was making between paucity, in terms of a moral and material existence, and criminality. While these characterizations exposed their social prejudices about the lower classes, it also articulated a position of frustration with the diverse ways in which youth challenged the norms of the family, the social mores in the city, education, and work. David's and Jesús's criminalized behaviors—homosexuality and the call to *huelga*—reflected the fears of social distortion produced by the pressures of demographic change and increasing number of young, indigent street workers and orphans in the capital.

The social studies also reflect the methods of training and comprehensive lines of questioning that caseworkers studied at UNAM. For example, David A.'s narrative, produced by Esther Juárez, indicates that she had direct contact with neighbors who verified his help in doing odd jobs, and that she used much of David's own voice in telling his story, using quotations in the file document to mark the points where David described how he was sexually assaulted in the tribunal. We can also deduce the fact that Juárez did not record the life history verbatim, but heard David's responses and then wrote the biography, with the palimpsest of his arrest for sexual deviancy and his history of trauma framing her account. Social workers, then, did not simply chronicle past events or document minor's responses, but tried to tell a story about young people, tried to make sense out of their behaviors, and, with or without their help, attempted to find a causal relationship between their social world and their acts of juvenile crime.

Similarly, in the case of Jesús, the detailed knowledge about family illness and parental work history indicates that the caseworker spoke either to the mother or aunt directly, and the record of his mother's stable and suitable work history seemed to explain that the defect was less in child-rearing and more in a damaged inheritance from an alcoholic father. Social workers offered their educated opinions on the reasons for bad conduct and delinquency, and these were then passed along to other clinics and halls of the court in the minor's file. Social workers had access to the homes, work, jobs, schools, and neighborhoods of young people more than any other specialist of the juvenile court, or state institution for that matter. It was made clear that these agents of the state were representative of the state's authority in public and private ways, seemingly without boundaries.

Conclusion

Reading against the grain of the social workers' narratives illustrates how the meaning and uses of juvenile delinquent life histories became foundational, contradictory, and multivalent texts in state formation, serving as both scientific evidence of the origins and consequences of transgressive behavior and as a scientific measure of social difference. The narratives also demonstrate how the welfare state produced modern forms of authority in three critical ways: in its institutional spaces, in the streets, and in the body of knowledge that was built on youth from the popular classes.

Though the possibilities for social inclusion of youth from the popular classes in the capital were limited to the informal sector, where work in city streets could place them "in danger of perversion," we can find instances where young people recognized the embryonic structures of citizenship that were tied to their work, friendships, education, and family life, and, in the absence or instability of any or all of these crucial pillars of society, found unapproved outlets to meet their basic needs and satisfy their youthful desires. Rather than seeing their "disobedience" as a universal symptom of puberty or growing up in the modern city, I contend that the strategies they might have shared—lying, pickpocketing, truancy, running away—with other adolescents across regional and national boundaries belong to a specific historical context. As much as reformers found problems with absentee parents, the transmission of "bad" traits, lack of access to education, and the burden of labor for poor and working class youth, there was little effort to understand why boys looked to each other for protection, friendship, education, and survival. As a history of *mentalités*, the sociological method of interviewing, once deconstructed, allows us to see how specialists in social work of the juvenile courts in Mexico shared beliefs about criminality and the rationalization of social groups that were developed within a transnational milieu based on a unified methodology with a local translation. The juvenile court places us at the site of the social investigators' efforts to build their profession and modernize authority in a rapidly changing urban environment, with much of that change, no doubt, coming from the youngest historical actors in the capital city.

NOTES

1 Census records show that in 1940, minors between the ages of 10 and 18 comprised a third of the inhabitants of the federal district; by 1970 nearly half of its population were under 15 and 56.7 percent were less than 20 years of age. See J. M. Pujol, "The Population of Mexico from 1950 to 2025: Demographic Indicators for 75 Years," in *Demos* 5, nos. 4–5 (1992). Also see Octavio Mojarro, Juan García, and José García, "Mortality," in *The Demographic Revolution in Mexico, 1970–1980*, ed. Jorge Martínez Manautou (Mexico City: Siglo XXI Editores, 1982), 378; and "Mortalidad infantil en México, 1990. Estimaciones por entidad federativa y municipio," in *XI Censo General de Población y Vivienda, 1990* (Mexico City: Siglo XXI Editores, 1992).

2 See Patience Schell, *Church and State Education in Revolutionary Mexico City* (Tucson: University of Arizona Press, 2003); Patricia Verinsky and Sherry McKay, introduction to *Disciplining Bodies in the Gymnasium: Memory, Monument, Modernity*, ed. Verinsky and McKay (London: Routledge, 2004), 2, 3–8; and Mary Kay Vaughan, *Cultural Politics in Revolution: Teachers, Peasants, and Schools in Mexico, 1930–1940* (Tucson: University of Arizona Press, 1997).

3 Elena Azaola Garrido, *La institución correccional en Mexico: Una mirada extraviada* (Mexico City: Siglo XXI Editores, 1990), 398.

4 Ann Laura Stoler, *Along the Archival Grain: Epistemic Anxieties and Colonial Common Sense* (Princeton, NJ: Princeton University Press, 2009), 21–23.

5 Claire Blencowe, Julian Brigstocke, and Leila Dawney, "Authority and Experience," in special issue on authority, *Journal of Political Power* 6, no. 1 (2013). The entire special issue addresses the themes laid out by Blencowe, Brigstocke, and Dawney.

6 José Angel Ceniceros and Luis Garrido, *La delincuencia infantil en Mexico* (Mexico City: Ediciones Botas, 1936).

7 Ibid., 10–18.
8 Donna Guy, "Pan-American Child Congresses, 1916–1942: Pan-Americanism, Child Reform, and the Welfare State," *Journal of Family History* 23, no. 3 (July 1998).
9 For a discussion of these institutional and organizational relationships in building the professional class of social work for women, see Nichole Sanders, "Gender, Welfare, and the 'Mexican Miracle': The Politics of Modernization in Postrevolutionary Mexico, 1937–1958" (PhD diss., UC Irvine, 2003).
10 Jeroen J. H. Dekker, "Children at Risk in History: A Story of Expansion," *Paedogicia Historica* 45, nos. 1–2 (February–April 2009): 19.
11 Dekker, "Children at Risk in History." On the expansion of the juvenile justice system and the parallel growth of childhood endangerment, or "the youth problem," see Ruth M. Alexander, *The "Girl Problem": Female Sexual Delinquency in New York, 1900–1930* (Ithaca, NY: Cornell University Press, 1995), and Mary E. Odem, *Delinquent Daughters: Protecting and Policing Adolescent Female Sexuality in the United States, 1885–1920* (Chapel Hill: University of North Carolina Press, 1995).
12 Aída Valero Chávez, "Apuntes sobre la genesis del trabajo social mexicano," in *Manual del trabajo social*, ed. Manuel Sánchez Rosado (Mexico City: UNAM, School of Social Work, 2004 [1999]), 14, 32.
13 Valero Chávez cites María Luisa Flores González, "La asistencia social en México," in *Tercer Foro Nacional de Trabajo Social* (Mexico City: Escuela Nacional de Trabajo Social, UNAM, 1982); see Valero Chávez, "Apuntes sobre la genesis," 12.
14 Sanders, "Gender, Welfare, and the 'Mexican Miracle'," 121. In 1959 several UNAM students spent five months at the University of Texas–Austin studying contemporary issues in personality development, mental health, and psychometric testing. They all had been students of Wayne Holtzman who was a professor of psychology at UT and had developed the inkblot for Mexican clinicians and had conducted cross-cultural analysis of personality traits.
15 Ibid., 25.
16 Ibid., 32.
17 Ibid.
18 Chávez, "Apuntes sobre la genesis." See also Lucio Mendieta y Nuñez, "La enseñanza de la sociología," in *Estudios sociológicos*, Primer Congreso Nacional de Sociología (Mexico City: Asociación Mexicana de Sociología, 1950), 37–48; Antonio Caso, *Sociología* (Mexico City: Porrúa, 1945); Oscar Uribe Villegas, *Técnicas estadísticas para investigadores sociales* (Mexico City: Universidad Nacional de Mexico, 1957).
19 Diego Ezekiel Pereyra, "A Review of Sociological Textbooks in Argentina and Mexico (1940–1960)," *Current Sociology* 56, no. 2 (2008): 267–287.
20 The core curriculum for first-year students consisted of courses in Mexican sociology, economics, the study of positive law, theories of social work, and psychology; second-year coursework included criminology, paidology (study of child

behavior and development), hygiene, general medicine, theory and practice of social work (part I), and instruction in children's sports; the third phase of social work education consisted of statistics, administrative organization, pathological psychology, puericulture (hygienic care of children including prenatal study), nutrition, and theory and practice of social work (part II). From Eli Evangelista, *Historia del trabajo social en México* (Mexico City: UNAM, School of Social Work, 1998), 92, 93.

21 Ibid., 119–124.

22 Marie-Christine Leps argues that with the emergence of positivist criminology— the study of "homo criminalis" as an object in the field of empirical, scientific knowledge rather than the study of the actions of the volitional subject—the development of mass media in the same period, and the rise of the novel and other popular literature, a new discourse of criminality was born. See Leps, *Apprehending the Criminal: The Production of Deviance in Nineteenth-Century Discourse* (Durham: Duke University Press, 1992). See also Piers Beirne, *Inventing Criminology: Essays on the Rise of Homo Criminalis* (New York: SUNY Press, 1993); Robert M. Buffington, *Criminal and Citizen in Modern Mexico* (Lincoln: University of Nebraska Press, 2000); Pasquale Pasquino, "Criminology," in *The Foucault Effect: Studies in Governmentality with Two Lectures by and an Interview with Michel Foucault*, ed. Graham Burchell, Colin Gordon, and Peter Miller (Chicago: University of Chicago Press, 1991). Early practices of measurement and identification, specifically Bertillonage, as nodes of surveillance and rationalization of groups were utilized to varying degrees among scientists in postrevolutionary Mexico, and they became a constituent element of criminogenic studies that took center stage at subsequent national congresses. Oscar Uribe Villegas discusses these influences in "Anotaciones del Quinto Congreso Internacional de Defensa Social," *Revista Mexicana de Sociología* 21, no. 1 (January–April 1959), 329–349. On criminogenics and the federal district, see Norman Hayner, "Mexico City: Its Growth and Configuration," *American Journal of Sociology* 50, no. 4 (January 1945): 295–304.

23 Nancy Leys Stepan, *The Hour of Eugenics: Race, Gender, and Nation in Latin America* (Ithaca, NY: Cornell University Press, 1991), 57, 58.

24 Alfredo M. Saavedra, *Manual del trabajo social* (Mexico City: UNAM, 1953), 13.

25 Pauline Young, *Interviewing in Social Work: A Sociological Analysis* (New York: McGraw Hill, 1935), 18, 21.

26 Vivien Palmer, *Field Studies in Sociology: A Student's Manual* (Chicago: University of Chicago Press, 1928), 23.

27 Mary F. Deegan, "The Chicago School of Ethnography," in *Handbook of Ethnography*, ed. Paul Atkinson, Amanda Coffey, Sara Delamont, John Lofland, and Lyn Lofland (London: Sage, 2001), 3.

28 Palmer, *Field Studies in Sociology*, 170.

29 Lizbeth del Carmen Pérez Irabién, "Orentaciones para el estudio de casos en los tribunales para menores," master's thesis for licensure (Mexico City: UNAM, 1961), 23–25.

30 Saavedra, *Manual de trabajo social*, 180–181.

31 In Lee Honeycutt's elucidation of Mikael Bakhtin, he stresses the importance of
considering how the vestiges of past conflicts and meanings make their way into
language: "Language is not a neutral medium that can be simply appropriated
by a speaker, but something that comes to us populated with the intentions of
others. Every word tastes of the contexts in which it has lived its socially-charged
life. Not only are there social dialects, jargons, turns of phrase characteristic of
the various professions, industries, commerce, of passing fashions, etc., but also
socio-ideological contradictions carried forward from various periods and levels
in the past. . . . Words bring with them, contexts." See Lee Honeycutt, "What Hath
Bakhtin Wrought? Toward a Unified Theory of Literature and Composition,"
master's thesis, University of North Carolina–Charlotte, 1994, chapter 2; accessed
November 29, 2010, www.public.iastate.edu.

32 This "panorama" of the social history, as described by Alfredo Saavedra, was
needed to provide the most intimate view of the boy or girl in question. In the
2,170 case studies sampled, almost all cases asked these questions, though each
social worker assigned to the case determined the breadth of detail in the report,
so in some cases answers reflect a simple "yes" or "no" or "I do not know" answer
from the minor or interviewee, while in other cases the answers are lengthier and
include the opinions of the caseworker. Saavedra also notes the importance of
developing this comprehensive knowledge as part of the social workers' investigations; see Saavedra, *Manual de trabajo social*, 153–160.

33 Ibid.

34 Young, "Las Tecnicas de la investigación social," 245.

35 "David A.," Archivo General de la Nación (AGN), Consejo Tutelar para Menores
Infractores (CTMI), vol. 187, file 33666. The last names of minors in the juvenile
court have been intentionally omitted.

36 "David A.," AGN, CTMI, vol. 187, file 33666.

37 "Jesús R.," AGN, CTMI, vol. 229, file 17216.

38 "Jesús R.," AGN, CTMI, vol. 229, file 17216.

3

The Search for Juvenile Delinquency in Colonial Zanzibar, East Africa

CORRIE DECKER

Unlike most other areas of the world during the first half of the twentieth century, juvenile delinquency never posed a serious problem for the British colonial administration in the Zanzibar Islands of East Africa.[1] The first authorities to deal with conflicts involving children and youth were the *masheha* (singular, *sheha*; local chiefs or elders) and the *mudirs* (urban officials who oversaw the *masheha*). Zanzibar's legal developments kept pace with British imperial interventions and the topic of juvenile delinquency frequently entered official discourse during the 1930s and 1940s. However, the actual number of juvenile offenders, those processed through the courts and prisons, was numerically insignificant during the colonial era (1890–1963). Thus, the British colonial state consistently refused to commit resources to juvenile justice. This does not tell the whole story, though. Officials in Zanzibar were willfully blind to both the extent of the problem of troubled youth and the social and economic dimensions that contributed to it. A close look at the debates about juvenile delinquency in colonial Zanzibar—the extent of the problem, its causes, and potential solutions—illuminates what British colonial officials could not see: that the problem did exist and that it was a symptom of the long-standing class and ethnic inequalities on the islands.

Scholars of juvenile justice have identified the turn of the twentieth century, the Century of the Child, as the beginning of formal state interventions in juvenile justice. In the United States, officials relied on informal avenues of dealing with difficult children and teens before juvenile courts and detention centers were in place. David Wolcott argues that before the establishment of juvenile courts in Detroit, police took advantage of the ambiguity of the law to separate juveniles from adults and direct them toward informal, protective services rather than adult prisons and courtrooms.[2] In Zanzibar, even after the Juvenile Offenders Ordinance passed in 1935, the juvenile courts were a secondary medium of discipline. Zanzibar was a legally pluralistic society, and before children and youth encountered colonial penal institutions they were dealt with by local chiefs or Islamic legal representatives (*masheha* and *mudirs*).[3] The formality of the juvenile justice system did not supplant the indigenous methods for disciplining children and youth.

This approach contrasts with those of British settler colonies. The juvenile criminal system in Kenya and South Africa, for example, took an aggressive stance toward juvenile delinquency and presumed that young criminal Africans were intellectually inferior to whites and would only respond to corporal punishment.[4] The methodical, eugenicist approach in Kenya and South Africa did not inform Zanzibari policies and practices. In contrast to these territories, Zanzibari boys and girls faced local officials (*mudirs* and *masheha*) before they appeared before colonial officers. Some scholars might view this as a more passive, laissez-faire approach to juvenile justice, but this was not the intention of the British colonial administration of the time.[5] When compared to juvenile justice philosophies in place in neighboring Kenya, for example, the lack of intervention in Zanzibar was not due to a British colonial philosophy of noninterference. Rather, officials in Zanzibar viewed the problem of juvenile delinquency as virtually nonexistent precisely because indigenous authorities dealt with these individuals before the colonial administration ever knew they existed.

In colonial Africa, juvenile delinquency was considered a by-product of urbanization and "detribalization" during the 1920s and 1930s.[6] Schooling, along with the Boy Scouts and Girl Guides, was the first systematic form of colonial intervention designed to control the behavior of children.[7] This tactic was modeled after nineteenth-century British policies such as universal schooling that sought to remove children from the workplace and urban streets.[8] The Youthful Offenders Act of 1854 identified juvenile delinquents as a separate legal category and criminalized destitute children.[9] British class ideologies and colonial race politics combined to stigmatize African children caught in the colonial legal apparatus.

Juvenile delinquency in colonial Zanzibar was loosely considered an urban issue. Zanzibar Town, which was "notorious for its immorality,"[10] rapidly expanded in size and population during the first few decades of the twentieth century.[11] Colonial officials believed that urban brothels, cinemas, and dance and music halls contributed to the lack of discipline among boys, but many of these subcultures dated back to the precolonial period when the city held more prominence in the Indian Ocean region.[12] From the time Zanzibar became the center of Omani plantations in the early nineteenth century, wealthy landholding families, including children, periodically moved to and from their urban and rural residences. The children of slaves, domestic servants, foodsellers, and others also frequently traveled between towns and villages with their parents or guardians. Europeans unfamiliar with this history of fluidity between urban and rural spaces on the island argued that the unsanitary and unsavory character of Zanzibar Town was especially dangerous for children.[13] The commandant of police stated in 1932, "It must be remembered that an uneducated child at large in a town is a potentially greater danger than an uneducated child in his own village."[14] The rural child became a threat once he was out of the control of his elders, a common fear about "detribalized" youth in colonial Africa.[15] Whereas, in places like Kenya and South Africa, the state went to great lengths to discipline and control juvenile delinquents, concerns about detribalization and the rise of youth in the towns did not preoccupy officials in Zanzibar to the same degree.[16] Comparison between the visibility of "vagrant" youth in Nairobi and Johannesburg and their invisibility in Zanzibar Town points to the very different colonial politics at work in settler versus nonsettler colonies, as well as the exceptionality of the Zanzibar case. At the same time, there was no distinct culture of urban juvenile delinquency in Zanzibar, certainly not to the extent that existed in settler colonies.[17] The racially tinged arguments about African degeneracy in colonial towns did not hold water on the Zanzibar Islands.

When and where children and young people were criminalized depended on local concepts of ethnicity and class. Omani rule prevailed on the Zanzibar Islands (Zanzibar and Pemba) for much of the nineteenth century, and the Arab sultans retained nominal power under the terms of the British Protectorate. The sultans and other landowners had grown wealthy off the East African slave trade and the islands' clove plantations fueled by slave labor. British colonialism resulted in the abolition of slavery on the islands, followed by widespread social and economic reorganization.[18] The ethnic composition of the islands' urban and rural communities was diverse and constantly in flux.[19] The tendency of the British administration and many Zanzibaris to oversimplify Zanzibar's ethnic categories into "Arabs" and "Africans" washed over this complexity and ignored the long history of intermarriage between indigenous islanders, those from the mainland, and Arab and other immigrants.[20] It also grouped indigenous landowning families with former slaves and their descendants to the chagrin of many. The categories "Arab" and "African" became euphemisms for the former ruling elites and their subjects (both slave and free), respectively. Ethnicity, and its corresponding class connotations, determined which children were identified as in need of intervention and which were ignored by the state.

Zanzibar's juvenile delinquents were always boys. Unlike other areas where concerns about girl hawkers and other disobedient girls arose, the Islamic gender segregation practices in Zanzibar meant that generally girls were not to be seen in public, and, if they were, they were covered and chaperoned.[21] At least that was the case with elite girls. Other girls might be seen about town working as domestic servants, market sellers, and laborers, but they seldom appear in the records. For most of the colonial era, the discourse on Zanzibari girls homes in on their need for education and protection from Islamic patriarchy.[22] In fact, one aspect of the 1935 Juvenile Offenders Decree, the first comprehensive juvenile justice legislation in Zanzibar, applied directly to girls—the stipulation that children in need of "care and protection" be handed over to a "fit person."[23] Because this part of the ordinance was intended to protect girls from early marriage and forced prostitution, it prevented the colonial state from seeing the ways in which boys, too, could be in need of "care and protection." Being invisible to the state prevented poor and homeless boys from accessing the kind of help the state provided for girls.[24]

Disciplining Youth through Schools and Courts

Before juvenile courts came into existence, the colonial administration sought to discipline "town boys" through the government schools.[25] In the early twentieth century, the term "town boys" referred to the offspring of wealthy Arab landowners who lived in Zanzibar Town off the profits they made from large clove farms and other plantations in the rural areas. In 1917, the British resident, as the colonial governor in Zanzibar was called, wrote that "an Arab boy does nothing but loaf." Complaining that parents provide their sons with concubines "when they are mere children" and that boys spend their money on "drink and evil companions," he directed his criticism toward both elite urban boys and the parents who were unable or unwilling to discipline them. The government schools sought to clear these boys from the streets and train them for positions in the administration.[26] In contrast to urban elite Arabs, the majority of Zanzibar's population (about 90 percent according to estimates of the time) consisted of the "Swahili or Native Zanzibari" (or "African" in colonial discourse), whom the British resident described as the "manual labourer of the country." This statement collapsed the distinction between former slaves brought to the islands from the mainland and indigenous Zanzibari farmers, merchants, and laborers. Colonial officials urged that the young African also required education, but his curriculum was geared toward training that fit his "normal pursuits."[27]

The class distinction between Arabs and Africans was reinforced in the different education policies designed for urban and rural children, though there was no direct correlation between ethnicity and geography. The first government boys' school, opened in 1905, emerged out of collaboration between the British government and Sultan Ali bin Hamud and was, at first, reserved for Arabs only. African students were gradually accepted into the schools, but the majority of teachers and administrators overseeing boys' schools were Arabs raised and educated in Zanzibar Town. From the simplified colonial perspective, urban boys were the sons of elites who were to become high-ranking government officials, schoolteachers, and other professionals whereas rural boys were the sons of laborers who would become clove pickers, small farmers, and fishermen, as well as "carpenters, blacksmiths, rope-makers . . . , masons, village shop-keepers, boat-builders . . . , tailors, traders, hawkers, overseers, seedy-boys on His Majesty's Ships, police, *askaris* [soldiers] of the King's African Rifles, private servants, Mosque Attendants, etc."[28]

During the first few decades of the twentieth century the government schools suffered from a lack of support from parents and children.[29] The schools offered free tuition through the primary course, yet they remained unpopular, especially in the villages.[30] Compulsory education for boys between five and nineteen years of age was introduced in 1921 to address the issue. In actuality, this only applied to the schools in Zanzibar Town and Chake Chake, the two largest towns, with a full staff and the support of local officials.[31] Compulsory education was a drastic measure and one impossible to realize because the government education system was still in its infancy. Had all of the boys in the protectorate abided by the law, the government would have had to immediately provide dozens of new schools. The law was a discursive statement of state power rather than a demonstration of the state's actual ability to direct and control urban male youth.

As a warning to parents, the names of truant schoolboys were published in the *Official Gazette*, but the police did not have the staff to go after them.[32] Between 1921 and 1924, only one boy was forcibly brought to school by the police.[33] Still, the tactic worked among the Arab elite. Arab parents in town agreed to force their boys to attend the Central Government School if the government agreed to run separate "Arab" from "African" classes and exempt their sons from the decree. By 1927, a significant number of urban Arab boys were attending schools and continuing on to the higher grades, though the upper classes of the African sections remained largely unattended.[34]

By the 1920s, undisciplined Arab boys were sent to the schools and African urban youth were increasingly sent to the courts to face their "crimes." Children and adolescents were fined, flogged, or sentenced to imprisonment for "landing without passport," engaging in "disorderly conduct," "gambling in a public place," being "a prohibited immigrant," "creating a disturbance in a public place," committing an "unnatural offence" (sodomy), trespassing, being drunk or in possession of alcohol, as well as the more serious theft, robbery, and violent crimes.[35] Many of these infractions reinforced the notion that lower-status and village boys did not belong in the town unless they had a legal work contract. The only educational proposal put forth for such boys living in town was the "industrial school" or "reform home."[36] Poor, "vagrant" boys appeared to some officials as a "serious social menace" because they were homeless, too young to work, and had the "inclination of earning their own living." They were on their way to becoming "habitual criminals."[37] These youths appeared to have no parents or morals and no interest in government schools.

The distinction between the obedient Arab schoolboy and the African vagrant rested on the question of labor. The education and juvenile justice policies directed Arab elites toward managerial positions and nonelites toward agriculture and other forms of manual labor. One reason for the lack of interest in government schools among Africans had to do with the fact that most government jobs were reserved for Arabs. This realization drove Africans to leave school and find work or other sources of income.

The labor issue preoccupied officials from the early colonial era. The Regulation of Adult Male Persons Decree of 1910 and the Native Labour Control Decree of 1917, for example, legalized compulsory labor and sought to transform "vagrants" into workers.[38] Yet these laws applied to adult men, not juveniles. The first laws directed at youth, other than those relating to general education, were the Apprentices Decree and the Reformatories Decree, both passed in 1926.[39] The Apprentices Decree regulated apprenticeships for young people between the ages of nine and sixteen. One section of the Apprentices Decree stated that the director of education had the right to order school officials to apprehend and return any apprentice who absconded from an institution or place of instruction, which fell in sync with the Compulsory Education Decree.[40] The Reformatories Decree was intended to deal with "youthful offenders and youthful vagrants" under the age of fourteen.[41] It laid out the terms under which an official could legally commit a child to a reform school. This was largely imaginary because there were no reformatories in Zanzibar.

It was not until the Juvenile Offenders Decree came onto the books in 1935 that Zanzibar established the juvenile courts and an official policy for dealing with children and youth who committed crimes. The law specified only that a "child" (someone under the age of fourteen) or a "young person" (someone between fourteen and sixteen years of age) had to appear before a juvenile court, which was defined as a court appointed by the chief justice that had to meet either in a different building or room, or at a different time, than the ordinary court. In Zanzibar, no official "juvenile court" existed, but the standard courtroom would transform into a juvenile court if a person sixteen years of age or younger came before the judge. There were other stipulations for juveniles, for example, journalists were not allowed to take photographs of young offenders or publish the names of children and youth in the newspapers. In essence, the juvenile court was an ad hoc institution that came into existence only when considered necessary. It is worth noting that this law appeared only one year after Zanzibar's Penal Code was reformed. The 1935 law was a reflection of both the child advocacy movement in Britain and judicial reform on the islands. Other stipulations of the Juvenile Offenders Ordinance could not be implemented because Zanzibar did not have juvenile detention centers. Still, the 1935 law was a turning point in identifying and managing the "juvenile offender." Modeled after Britain's 1933 Children and Young Persons Act, the decree dealt with both "juvenile offenders" and "children and young persons in need of care or protection."[42] The decree prohibited children under fourteen from being sentenced to imprisonment and discouraged the imprisonment of those under sixteen if they could be dealt with "by probation, fine, corporal punishment, committal to a reformatory or industrial school, or otherwise."[43] These rules did not apply to children who committed "grave" crimes such as homicide or who were otherwise dangerous and needed to be detained, though no death sentence could be given in these cases.

The Juvenile Offenders Decree discursively connected poverty to delinquency in Zanzibar. Children found "begging," "wandering," or "destitute," as well as those in care of a parent or guardian with "criminal habits," could be taken into custody or committed to the care of a "fit person or institution named by the Court," or both.[44] The colonial administration claimed the right to hold these children in "legal custody," though the decree included the caveat that the sultan could make additional rules regarding the detention and treatment of juveniles.[45]

Despite the emergence of juvenile justice legislation in the 1930s and the subsequent establishment of juvenile courts, most young offenders faced the same fate as those who came before them. They continued to be sentenced to flogging, fines, or short-term imprisonment. Throughout the 1930s, 1940s, and 1950s, the debate about whether or not to establish a reformatory or approved school in Zanzibar surfaced and resurfaced. Most officials played down the extent of the juvenile delinquency problem. By the late 1940s, after a reform school opened in

Tanganyika on the mainland, the most serious juvenile offenders from Zanzibar were sent there. Many of the rules laid out in the Reformatories Decree, the Juvenile Offenders Decree, and subsequent legislation thus never came into effect.

The "Very Small" Problem of Juvenile Delinquency

From the time of the Juvenile Offenders Decree of 1935 to the 1950s, officials repeatedly considered proposals to establish a reformatory for juvenile delinquents. The push for this plan came partly from officials in the Colonial Office who argued that juvenile offenders needed to be separated institutionally from both adults and nondelinquent children. In the early 1940s, juvenile offenders sentenced to imprisonment were often stationed at the same work camps where adult prisoners worked, though Zanzibari officials ensured the two groups did not mingle.[46] Zanzibar's chief justice and commissioner of police put additional pressure on the government to build a reformatory.[47] In 1947, a Juvenile Justice Committee was appointed to investigate the issue. Beyond concerns about contact between juvenile delinquents and "habitual criminals," they concluded that the best solution would be to provide a "School for Truant Children" rather than a correctional facility so as not to stigmatize the boys.[48]

Despite these endorsements, the administration could not muster the funds for the institution. Officials argued that were too few juvenile offenders to justify the cost. In 1935, for example, the number of cases per year in Zanzibar was "very small," only fifteen, and the numbers seemed to be falling.[49] Of these, only about five or six were sentenced to imprisonment. Based on these data, the attorney general believed that the expense of a reformatory was too high to reasonably consider the plan.[50] The same arguments, and similar statistics on the annual number of juvenile offenders sentenced to imprisonment, were repeated during the 1940s. Even some of those who strongly advocated the project were pessimistic about the likelihood of it coming to fruition.[51]

Other proposals surfaced. Though missions were historically unpopular in the predominantly Muslim Zanzibar Islands, the administration appealed to the Friends Industrial Mission on Pemba to run a reform school in 1932. As one of the first missions on the islands to offer accommodation and education to freed slaves, the Friends mission had a history of dealing with boys who lived away from their parents and who engaged in mischief, such as petty theft.[52] During the negotiations, the missionaries asked if they could proselytize among the boys.[53] The Executive Council, of which the sultan was a member, "strongly opposed" this type of religious instruction and told the missionaries they could neither preach Christianity nor obstruct any Muslim from engaging in his daily prayers.[54] The scheme was subsequently abandoned in 1933.

One experiment that did seem to work was the Police Department's Watoto Club (Boys' Club), an informal organization based in Malindi, at the north end of Zanzibar Town, started in the early 1930s.[55] The club was equipped with cooking and sleeping facilities and claimed to direct boys away from dangerous illegal activities on the town streets. Pleased with the apparent correlation between a reduction in juvenile crime and the existence of the Watoto Club, the commissioner of police suggested the club could be used as a place to temporarily detain a child or young person awaiting transfer to a reformatory. He offered to expand the club into a reformatory if the government could provide an annual grant of thirty pounds, the amount it would cost to send a boy to a reformatory in Kenya. In exchange, "the club would be able to look after, feed, and educate convicted juveniles."[56] The administration refused to commit recurring funds for the purpose, and the Watoto Club remained a small program for boys in the neighborhood until it closed permanently in 1947.[57]

In 1934, the government inquired into sending boys to reformatories in Kenya and Tanganyika, but the Kabete Reform School in Kenya did not have the room and Tanganyika had not yet established an approved school.[58] As a result of these failed schemes, the worst young offenders were sentenced to imprisonment and work in prison camps.[59] Still, the top administrators would not budge on their stance not to cover expenses for a reformatory and continued to insist that the numbers of juvenile delinquents on the islands was "very small."

Was juvenile delinquency really that insignificant in colonial Zanzibar? The answer depends on where one looked for "offenders." At the height of these debates in 1947, the registrar at the High Court noted that the resident magistrate had recently seen several boys "sleeping out in the streets by the police" and urged that they were "badly in need of special care and attention, if they are not to degenerate into criminals." This opened the door to his most biting criticism of the existing legislation, mainly that it considered "not having any home or settled place of abode or visible means of subsistence" an "offence." The proposed School for Truant Children, the registrar implored, was "not designed to meet the case of the juvenile delinquent but to meet that of the juvenile in need of care and protection."[60]

Two conclusions emerge from these points. First, the number of those who might have been considered "juvenile delinquent" according to the law was much larger than the records indicated. And, second, officials sometimes found it difficult to draw a line between the criminal and the destitute. Though the police and court officials had a legal obligation to deal with children who were "in need of care and protection," it is very likely that a poor child who came before the court but did not commit a serious crime was either acquitted or released on surety of "good behaviour," and therefore did not count in the books as a "delinquent."[61] Perhaps most officials did not take notice of the homeless groups of boys who wandered the streets of Zanzibar Town, a sight that in Nairobi or Johannesburg would have sparked fears of anticolonial uprisings and rampant criminality. Though "vagrant" boys were considered "offenders" by law, as long as folks did not feel they posed a threat they were likely left alone, which, in turn, created the illusion that there was no real problem of juvenile delinquency in Zanzibar.

A brief look at the court systems on the islands provides further insight into the small numbers of juvenile offenders. Colonial Zanzibar was a legally pluralistic society with a system of Islamic courts under the charge of *kadhis* (Islamic judges) and British courts under the authority of colonial magistrates and, ultimately, the chief justice of the High Court. In addition, there were somewhat informal district courts overseen by the *mudirs* (Zanzibari district officials appointed by the government) that had jurisdiction over "petty criminal cases."[62] The *kadhi* courts were based on local interpretations of *shari'a* (Islamic law). Initially during the colonial era, they had full jurisdiction over cases, but many of their functions were gradually taken over by the colonial courts. By 1930, they could no longer oversee criminal cases, nor high-stakes civil cases, and they were basically limited to "divorce and small disputes."[63] The British courts had the final say on any case that went to appeal. This judicial network, however, does not explain what people actually did when a child allegedly committed a crime.

Before a case involving a child would come before the *mudir, kadhi,* British judge, or even the police, the victims of the crime might have consulted the *sheha* (plural, *masheha*), the locally appointed elder or headman. During the nineteenth century, the *masheha* acted as a legislator, judge, and administrator, but by the end of the century the *kadhis* and *mudirs* had usurped much of the traditional authority of the *masheha*.[64] Still, as British colonial administrator W. H. Ingrams put it, the *masheha* acted "as a kind of glorified policeman, and he [had] statutory police powers of arrest," which meant he could very well have been the first "official" contacted in the event of a crime.[65] Some *masheha* wore a distinct uniform, including a badge, and settled disputes involving trespassing, theft, and minor assault.[66] In matters involving juveniles, the child's elders were generally the first authorities consulted as there was a tendency during the colonial era for a family not to air its dirty laundry in public.[67] In all likelihood, the primary reason Zanzibar's numbers of juvenile delinquents was so "very small" was that most cases of child criminality or misbehavior were dealt with by this community infrastructure for dispute resolution.

Some of this information about traditional dispute settlement came to light thanks to the work of the committee appointed to examine the problem of juvenile delinquency in 1947. Whereas Indians and Arabs tended to consult with the Indian Association and the Arab Association, respectively, on such matters, the committee noted that Africans often approached the *masheha*, members of the "Ng'ambo[68] Council, Police Officers and Tribal Headmen" first.[69] The fact that *masheha* rarely appear in official documentation on juvenile delinquency suggests that the colonial administration was willfully ignorant about juvenile cases outside the towns, where *masheha* had more influence. This, combined with the concentration of police and others reporting to the central colonial administration in Zanzibar Town, contributed to the disproportionate focus on urban delinquency. What they did not fully understand, however, was the extent to which conditions in the rural areas intertwined with the problem of "vagrant youth" in Zanzibar Town.

Ali Shariff Mussa, the African representative from Pemba Island appointed to the Legislative Council in 1947, explained what he considered the root causes of juvenile delinquency. There are certain "people of the town," he explained, who go to the plantations and offer to raise and educate a child. Mussa continued,

> The poor ignorant man of the shamba [farm] gives him [the child] because he thinks that it is true that his child is taken to be brought up mannerly. . . . But it is not so. That child . . . becomes a servant of the house. He is given a bucket or a tin to fill water inside, and is given a tray of confectionary or fried fish, and if the child is a girl she is given, besides these works, jasmine to sell, and many other sufferings reach them. These mishaps fall on both male and female.

He warned that if nothing was done about this problem, it would soon result in the outcome of "bad children and bad subjects." His statement that both girls and boys were affected may have been a strategy to grab the attention of officials as to the gravity of the situation.[70]

Mussa blamed both those claiming to be "tutors" for their dishonesty and the parents for being "ignorant." At the same time, he provided some context for understanding the circumstances under which a parent was willing to give up custody of his or her son. There were other children as well, those between the ages of ten and thirteen who ran away from home or were sent to town to work as a house servant and upon arrival became "mischievous." All of these juveniles were products of poverty in the villages.

The phenomenon of rural children working in the town with or without the consent of their parents was confirmed by the *mudir* of Mkokotoni in 1948 when he presided over a case of a father demanding his child's wages.[71] Though the chief justice expressed alarm at the "the very unsatisfactory manner in which juvenile labour is recruited to work in the town of Zanzibar," he focused his criticism on the parents rather than on the system of trafficking and the reality of the desperate rural conditions that necessitated these situations. Following this incident, the provincial commissioner sent a notice to the district commissioners of Pemba and Zanzibar to keep a lookout for such cases and to notify the *sheha*, *mudir*, or police of incidents of "child absentees."[72] These children were considered village runaways to be tracked by the *masheha* and other local authorities. As concerned as they were about these cases, colonial officials did not connect them to incidents of urban juvenile delinquency.

By the late 1940s, the new Tabora Approved School in Tanganyika, a British territory on the mainland, accepted Zanzibari boys, and the door to discussions of a reform school on the islands was closed for good. Being sent to the Tabora School was arguably worse than any other punishment. It meant years of complete separation from a boy's family and community. Tabora was about a three-day journey from Zanzibar. Parents who wanted to visit their sons would have to take a four- or five-hour boat ride from the islands to Dar es Salaam on the mainland, and then travel 900 to 1,000 kilometers (about 560 to 620 miles) on mostly unpaved roads to the far western region of Tanganyika. This was an impossible trip for poor families. If a boy was sent to Tabora at the age of twelve, thirteen, or fourteen and sentenced to stay there until he was eighteen, as occurred in many cases, that meant four to six formative years during which he was absent from home, years during which he was surrounded by boys from all over Tanganyika who spoke other languages and practiced other religions. During those six years the Zanzibari boy might get to see his parents once or twice, if at all.

New rules regarding sentencing to an approved school (Tabora) came into effect in 1946, and the juvenile court was now required to "obtain reports as to the child's past history before making an approved school order." This decision was then "vetted" by the High Court and the British resident.[73] This did not prevent judges from sentencing boys as young as twelve years old to several years' detention at the approved school for crimes such as breaking and entering with an attempt to commit a felony, stealing from a government official, and escaping custody.[74] The chief justice stated that it was only after attempts to supervise the juvenile under the care of a probation officer failed that the court took up the question of sending a boy to Tabora. He urged that parents be required to contribute "towards the maintenance of the child in the approved school" because he did not want this legislation to become "an easy means of throwing off all their parental responsibilities."[75] It never occurred to him or the other officials discussing these cases that the parents might not want their children to be sent so far away. At least if their children lived in Zanzibar Town, they would be able to visit them on a regular basis.

Throughout these debates about juvenile delinquency, from the schools to the courts to undocumented cases of child labor, British officials always blamed parents, whom they considered apathetic, inept, or greedy and who seemed to put their interests before those of their children. These cases were symptomatic of rural poverty. Officials ignored these issues and played down the problem of delinquency not only because they were uninvolved in the initial disputes but also because they refused to recognize the underlying causes. The "very small" problem of juvenile delinquency was in fact a symptom of the very big problem of economic hardship across the islands. Had the state gone after all of the children targeted in the 1935 Juvenile Offenders Decree, including those in need of "care and protection," the problem of rural and urban poverty would have been undeniable.

The 1940s was a time of food rations and ethnic conflict, which intensified in the postwar era. Though officials understood little about indigenous forms of dispute settlement and concepts of child rearing, the fundamental problems of economic scarcity, malnutrition, and disease were common knowledge.[76] Zanzibar's agricultural labor system was not the only legacy of slavery.[77] It was far easier to hone in on "parental apathy," the same explanation given for juvenile delinquency among wealthy Arabs in the early twentieth century, than to address the more systematic inequalities that existed around ethnicity, class, and the abundant opportunities for education and social mobility in town compared to the lack of these resources in the villages. The inability of the colonial administration to see the cases that made it only as far as the elders or *masheha* allowed them to understate the problem of juvenile delinquency and place the onus of responsibility on parents. British officials were content to let the *masheha*—and, if need be, the *mudirs*—deal with troublesome youth if it meant they did not have to fork over the funds to build a reformatory.

Conclusion

In 1950, the United Nations disseminated a twenty-three-page questionnaire for its survey on the treatment of juvenile delinquents, another call to action that Zanzibari officials dismissed.[78] When it became clear that East African colonies like Zanzibar were not abiding by British or international standards, the Colonial Office organized two conferences on juvenile justice in the region, one in Dar es Salaam in 1953 and the other in Uganda in 1956. These conferences stressed many of the same orders that had come down from the Colonial Office since the 1930s, mainly to separate juveniles from adults in detention and provide reformatories for rehabilitation. Zanzibar avoided these issues by repeating the mantra of the insignificant numbers of juvenile delinquents and by relying on the Tabora School to take in the most difficult children.

As the international community ramped up its call for intervention, the discourse on juvenile delinquency failed to gain traction in Zanzibar. This issue appeared inconsequential compared to the ethnic and class tensions that prevailed during the "time of politics" (1957–63) leading up to Zanzibar's independence.[79] During the early 1960s, the newly independent socialist state implemented institutions such as the Young Pioneers to control and discipline young people. Members of the youth wings of ruling political parties on the islands and the mainland also policed the behaviors of teenagers.[80] They took on the responsibilities of the *masheha* and *mudirs* to discipline Zanzibari youth before they came before police officers and courts. The state was more directly involved in the management of adolescents, but once again not through the juvenile court system. Officials failed to understand that juvenile delinquency (or the lack thereof) was a barometer of politics. More work needs to be done on the criminal processing of children and youth during the early nationalist era to assess how and why, like the young Zanzibaris of the previous era, they were beyond the scope of the state. The stories of troubled youth do exist if we know where to look.

NOTES

1 In addition to the other chapters in this collection, see Margaret K. Rosenheim, Franklin E. Zimring, David S. Tanenhaus, and Bernardine Dohrn, eds., *A Century of Juvenile Justice* (Chicago: University of Chicago Press, 2002); Sarah Fishman, *The Battle for Children: World War II, Youth Crime, and Juvenile Justice in Twentieth-Century France* (Cambridge: Harvard University Press, 2002); Anthony M. Platt and Miroslava Chavez-Garcia, *The Child Savers: The Invention of Delinquency*, expanded 40th anniversary ed. (New Brunswick, NJ: Rutgers University Press, 2009).

2 David Wolcott, *Cops and Kids: Policing Juvenile Delinquency in Urban America, 1890–1940* (Columbus: Ohio State University Press, 2005).

3 Kristin Mann and Richard Roberts, eds., *Law in Colonial Africa* (Portsmouth, NH: Heinemann, 1991).

4 David Killingray, "The 'Rod of Empire': Debate over Corporal Punishment in the British African Colonial Forces, 1888–1946," *Journal of African History* 35, no. 2 (1994): 201–216; Chloe Campbell, "Juvenile Delinquency in Colonial Kenya, 1900–1939," *Historical Journal* 45, no. 1 (2002): 129–151.

5 See, for example, Franklin E. Zimring and Máximo Langer, "One Theme or Many? The Search for a Deep Structure in Global Juvenile Justice," in *Juvenile Justice in Global Perspective*, ed. Franklin E. Zimring, Máximo Langer, and David S. Tanenhaus (New York: New York University Press, 2015).

6 Clive Glaser, *Bo-Tsotsi: The Youth Gangs of Soweto, 1935–1976* (Portsmouth, NH: Heinemann, 2000); Campbell, "Juvenile Delinquency"; Laurent Fourchard, "Lagos and the Invention of Juvenile Delinquency in Niger, 1920–60," *Journal of African History* 47 (2006): 115–137; Paul Ocobock, "'Joy Rides for Juveniles': Vagrant Youth and Colonial Control in Nairobi, Kenya, 1901–52," *Social History* 31, no. 1 (February 2006): 39–59; and Heather Ellis, ed., *Juvenile Delinquency and the Limits of Western Influence, 1850–2000* (New York: Palgrave Macmillan, 2014).

7 Campbell, "Juvenile Delinquency"; Timothy Parsons, *Race, Resistance, and the Boy Scout Movement in British Colonial Africa* (Athens: Ohio University Press, 2004).

8 Jane Humphries, *Childhood and Child Labour in the British Industrial Revolution* (New York: Cambridge University Press, 2010).

9 Harry Hendrick, *Child Welfare: England 1872–1989* (London: Routledge, 1994), 24, 174. The first reformatory school in Britain was actually designed for the poor. See Peter King, *Crime and Law in England, 1750–1840: Remaking Justice from the Margins* (New York: Cambridge University Press, 2006), 73–164.

10 Zanzibar Education Department Annual Report (hereafter ZEDAR) 1927, 19.

11 Laura Fair, *Pastimes and Politics: Culture, Community, and Identity in Post-Abolition Urban Zanzibar, 1890–1945* (Athens: Ohio University Press, 2001), 15–16.

12 ZNA AB 61/34, R. T. Coryndon, High Commissioner to Secretary of State for the Colonies, October 19, 1923. On the nineteenth-century cosmopolitanism of Zanzibar and other East African coastal cities, see Jeremy Prestholdt, *Domesticating the Empire: African Consumerism and the Genealogies of Globalization* (Berkeley: University of California Press, 2008).

13 William Cunningham Bissell, *Urban Design, Chaos, and Colonial Power in Zanzibar* (Bloomington: Indiana University Press, 2011).

14 ZNA AB 61/34, Commandant of Police notes, October 13, 1932.

15 Campbell, "Juvenile Delinquency," 131.

16 See, for example, Ocobock, "'Joy Rides for Juveniles,'" and Glaser, *Bo-Tsotsi*.

17 For juvenile delinquency and crime in South Africa, see Glaser, *Bo-Tsotsi*; Robert Morrell, "Of Boys and Men: Masculinity and Gender in Southern African Studies," *Journal of Southern African Studies* 24, no. 4 (1998): 605–630.

18 Elisabeth McMahon, *Slavery and Emancipation in East Africa: From Honor to Respectability* (New York: Cambridge University Press, 2013). Abolition was a slow, gradual process that began in the nineteenth century and was not complete until 1909 when all legal forms of slavery ceased to exist.

19 Laura Fair devotes a considerable section of her introductory chapter to the fluidity of ethnic categories and people's identification with them. Fair, *Pastimes and Politics*, 28–55.

20 For a history of this polarization of racial identity in Zanzibar, see Jonathon Glassman, *War of Words, War of Stones: Racial Thought and Violence in Colonial Zanzibar* (Bloomington: Indiana University Press, 2011).

21 On the criminalization of girl hawkers in Nigeria, for example, see Abosede George, *Making Modern Girls: A History of Girlhood, Labor, and Social Development in Colonial Lagos* (Athens: Ohio University Press, 2014).

22 Corrie Decker, *Mobilizing Zanzibari Women: The Struggle for Respectability and Self-Reliance* (New York: Palgrave Macmillan, 2014). Under the 1934 Penal Code, for example, no man could have intercourse with a girl unless she had both reached puberty and the age of thirteen.

23 ZNA AX 10/5, Return of Criminal cases in the juvenile court Pemba 1953–64.

24 For more on child marriage, see Elke Stockreiter, "Child Marriage and Domestic Violence: Islamic and Colonial Discourse on Gender Relations and Female Status in Zanzibar, 1900–1950s," in *Domestic Violence and the Law in Colonial and Postcolonial Africa*, ed. Emily Burrill, Richard Roberts, and Elizabeth Thornberry, 138–158 (Athens: Ohio University Press, 2010).

25 Most Zanzibaris were Muslim, so the missionary schools mainly catered to former slaves and the few others willing to convert to Christianity.

26 Glassman, *War of Words*, 42. Glassman argues that colonial education transformed the Arab elite into a "secular intelligentsia" (75–91).

27 UKNA CO 618/18 1917, Vol 2, British Resident Pearce to Secretary of State for the Colonies, October 1, 1917.

28 Ibid.

29 UKNA CO 618/55/19, British Resident Rankine to Secretary of State for the Colonies, January 16, 1933.

30 Roman Loimeier, *Between Social Skills and Marketable Skills: The Politics of Islamic Education in 20th Century Zanzibar* (Leiden: Koninklijke Brill NV, 2009).

31 UKNA CO 689/9, Compulsory Education Decree, 1921. Girls were excluded from the legislation. Government girls' schools were available until 1927.

32 UKNA CO/689/9 1921, *Official Gazettes*: July 18, 1921, 278, Government Notice No. 87; UKNA CO/689/18 1926, May 22, 1926, 358, Government Notice No. 94; UKNA CO/689/19 1927, May 20, 1927, 481, Government Notice No. 83.

33 ZEDAR 1929, Appendix II.

34 ZEDAR 1927, 8.

35 ZNA AB 61/34, Statement of Juveniles Dealt with by Court during 1925–34.

36 ZNA AB 61/34, E.G. Fish, Commissioner of Police to Chief Secretary, May 17, 1943.

37 ZNA AB 61/34, Judge, H.B.M. Court, to J. H. Sinclaire, Acting High Commissioner, Zanzibar, August 16, 1923.

38 UKNA CO 618/20 1919 v2, Acting British Resident, Sinclair, to High Commissioner, Nairobi, May 3, 1919. George Hadjivayanis and Ed Ferguson, "The Development of a Colonial Working Class," in *Zanzibar under Colonial Rule*, ed. Abdul Sheriff and Ed Ferguson, 188–219 (Athens: Ohio University Press, 1991).

39 There were additional restrictions placed on the labor of children and youth in the 1932 Employment of Women, Children, and Young Persons (Restriction) Decree. UKNA CO 842/2, Zanzibar Decrees, 1932–36.

40 UKNA CO/689/18, Zanzibar *Official Gazette*, August 14, 1926, 524–525.

41 UKNA CO 689/18, Zanzibar *Official Gazette*, February 27, 1926, 157, The Reformatories Decree, 1926 (Decree No. 4 of 1926).

42 ZNA AB 61/35, The Children and Young Persons Act 1933. Juvenile Offenders; UKNA CO 842/2 Zanzibar Decrees 1932–36, Juvenile Offenders Decree, 1935.

43 ZNA AB 61/36, Juvenile Offenders Decree, 1935, 6.

44 Sections 10–11 of the Juvenile Offenders Decree, 1935.

45 Sections 13–14 and 18 (3) of the Juvenile Offenders Decree, 1935.

46 ZNA AB 61/34, British Resident to Chief Justice, quoting the Superintendent of Prisons, September 7, 1943.

47 ZNA AB 61/36, Chief Justice to British Resident, June 18, 1943; ZNA AB 61/34, Commissioner of Police E.G. Fish to Chief Secretary, May 17, 1943.

48 ZNA AB 61/39, Juvenile Delinquents, 1947–55.

49 ZNA AB 61/34, Commissioner of Police to Chief Secretary, July 25, 1936.

50 ZNA AB 61/36, Attorney-General's Notes on the Juvenile Offenders Bill, January 35, 1935.

51 ZNA AB 61/39, Chief Justice, extract from letter dated July 4, 1950.

52 McMahon, *Slavery and Emancipation*, 132.

53 ZNA AB 61/34, H.E. Heath to Chief Secretary, July 23, 1932.

54 ZNA AB 61/34, Extract from the Minutes of a Meeting of the Executive Council held on Tuesday, August 2 1932; Director of Education to Commandant of Police, August 11, 1932.

55 ZNA AB 61/34, Commissioner of Police to Chief Secretary, April 14, 1934.

56 ZNA AB 61/34, Commissioner of Police to Chief Secretary, July 25, 1936.

57 ZNA AB 61/36, Chief Secretary to Registrar, High Court, May 28, 1947.

58 ZNA AB 61/34, Colonial Secretary of Kenya to Chief Secretary, Zanzibar, June 23, 1934; Chief Secretary, Tanganyika to Chief Secretary, Zanzibar, July 25, 1934. The Kabete Reformatory was established in 1909 and was one of the institutions through which colonial officials developed theories about race and mentality. See Chloe Campbell, *Race and Empire: Eugenics in Colonial Kenya* (Manchester: Manchester University Press, 2007), 47.

59 ZNA AB 61/34, Commissioner of Police to Chief Secretary, May 17, 1943.

60 ZNA AB 61/36, Registrar, High Court to British Resident, June 27, 1947.

61 A significant portion of juvenile court cases were "dismissed" or were handed over to a parent or guardian on surety of good behavior.

62 Elke Stockreiter, "Tying and Untying the Knot: *Kadhi*'s Courts and the Negotiation of Social Status in Zanzibar Town, 1900–1963" (PhD diss., School of Oriental and African Studies, University of London, 2008), 22.

63 McMahon, *Slavery and Emancipation*, 73.

64 Stockreiter, "Tying and Untying," 18, 48–51.

65 W. H. Ingrams, *Zanzibar: Its History and Its People* (London: Stacey International, 2007 [1931, H. F. G. Witherby]), 252.

66 Ibid., 267. See also McMahon, *Slavery and Emancipation*, 128.

67 Erin Stiles, *An Islamic Court in Context: An Ethnographic Study of Judicial Reasoning* (New York: Palgrave Macmillan, 2009), 132.

68 Ng'ambo was the middle- and working-class section of Zanzibar Town.

69 ZNA AJ 10/4, Report of the Committee to Examine the Problem of Juvenile Delinquency, 1948.

70 ZNA AB 61/39, Ali Shariff Mussa to Resident Magistrate, Juvenile Court, 1950. Mussa was the African representative from Pemba appointed to the Legislative Council in 1947.

71 ZNA AB 61/39, Chief Justice, High Court to British Resident, June 30, 1948.

72 ZNA AB 61/39, Acting Provincial Commissioner to District Commissioner, Pemba and District Commissioner, Zanzibar, October 7, 1947.

73 ZNA AB 61/36, Chief Justice to Registrar, High Court, January 16, 1947.

74 ZNA HC 22/4, Juvenile Court Case No. 30 of 1948 and other cases in ZNA AB 61/34, Reformatory for Juvenile Offenders 1916–47; ZNA AX 10/2 Returns of the Juvenile Court, Pemba 1948–53.

75 ZNA AB 61/36, Chief Justice to Registrar, High Court, January 16, 1947.

76 Beginning in the mid-1930s, colonial officials conducted surveys of rural agricultural communities that examined incidents of malnutrition and disease among schoolchildren (Decker, *Mobilizing Zanzibari Women*). Of course the question of labor and the economic health of the plantation economy had always preoccupied British officials.

77 Frederick Cooper, *From Slaves to Squatters: Plantation Labor and Agriculture in Zanzibar and Coastal Kenya, 1890–1925* (Portsmouth, NH: Heinemann, 1997); Hadjivayanis and Ferguson, "The Development of a Colonial Working Class." Cooper and Hadjivayanis and Ferguson focus on the structural legacies of slavery in the colonial economy, but the interpersonal dynamics between parents and "tutors," and the transfer of children from the homes of the poor into the homes of the wealthy as servants, are also reminiscent of nineteenth- and twentieth-century relationships between slave families and their owners. See Bernard Freamen, "Islamic Law and Trafficking in Women and Children in the Indian Ocean World," in *Trafficking in Slavery's Wake: Law and the Experience of Women and Children*

in Africa, ed. Benjamin Lawrance and Richard L. Roberts, 121–141 (Athens: Ohio University Press, 2012).

78 ZNA AB 61/39, United Nations questionnaire on the treatment of juvenile delinquents, April 11, 1950.

79 Glassman, *War of Words*, 153–154.

80 Thomas Burgess, "Cinema, Bell Bottoms, and Miniskirts: Struggles over Youth and Citizenship in Revolutionary Zanzibar," *International Journal of African Historical Studies* 35, nos. 2–3 (2002): 287–314; Andrew Ivaska, *Cultured States: Youth, Gender, and Modern Style in 1960s Dar es Salaam* (Durham: Duke University Press, 2011).

PART II

Policing and Punishing Youth Crime

4

Youth Consciousness, Delinquency, and the Montreal Miracle

TAMARA MYERS

The 1940s provide an intriguing landscape for the study of juvenile crime rates and responses. For Allied nations, these years were turbulent ones of change and innovation set against the backdrop of war, victory, and early postwar reconstruction and renewal. The scholarship on juvenile justice has long acknowledged how war has been productive of delinquency, delinquents, and youth work.[1] As James Gilbert noted in his classic study, "From the middle of World War II, a great many Americans, led by federal law-enforcement officials, concluded that broken families, mobility, and absent working mothers had caused a spurt in delinquent behaviour."[2] Other Allied nations like Britain and Canada, and occupied France, similarly experienced an exceptional growth in delinquency with a concomitant expansion in juvenile justice apparatuses and agendas. Wartime developments in both delinquency and juvenile justice set a pattern that persisted long after soldiers came home, as youth problems became a constitutive feature of postwar society. As Gilbert and Mary Louise Adams note for the United States and Canada, respectively, the discursive moral panic over criminal youth began during the war but peaked, in fact, in the early postwar years, with very real implications for the policing of young people.

During wartime and in its tragic wake, young people came to represent the promise of a better tomorrow. As a powerful symbol of the future, children and youth were often associated with innocence, casting their deviant behavior in a particular light: experts and the media alike insisted that delinquency was a product of contemporary society's ills and the individual's environment. But if the causes were understandable—linked often to war's dislocating effect—the consequences of delinquency were thought to be monumental. For example, in an illustration in an American social work journal, *Survey Mid-monthly*, two giant young people stand in a city about to be consumed by a wave of criminality crashing down on it. This flood threatened not only the girl and boy but also the fundamental building blocks of society, represented in the picture as the church.[3] A parallel set of imagery likened juvenile problems to a contemporary plague.[4] Both the natural disaster and the disease metaphors assigned children underscored their vulnerability; saving the children from these external forces and from themselves became the clarion call of youth work, especially with boys, in these decades.

At mid-20th century North American police officers both joined and led a movement to creatively rethink solutions to rising juvenile crime rates. While law enforcement had a vested interest in contributing to the panic over out-of-control youth, juvenile squads were also at the forefront of resolving the problem by emphasizing their own innovative youth work. Their solutions built on social and moral reformers' attempts to improve modern boyhood in the 19th century that found expression in the 20th century through myriad boys' clubs, Boy Scouts, and the like, that often relied upon recreational activities and sports for their remedial effect.[5] As law enforcement made the shift to delinquency prevention schemes, it reinvented itself vis-à-vis youth—from being on the sidelines during the heyday of the juvenile court movement to being captains of delinquency prevention starting in the mid-1930s and continuing through the next two decades. This soft authority approach had multiple consequences: it called on police officers to embrace contemporary child psychology and "boyology" (or the science of boys)[6] and their own identities as coaches and teachers; it helped reconstruct the image of cops in the eyes of youth; it gave youth who joined a chance at belonging; and for those who didn't or couldn't join, the specter of disenfranchisement and dropping out became all the more real. By the early 1950s, Montreal's police department developed a reputation as a result of the apparent stunning success of its delinquency prevention program: it had achieved a miracle in reversing the upward trend in youth crime.

This chapter explores the 1940s juvenile crime wave (as conjured in statistics, anecdotes, and expert pronouncements) and the approach taken by some municipal police forces to arrest its unrelenting rise. Using the case of Montreal's youth crime prevention campaign, it explores the contours and meaning of a child-centered, or youth-conscious, approach to delinquency that insisted on the identification of juvenile delinquents as "innocent" young people, an essentialized state that was selectively applied to certain children and youth. This approach reveals a central paradox of juvenile justice: that in prevention/protection-oriented regimes youth are subjected to extensive surveillance and training, coercion and conformity, which results in some of those youth gaining access to liberal citizenship. Ultimately, it assesses the "miracle" of Montreal as mostly media hype that celebrated police officers moving into the realm of youth recreation programming.

Behind the Raging Rates of Delinquency

During the Second World War, Britain's Allies anxiously received news about that country's experience of peril. Threats to the home front, beyond enemy bombs, included a war-related spike in juvenile crime.[7] This news of British home front trouble seemed to prophesy imminent delinquency problems in other nations further removed from conflict zones. The North American media explained youth's antisocial behavior as a product of high employment, relative freedom, and excitement, on the one hand, and blackouts, absent parents, and ever-present death and destruction, on the other.[8] News stories of errant children and wild youth were translated onto the silver screen by Hollywood, which produced an excess of cautionary youth tales through the 1940s and into the 1950s.[9] At the conclusion of the war, juvenile crime was recognized as one of the war's worst consequences.[10]

Picking up on problems in Britain and those portrayed in contemporary movies, Canadian news media also reported a "sense of unrest and unsettlement" among its youth.[11] It was not difficult to find proof that youth were out of control: nationwide, the number of juvenile delinquents, according to the Dominion Bureau of Statistics, rose from under 10,000 at the beginning of the war to almost 14,000 in 1942. In that year, vulnerable and delinquent children were making headline news in Canada and by 1944 its largest city, Montreal, experienced a full-blown juvenile crime wave.[12] The number of children appearing before Montreal's juvenile court judge increased by 20 percent in the early years of the war (from 2,979 in 1940 to 3,680 in 1942). Many parents and guardians of these children and youth claimed an inability to control and contain their charges.[13] For their part, the Montreal police arrested 1,063 minors in 1941; this number climbed to 2,632 in 1943, and spiked at 3,130 in 1944 before easing to 2,918 in 1945 [14]

At the conclusion of the war—as families were reconstituted or left to face the absence left by fallen fathers[15]—the delinquency problem did not fade. Rather, as reported in the Canadian police press, delinquency raged across North America and Europe.[16] "Canadian youth has never been so insolent, and so defiant," according to the Ontario prisons and reformatories annual report for 1947.[17] This juvenile problem would continue to plague authorities through the 1950s. At the same time, these numbers accompanied a discursive construction of children as sacred property, elevating local problems to national import and underscoring the issue's urgency.[18]

Noting the long-term trends in numbers of arrested kids, Montreal's anomaly is actually the great *rise* of arrests in 1943–44. An explication of the mechanisms and processes that helped to create and quell the surge in delinquency requires some attention. Beyond the usual media-identified causes for delinquency, such as family breakdown and neglectful parenting, its wartime rise can certainly be attributed to an altered landscape; war on the home front created more opportunities for youth in terms of work and mobility, for example, but there were also structural changes to policing that helped produce higher numbers. Taking Montreal as an example, there were specific reasons for delinquency rates to rise that were only tangentially related to wartime: a new youth squad was established officially in 1941; the provincial government raised the official age of the category juvenile delinquent from 16 to 18 in 1942; and a citywide juvenile nocturnal youth curfew was established in 1942.

The dramatic increase in juvenile arrests in the mid-war years therefore had multiple causes. The 1942 juvenile curfew law certainly accounts for part of this increase: passed in late 1942, it was a direct product of the early war years' anxiety over the absence of masculine presence on the home front with men serving overseas and the related (and alleged) distraction of mothers. "Sunset" offenses—curfew (applying to children under 14 years of age) and vagrancy/loitering by night (for those 14 years and older)—show the most dramatic increases. In 1942 the police recorded just 85 arrests (70 boys and 15 girls) for loitering, but by 1944 this had swelled to 899 arrests (808 boys and 91 girls), including 632 boys for loitering at night.[19] Other offenses that account for the boom in delinquency arrests include public disorder and theft. Both of these can be characterized as typical boy offenses. The number of boys arrested for disturbing the peace more than doubled from 190 in 1942 to 391 in 1944, while those charged with theft rose just over 65 percent in the same period, from 271 to 414.[20] The press blamed absent fathers and working mothers, gangster cinema, and "prosperity delinquency" for the rise in youth trouble.[21]

Another potential cause of the swelling numbers relates to the fact that in 1941 the Juvenile Morality Squad officially began its work with a team of five constables. By the war's end the squad would number 13 with this climbing to 80 by the early 1950s. The squad's impact on numbers can be seen clearly in the case of the curfew by-law. In the debates over implementing the curfew law, Montreal's police chief admitted to *La Presse* in September 1942 that he had lost so many men to the armed forces that he had only 150 men on the streets at night; the implication was that few of the 100,000 children in the city would be subject to policing.[22] The annual reports of the police department show that in 1944 only 147 children were arrested for violating by-law 1715 on curfew. In the same report, the return of the Montreal Juvenile Morality Squad recorded an astonishing 6,967 stopped and interrogated for the same offense.[23]

The structural causes of the delinquency surge—older youth included in delinquency statistics, the curfew law, and a youth squad targeting young offenders—ought to have resulted in a continuation of elevated numbers after war's end. Yet the numbers of children and youth arrested declined in the postwar period: in 1946 arrested juveniles numbered 1,601 and this number would remain below 2,000 for a decade.[24] How was this possible? Simply fewer "bad" kids, an easier adjustment to peacetime, and a more well-behaved generation? Perhaps. Another answer emerges if we turn back to the police annual reports and look beyond the arrest statistics, to those numbers and statements that address the Montreal police youth squad's interaction with children and youth. The Montreal Police Department's youth squad reports suggest the police response to youth expanded—even exploded over the 1940s—with more young people falling under the gaze of policemen and women. That is, the prevention techniques that took off in the mid-1940s led to a larger scale of interaction with children and youth, and a highly public and seemingly "new" approach to children and youth meant that fewer youth were technically arrested but the surveillance intensified.

The Montreal Miracle

Montreal's ability to buck the upward trend in postwar delinquency was partly a careful media construction. In 1949 the international press lauded the work of the Montreal police force in stopping the "rising tide" of delinquency. That year, a Swiss journalist, allegedly reporting from the streets of Montreal, told the story of a gang leader called Archie. This youth and his band of "little rascals" attacked a corner grocery store, smashing the front window.

At the sight and sound of breaking glass Archie fled the scene, only to be stopped in his tracks by a police officer. According to the photo-story, this officer did not take him to a cell but to a "welcoming place" where he would be with boys his own age. Rather than prison, reform school, or even a scolding, gang leader Archie was given a membership card to the Police Club for Boys.[25] According to this journalist, the "miracle" of Montreal—the decline in the juvenile crime problem, in fact, the *reversal* of the trend—was causally related to the so-called direct method of dealing with delinquency: a rejection of corrections (including the juvenile court process and especially incarceration) and a full-scale embrace of crime prevention methodology. According to those responsible for the police boys' club, this tack had resulted in an astonishing feat: Montreal's juvenile delinquency rates had declined by 50 percent.

In an era that demonized the delinquent and raised delinquency to the level of an international emergency, it's perhaps not surprising that such a drop in the delinquency rate was labeled the "Miracle of Montreal."[26] An expansive, highly coordinated crime-prevention strategy apparently reversed the city's juvenile delinquency rise as it fundamentally altered the relationship of police to children and youth. As the story was told to the press, one man, Detective-Sergeant Ovila Pelletier, delivered the city from the crisis of youth, by tackling *incipient* delinquency. Pelletier effectively challenged previous understandings of the police role in combatting delinquency, borrowing from social work and youth squad practices in other cities. Pelletier's experiment was mounted as resounding proof that such schemes could work.

North American police forces slowly turned toward crime prevention in the 1910s and '20s, instituting piecemeal athletic or recreational programs for boys considered high risk to offend. In so doing they were joining a club movement made popular by the Boy Scouts and the Young Men's Christian Association that were founded to encourage character building and physical fitness among boys as a response to the industrial society's "overcivilizing" of men, leaving them "sedentary and weak."[27] They were also borrowing ideas from prominent contemporary sociologists, like Chicago's Clifford Shaw, that produced the Chicago Area Project in the interwar years, a community-based delinquency-prevention experiment that focused on recreation for youth, mediation for gangs, and grassroots community renewal.[28] Chief August Vollmer of the Berkeley, CA, police department was best known for his efforts to wed the ideas of sociology, psychology, and social work with the policing of young people. In the 1910s and '20s he championed the notion that police officers should intervene in the lives of "predelinquents," influence the environment in which they were growing up, and connect them with relevant social agencies, so as to interrupt the production of delinquents and criminals.[29] What stands out among these early prevention programs is the determination to steer youth away from the juvenile court system and corrections; as Elisabeth Lossing of the Berkeley Crime Prevention Division argued, "we . . . try to save our predelinquents and juvenile delinquents the necessity of Juvenile Court action."[30]

Crime prevention programs led urban police forces to a central position in youth work although its development was slow and uneven. As David Wolcott demonstrates for Chicago, Detroit, and Los Angeles, how these prevention programs played out depended on many factors, including police leadership, the perceived nature of delinquency, and who was allegedly at risk and committing crimes. As Wolcott has shown, even with the emergence of Progressive Era juvenile courts some city police, like those in Chicago, remained antagonistic to youth and meted out arbitrary and sometimes brutal justice.[31] Early 20th-century Chicago cops used intimidation and violence in their dealings with youth on the streets and in custody, defending these actions as teaching lessons to kids who needed it. Stories of cops threatening with weapons, exacting bribes, and committing physical and emotional abuse go some distance to explaining why youth mistrusted police authority that was embodied by the bullies and corrupt officers of urban forces.[32] Not all police forces deserved a reputation like Chicago's, yet ambivalence toward juvenile delinquents was common and persistent: police harassed young people who simply appeared to be up to no good on city streets, and enforced the law through informal discipline and rough justice. We find a similar situation in Canada: the complexity of the cop-child relationship and the uneasy contemporary reception of the rough justice meted out to kids acting out. By the 1940s delinquency prevention in cities like Montreal seemed to have resolved this ambivalence.

Over the course of the 20th century municipal police forces would engage schools, welfare agencies, and youth organizations, as they developed delinquency prevention programs. Rather than seeing this development as an opportunity to become part of the juvenile justice movement the police sought to correct what was increasingly clear—the juvenile justice system's limited success in the realm of protecting children and preventing crime.[33] Wolcott argues in his study of policing youth from 1890 to 1940 that whereas the juvenile court movement of the turn of the century had effectively "marginalized" the police in the regulation of juveniles, the adoption of crime prevention measures created the possibility of creating a new role—and I would argue, a new identity—for police in the campaign against delinquency.[34]

Prevention required that the police reinvent themselves in the eyes of young people and offer something that kids wanted. In the mid-1940s, experts on juvenile delinquency and prevention noted that police forces required a fundamental change in approach to quell the delinquency problem. The director of the Federal Bureau of Investigation, J. Edgar Hoover, frequently spoke on the war against delinquency and his words were repeated in the North American police press. Hoover's message was partly alarmist—decrying the surging crime rate, especially among minors during the war—but also encouraging and prescriptive: "We must adopt a new attitude towards children as well as towards law." His words suggest that the foundational youth policing efforts had not gone far enough, that the police needed to take the situation further. In relation to juvenile crime Hoover condemned the home that produced the next generation of criminals and advocated that preventive officers be intermediaries between the child and its home.[35] A much-noted authority on the 1940s delinquency problem and chief of the Milwaukee Police Department, Joseph Kluchesky, likewise denounced parental shortcomings and advocated for a greater role for policemen and women in youth crime prevention. In intervening (or playing intermediaries), Kluchesky argued, police could reverse the bad attitude toward authority that children absorb from their disgruntled mothers and fathers.[36] We find this perspective in the Canadian police press also, which warned of the cost of parents teaching children to fear police: "Such fear . . . leads to dislike and suspicion of the police. With that comes a breakdown in law and order."[37] In a piece of propaganda from 1946, Canada's National Film Board's 11-minute film, *The Policeman*, shows a doubtful and nervous "Freddie" learning to trust a policeman and see for himself how police officers were actually community workers.[38]

A system predicated on befriending children, youth policing often functioned to keep children out of the court system. This prevention orientation and the concomitant youth consciousness took several forms and represented a qualitative change in the approach to young people.

"More Head Work," Less Intolerance of Youth: Crime Prevention at Mid-20th Century

The mid-1940s article in the *Constables Revue* (Montreal), "Juvenile Crime, a Social Evil," was accompanied by a reprinted *Survey Midmonthly* illustration summing up the prescriptive role for postwar police. The caption read, "Less violence, more head work." In the first diagram a large fist is threatening a boy; in the latter box a policeman is shown demonstrably giving advice to a youth. The image couldn't be clearer: the once brutal orientation of police (where force ensured a disciplined public) should be replaced with understanding and good will toward young people. This transformation was predicated on reaching those young people who were redeemable and deserving and who could avail themselves of what the police offered.

In Montreal, youth policing emerged in the late 1930s. It began with just a handful of officers assigned to juvenile cases and developed into the Juvenile Morality Squad (JMS), then into its own bureau in 1946 and finally it was renamed the Juvenile Delinquency Prevention Bureau in 1950, years after it was thus nicknamed. The Juvenile Morality Squad had its heyday in the 1940s and 1950s, growing in numbers and importance as it targeted the twin and intertwined problems of immorality and youth. Like New York City's example, Montreal youth policing incorporated a fundamental emphasis on extracurricular athletics clubs for youth. The case of Montreal's youth policing provides an excellent example of the profound changes in urban policing and antidelinquency work that helped reshape youth's relationship to authority and the position of minors in society.

By 1946 the first phase of the JMS plan to eradicate delinquency was well under way. Places of youth corruption were under surveillance and Montreal delinquents' hangouts and habits were well known by the squad.[39] A curfew law enabled the squad members to interrogate any child on the street at 9 p.m., regardless of age. It now shifted its emphasis toward delinquency prevention, allegedly making "correction . . . a secondary factor."[40] In fact, the JMS message was often that if even one child landed in jail, they had failed. This second phase of youth police work launched police toward eliminating the causes of delinquency. In this phase, child-friendly police would self-present as youth workers and insist on collaborating with other youth organizations to avert delinquency.[41]

From his own long experience of antidelinquency work, the squad and bureau leader, Ovila Pelletier, assembled several truisms: how a child spends his/her leisure time is critical in predicting delinquency; early detection of youth problems is essential for avoiding full-blown delinquency; youth police can and should instill in children a positive attitude toward authority; children must understand that the police are their friends, who are there to help and protect them; police must treat children with respect and consideration in order to win their trust. "Mutual understanding" between cops and kids, according to Pelletier, would lead to a decline in delinquency and a better society.[42]

Bureaucratic changes implemented in January 1946 facilitated Montreal's success in developing youth policing. Not only was the squad now its own Bureau with a separate physical space (since 1944)[43] and a reporting structure that connected the Bureau directly to the top of the police administration, significantly it had devised a radio system that allowed the members of the Bureau to take jurisdiction of all children who came into contact with the law within the city. Over the course of 1946 the Bureau's fleet of radioed cars grew to eight and personnel to 28 men. When a child was detained for committing an offense or infraction of municipal by-laws the police officer would immediately alert the Juvenile Morality Bureau, which would take over the case. In principle this meant that all children in conflict with the law would be dealt with by youth squad officers. In the case of minor infractions the child was often taken home.[44] Only these officers would be responsible for the paperwork on the child, which was now centralized, and for informing parents and of deciding whether to take him or her to the juvenile court. If the juvenile court route was taken, a Bureau "liaison" officer handled the report at the juvenile court.[45] This system design ensured that police could verify quickly and easily whether a child had been previously apprehended. This system meant an escalation in the number of children and youth coming into contact with the municipal police force.

The sports solution to the problem of errant and wayward kids became the *pièce de resistance* of Montreal's youth-conscious policing. In order to foster "better understanding between youngsters and policemen," the bureau officially opened Police Juvenile Clubs (PJC) for boys in 1947. These clubs added a new dimension to the city's network of organized activities for young people, which were largely church-based or denominationally based and arranged along linguistic and religious lines (for example, the YW/YMCAs and Catholic or parish youth groups). The PJC stands out in Montreal for initiating recruitment of members regardless of religion or language.[46] These secular organized activities claimed to offer a new site for boys' socialization where they would wear not gang colors but Police Department badges. Scattered around the city, the PJC provided boys aged 10–17 with leisure time activities,[47] especially the opportunity to play on hockey, basketball, volleyball, and softball teams. The idea was that under the supervision of policemen these team members would gain guidance and instruction in these sports, embrace team spirit, and at the same time acquire a sound appreciation of the friendly neighborhood policeman. Free equipment was issued, although boys playing hockey were to purchase a team sweater that sported the Police Juvenile Club logo and the Montreal Police Department flag. Police officers encouraged boys to visit their local police station where they were issued a membership card after taking a pledge to "be a good sportsman and be at all times a good law-abiding citizen."[48] Membership required that the young behave "honorably"; failure to follow the honor code could result in the retraction of membership. A juvenile court appearance was cause for membership to be cancelled. Through the PJC the police focused not on reforming juvenile delinquents but rather making the point that staying out of trouble had its rewards.

Boys were solicited to join Police Juvenile Clubs through radio broadcasts in both English and French. According to the article on the Montreal Miracle, in 1947 Ovila Pelletier launched a radio campaign to solicit membership and a stunning 42,000 came forward, growing the membership that year to 65,000.[49] By 1954 the PJC boasted 80,000 members.[50] That year there were 160 teams including football, volleyball, basketball, and hockey as well as boxing lessons, and self-defense and music classes. For their part, officers were selected for the Delinquency Prevention Bureau for their interest in boys and their facility in both English and French.

Police athletic and hobby clubs for youth sprung up across North American cities starting in the 1930s. Some cities managed girls' team sports, although when girls were considered, it was usually for other leisure clubs like crafts. Some police departments tailored their offerings to what they thought the boys most needed, including how to manage firearms. Boys' rifle clubs may seem somewhat unlikely in delinquency prevention programs but, according to the sergeant in charge, "[e]very healthy boy likes to shoot, and that this urge finds its perfect expression in rifle shooting."[51] Channeling boys' excess energy had long been a goal of community boxing clubs and the like; now the police similarly offered such opportunities. This "sports solution" demanded a high degree of child deference to police—a willingness to wear police colors rather than gang colors, and acquiescence to and acceptance of the hierarchy of power and authority, and undoubtedly coercion.

What did the boys get out of it? Boys were likely attracted to the PJC because it meant access to spectator sporting events as well as participatory team sports. Thousands of youth, for example, received free admission with their memberships in the PJC to see the Montreal Royals baseball team at the Delorimier Street Stadium or to the Montreal Forum to see hockey games.

In 1958 Detective Inspector Ovila Pelletier died suddenly at the age of 56, giving the press an occasion to appraise the Montreal Police Department's work with children and youth. Although the local press did not get nostalgic over the Montreal Miracle, it did emphasize how under Pelletier not only did juvenile delinquency seem tamed but youth's definition of the word "cop" had changed; the *Gazette* proposed that "for thousands of young Montrealers it has come to mean 'friend.'"[52] Pelletier, along with his colleagues responsible for preventing delinquency, had apparently transformed policing into "a positive, energetic force for good among the city youth."[53] Under his leadership the Montreal police force's youth police had endorsed the message and embraced the practice of "prevention," meaning youth protection not punishment. Laid to rest in 1958, Pelletier would be remembered as a great success and an "ami des jeunes," memorialized eponymously in a children's playground and with a trophy awarded annually to civic-minded girls and boys.[54]

Critiquing Prevention

This new prevention method caught the attention of many observers and was challenged from at least two angles, both related to the police usurpation of other professionals' youth work. In late 1948 an umbrella organization, the Montreal Council of Social Agencies, took note of the police organization advancing into the field of juvenile delinquency prevention. Operating since 1921, this agency had been concerned with studying and alleviating Montreal's social problems; chief among them was juvenile delinquency and child neglect. In the late 1940s the Council produced a report on police activities with youth. While undoubtedly biased as a source, the report on the Delinquency Bureau does provide us with some interesting details about, and the limitations of, the practice of police preventive programs.[55]

The Council's report was the result of "careful study" of police work and "correspondence with leading authorities in United States welfare organizations."[56] Concerning the "tours of inspection," the report stressed the vital role played by the police in making rounds through adolescent hangouts. The street patrol also seemed to conform to the role the police were supposed to be playing in making sure that youth obeyed municipal regulations. This work apparently led to a decline in the number of youth coming before the juvenile court, "allowing the time of the Judges and the Juvenile Court staff to be spent on more serious cases."[57]

Despite the positive press and popularity of the Police Juvenile Clubs the Council report exposed the negative effects of this prevention program. Too often the boys were encouraged to develop a taste for spectator sports where there was little supervision and questionable socialization. The report writers estimated that while the Clubs had thousands of members, only 500–600 boys actually participated in physical activity. As well, the literature from across the United States (for example, the Boys' Clubs of America and the National Probation and Parole Association) on the issue suggested that the police clubs for boys likely duplicated already established sporting clubs and gymnasiums.

A parallel set of complaints about preventive police work with youth came in the guise of a jurisdictional complaint launched in 1946 by the juvenile court workers. Ultimately, Pelletier and his colleagues won the dispute through a well-orchestrated public relations campaign, but the complaint reveals how the "Montreal Miracle" involved a true transformation of police work. The Delinquency Prevention Bureau had, after all, reduced juvenile delinquency at a time when other cities seemed powerless to do so. Yet over the course of doing so the police wildly overstepped their jurisdiction, according to Montreal Juvenile Delinquents' Court personnel who chose to complain in 1946 to the Quebec attorney general. As damning was the critique that the child-friendly ways were not always in the best interest of the child.

In early 1946 members of the Montreal Juvenile Delinquents' Court filed a complaint against the Juvenile Morality Squad's new system for managing arrested children. Rather than delivering children who committed major acts of delinquency to the juvenile court, as they had done in the past, police were now instructed to take children to the JMS where none other than Ovila Pelletier decided the outcome of the case. The complaint accused the police of usurping jurisdiction over processing juvenile cases. The police were allegedly breaching municipal regulations concerning police procedure by refusing to take all prisoners who are brought to the station and who have committed crimes to the appropriate tribunal "without delay."[58] The complaint extended to the cases that ended up before the juvenile court judge: even in these cases the police officers allegedly interfered with the gathering of information on the child and family, thereby overriding the jurisdiction of the court's probation officers.

The response from the office of the attorney general was a sign of the times. Not only did the government side with the Juvenile Morality Squad, it encouraged the court to make more room for the youth police in juvenile justice in Montreal. Many cases before the juvenile tribunal, Assistant Attorney General Léopold Désilets pointed out, concerned the frivolous rather than the serious, tying up valuable court time with the mere "peccadilloes" of the young. Calling for a spirit of collaboration, he asserted the JMS officers' right to protect childhood, instructed the juvenile court probation officers to consider the JMS members "volunteer probation officers," and to assist the JMS in any way necessary.[59]

Despite the social agency's concerns and the jurisdictional disputes about the new directions of policing in the late 1940s the JMS/Prevention Bureau continued with its mandate. It enlisted the media to advance its position. In 1954 the National Film Board of Canada's weekly television series, *On the Spot*, featured an episode on the Montreal Police Juvenile Clubs. In this news short, Pelletier proudly demonstrated how his PJC had quelled the "serious and tragic problem" of juvenile delinquency. Replete with images of boys happily focused on table tennis, volleyball games, and the like, the uncritical documentary provided ample evidence of the success of the police in preventive care for children.

In hindsight we can see other implications of the prevention program. By enabling an expanding youth squad to administer and judge juvenile delinquency cases, the juvenile court became preoccupied with serious juvenile crime. As David Wolcott shows for the Los Angeles Police Department, the diversion of predelinquents and younger delinquents away from the court system left older and often racialized youth in a system that would turn away from rehabilitation toward a "get tough" on juvenile crime approach.[60]

Conclusion

Juvenile delinquency's postwar rise stymied authorities in many large cities, except perhaps one: Montreal. Canada's largest and most cosmopolitan city did not seem to suffer the same escalation in youth crime that beset its counterparts in English Canada and in the United States. Not that the Montreal Police Department avoided the midcentury's imperative focus on children and youth. Quite the opposite, in fact: the astonishing 50 percent reduction in juvenile delinquency over the course of the 1940s, Montreal officers would explain, was the result of a "master plan of operation" to combat the roots of delinquency and involved a reconceptualization of the role of police officer in contemporary society.[61] Montreal's multipronged approach to juvenile crime was not unique to that city or to the 1940s—it simply seemed most effective there. Antidelinquency programs predicated on a thorough understanding of the child and an emphasis on crime prevention over correction had emerged and spread throughout North America in the preceding decades. What the delinquency panics of the 1940s and '50s provided was the impetus to expand, coordinate, and fully fund earlier police efforts at preventing delinquency.

Prevention work with youth necessitated the production of a particular construction of youth—one that was deserving of protection; that is, police "protection" was carefully meted out and exclusionary. The Montreal Miracle—the decline in juvenile delinquency—points to a radical shift in policing that targeted not delinquents per se, but good kids—or predelinquents, as they were sometimes called—to teach them to respect authority, reject delinquency, and exercise their otherwise idle minds and bodies. This reconfiguration of police activity to incorporate preventive programs with young people was an expression of changing ideas about the nature of children and childhood and furthered several trends in early 20th century policing including the hiring of women, the athleticism of police, and the use of laws such as juvenile curfew regulations to change behavior.

By midcentury many, mainly working-class, youth had contact with police during the course of a day or week. These were not the archetypical beat cops considered the "natural" enemy of children, but rather male authority figures one might associate with avuncular benevolence.

Although youth policing would open the door for greater numbers of women officers, the prevention programs' sports orientation along with postwar prescriptions of masculinity and fatherhood worked well here alongside police paternalism to help reconfigure the cop as emotionally caring and responsible for children. Male officers were encouraged to embrace their new identity through involvement in sports clubs for youth. Rather than mark a diminishment in the policing of youth, this new system projected law enforcement more thoroughly into the realm of childhood and adolescence as officers could be found in playgrounds, streets, and schools that spatially belonged to young people.

NOTES

1 Sarah Fishman, *The Battle for Children: World War II, Youth Crime, and Juvenile Justice in Twentieth-Century France* (Cambridge: Harvard University Press, 2002); Jeffrey A. Keshen, *Saints, Sinners, and Soldiers: Canada's Second World War* (Vancouver: University of British Columbia Press, 2004); Tamara Myers, *Caught: Montreal's Modern Girls and the Law 1869–1945* (Toronto: University of Toronto Press, 2006).

2 James Gilbert, *Cycle of Outrage: America's Reaction to the Juvenile Delinquent in the 1950s* (New York: Oxford University Press, 1986), 14.

3 Reproduced in the Montreal publication *Revue des agents de Police* (March 1946), 2.

4 "Juvenile crime has become a veritable plague not only in Montreal but in all large cities of the world," wrote medical-legal expert Dr. Rosario Fontaine in "La criminalité juvénile," *Revue des agents de Police* (March 1946), 2. Montreal police officer Ovila Pelletier described youth-oriented commercial leisure spots as "centres of infection." Det.-Sgt. A. O. Pelletier, "Campaign to Stamp Out Juvenile Crime," *Revue des agents de Police* 1, no. 1 (February 1946): 12.

5 For an excellent summary of these developments, see Julia Grant, *The Boy Problem: Educating Boys in Urban America, 1870–1970* (Baltimore: Johns Hopkins University Press, 2014), chapter 2.

6 Grant, *Boy Problem*, 11.

7 Keshen, *Saints, Sinners, and Soldiers*, 204.

8 Gilbert, *Cycle of Outrage*, 27.

9 Gilbert, *Cycle of Outrage*; Eric Schneider, *Vampires, Dragons, and Egyptian Kings: Youth Gangs in Postwar New York* (Princeton, NJ: Princeton University Press, 1999).

10 "La criminalité chez les jeunes est devenue un terrible fléau de nos jours," *La Presse* (October 19, 1945), 5.

11 John McLeish, "Youth Problems in Wartime," *Municipal Review of Canada* (July/August 1942), 7.

12 *Montreal Gazette*, January 22, 1941; June 15, 1942; March 1, 1944.

13 *Montreal Gazette*, March 11, 1944, 6.

14 City of Montreal, Police Department, Annual Reports (1945), "Grand Sommaire des Arrestations," 108.

15 Madga Fahrni, "The Romance of Reunion: Montreal War Veterans Return to Family Life, 1944–1949," *Journal of the Canadian Historical Association* 9, no. 1 (1998): 187–208.

16 See the *Canadian Police Gazette* and the *Canadian Police Bulletin*, both of which contained myriad stories of postwar delinquency problems and reproduced American, British, and Canadian press articles on delinquency.

17 "Canadian Youth Scored," *Canadian Police Gazette* (April 1947), 20.

18 This sense of children being valued on a national scale was connected to both wartime loss and the changing emotional role children played in society.

19 City of Montreal, Police Department, *Annual Reports* for 1942 and 1944. "Sunset offenses" is my category, which includes vagrancy or loitering by night and after the city's legal curfew.

20 City of Montreal, Police Department, *Annual Reports* for 1942 and 1944.

21 Rev. J. Dinnage Hobden, "Prosperity Delinquency," *Canadian Police Gazette* 17, no. 6 (September 1942), 12.

22 "Le problème insoluble pose par le couvre-feu," *La Presse*, September 11, 1942, 3.

23 City of Montreal, Police Department, *Annual Report*, 1944.

24 City of Montreal Police Department, Annual Reports (1953), "Grand Sommaire des Arrestations," 50.

25 *La Patrie Suisse* (Geneva) 50 (December 10, 1949).

26 "Le Miracle de Montréal," *La Patrie Suisse*, no. 50 (December 10, 1949): 1570–71.

27 Clifford Putney, *Muscular Christianity: Manhood and Sports in Protestant America, 1880–1920* (Cambridge: Harvard University Press, 2009); David I. MacLeod, *Building Character in the American Boy: The Boy Scouts, YMCA, and Their Forerunners, 1870–1920* (Madison: University of Wisconsin Press, 1983); Grant, *Boy Problem*.

28 Steven Schlossman and Michael Sedlak, "The Chicago Area Project Revisited," *Crime and Delinquency* 29 (July 1983): 398–462, at 415.

29 David Wolcott, *Cops and Kids: Policing Juvenile Delinquency in Urban America, 1890–1940* (Columbus: Ohio State University Press, 2005), 128–31. See also Elisabeth Lossing, "The Crime Prevention Work of the Berkeley Police Department," in *Preventing Crime: A Symposium*, ed. Sheldon Glueck and Eleanor Glueck (New York: McGraw-Hill, 1936), 237–63.

30 Lossing, "Crime Prevention Work," 252.

31 Wolcott, *Cops and Kids*, 120.

32 Wolcott, *Cops and Kids*, 122–24.

33 As William Bush explains, protected childhood had been on the agenda of reformers since the early 19th century; a century of policies and programs followed, yet the result was "abject failure." William S. Bush, *Who Gets a Childhood? Race*

and Juvenile Justice in Twentieth-Century Texas (Athens: University of Georgia Press, 2010), 5.

34 Wolcott, *Cops and Kids*, 127.

35 Det.-Sgt. O.-A. Pelletier, "Crime and Youth," *Revue des Agents de Police-Constables Review* 1, no. 3 (May 1946), 47. In this article Pelletier draws on the Chicago Area Project and Hoover's 1945 speech to the International Association of Police Chiefs.

36 Joseph Kluchesky, "Juvenile Delinquency," *Canadian Police Gazette* 20, no. 2 (May 1945), 4. See also Pelletier, "Crime and Youth," 48.

37 "The Policeman, Youth's Friend," *Canadian Police Bulletin* (September 1947), 34.

38 National Film Board of Canada, *The Policeman*, 1946. Producer Gudrun Parker.

39 Pelletier, "Campaign to Stamp Out Juvenile Crime," 12.

40 Det.-Sgt. O.-A. Pelletier, "Crime and Youth," *Revue des Agents de Police-Constables Review* 1, no. 3 (May 1946), 47.

41 Pelletier, "Campaign to Stamp Out Juvenile Crime," 12.

42 Pelletier, "Crime and Youth," 47.

43 In July 1944 the Bureau moved to a police station at rue Craig and rue Cartier. Julien White, personnel file, Letter to the Comité des Griefs, Syndicat des Fonctionnaires Municipaux, January 30, 1948, 2.

44 Ovila Pelletier, "Allocution," text of speech before the Annual Convention of the Association des chefs de Police et Pompiers de la Province de Québec, Chicoutimi, Québec, July 1946. Archives municipals de Montréal, Coupres de la presses, Bobine 113, Justice, Délinquance juvénile.

45 O.-A. Pelletier, "Le B.M.J [editorial]," *Revue des agents de Police/Constables Review* 1, no. 2 (March 1946), 1 and 23.

46 It is important to remember that Montreal comprised French-Canadian Catholics and Anglophones who might be Irish Catholic, Jewish, or Protestant. Tensions among these groups were familiar since the conquest of Quebec in 1759.

47 *Montreal Police Juvenile Guide*, no. 1 (November 1950): 79, 81.

48 *On the Spot* (with the Montreal Police Juvenile Club), National Film Board of Canada, 1954.

49 "Le Miracle de Montreal," 1570.

50 *On the Spot*.

51 *Canadian Police Bulletin*, June 1949. On boys and guns, see R. Blake Brown, "'Every Boy Ought to Learn to Shoot and to Obey Orders': Guns, Boys, and the Law in Canada from the Late Nineteenth Century to the Great War," *Canadian Historical Revue* 93, no. 2 (June 2012): 196–226.

52 Editorial, "To Teach and Not to Punish," *Montreal Gazette*, April 3, 1958, 8.

53 Ibid.

54 "Friend of Youth," *La Presse*, April 1, 1958, 6. Parc Ovila-Pelletier is in the east end of Montreal near the Olympic Stadium.

55 The Montreal Council of Social Agencies was a coordinating organization for English-speaking, non-Catholic social agencies that had its origins in the Montreal School of Social Work.

56 McGill University Archives, MO 2076, C30, file 520, "Juvenile Delinquency Prevention Bureau Study."

57 Ibid., 2.

58 ANQ-Q, E17 Correspondance du Procureur-general, file 1946–2121. Letter from Marcel Trahan to the Assistant Attorney General, Léopold Désilets, 7 February 1946.

59 ANQ-Q, E17 Correspondance du Procureur-general, file 1946–2121. Letter from L'Assistant-procureur general, no date.

60 Wolcott, *Cops and Kids*, 161–67.

61 Det.-Capt. A. O. Pelletier, "Delinquency Prevention," *Municipal Review of Canada* (March 1949), 13.

5

Supervising Freedom

Juvenile Delinquency in Paris and Boston in the Mid-Twentieth Century

GUILLAUME PÉRISSOL

"The quality of mercy is not strain'd, It droppeth as the gentle rain from heaven."[1] These words, which served as the motto of the Boston Juvenile Court (BJC) in the 1950s, could very well have been used for other juvenile courts in the United States or elsewhere, inasmuch as they reveal the era's optimistic faith in a nonpunitive system whose natural and primary role would be the protection of children. The quotation is taken from William Shakespeare's *The Merchant of Venice*, in the scene where Portia addresses the Jew Shylock, who has come to make a legal claim for a pound of his debtor's flesh. Portia defends clemency as opposed to the strict application of the law that he demands. Transposed to modern-day state apparatuses, this New Testament-like message would mean that the traditional repressive function of the law tends to be replaced by an ideological function expressed by love. Is it not the ultimate goal of juvenile justice to make the youths "work by themselves" without any violent intervention?[2]

Probation stands at the very core of such a system. Seven years after the first juvenile court was created in 1899 in Chicago, Édouard Julhiet, a reformer who had worked in the United States, presented the then little-known workings of the American juvenile courts in a famous lecture given in Paris.[3] He pointed out that a "typical court" was characterized by its specialization and, most notably, the practice of probation, the goal of which was "to abolish prison for children" (or at least the "common jail"), translating the English term by the peculiar phrase *liberté surveillée* (literally, supervised freedom).[4] In 1912, the French Parliament enacted a law establishing *tribunaux pour enfants* (juvenile courts) as well as providing for this new form of control outside the facility walls.[5]

On February 2, 1945, a law reaffirmed the court's educational vocation and heralded the veritable birth of juvenile justice with specialized juvenile judges established nationwide.[6] A lawyer who took part in preparing the law, Hélène Campinchi, insisted that probation was a "beneficent system."[7] Jean Chazal, a juvenile judge who enjoyed a high media profile after the Second World War, praised the juvenile courts' "judicial neo-humanism" and their reliance on probation: assisted by the *délégué à la liberté surveillée* (probation officer), the minor "learns what life and freedom are about while living freely."[8]

The American model of juvenile courts achieved rapid worldwide success in the twentieth century, with Boston and Paris becoming leaders in the field. There were local variations. In the United States itself, there was no single type of juvenile court. The responsibility for developing and administering juvenile justice fell to individual states, which resulted in discrepancies between principles and practices.[9] Though standards were drawn up at the federal level in 1923, they were not compulsory.[10] Massachusetts had often played a pioneering role in the judicial field. For example, in 1846 it created, in Westborough, the first public reform school. This reform school for boys was partly inspired by the Mettray Penal Colony in France, illustrating the long-standing movement of reform ideas and the transnational borrowing processes in the North Atlantic world.[11] And in 1906 Massachusetts also established the BJC.[12] This specialized court had jurisdiction over a limited area in Boston, principally the center of the city; elsewhere in Massachusetts, juvenile justice was dispensed by district courts during specific "juvenile sessions." This illustrates how different the judicial treatment could be even within the same state, since juvenile delinquency was above all considered to be an urban problem. Similarly, in France, before the 1945 law, juvenile courts existed only in certain cities. The Seine Juvenile Court was established in 1914 to serve the Seine *département*, an administrative division encompassing Paris and the surrounding suburbs, and managed to operate as a relatively specialized and autonomous body. It drove the development in France of a juvenile justice system, with its "disciplines" and services devoted to the reeducation of youths, ranging from specialized social services to child guidance clinics.[13]

Probation remains the primary means of applying the principle of loving one's neighbor, which, democratized and more or less dechristianized, played a unifying role in the creation of the model of juvenile courts by laying down the ideals of mutual understanding and exchange between subjects. The central role of probation was quickly noted by historians, who referred to prescriptive texts or had gained access to court archives, such as Steven L. Schlossman in his classic study.[14] Nonetheless, there is scant historiography on the subject, not to mention comparative history, which is virtually nonexistent with regard to comparative research between juvenile courts in France and the United States.[15] The comparative approach, however, can offer helpful insight into a number of questions. What conclusions can we draw from the rapid spread of juvenile courts and of the use of probation in the West and throughout the world? To what needs does this success correspond? What strategic positions does the strange notion of "supervised freedom" occupy in the judicial field, and beyond?

While drawing on new archival material, this chapter will focus on Boston and Paris in the mid-twentieth century, when America and France shared the same optimistic belief in employing the "more humane method" of juvenile courts. In the 1960s, juvenile justice—and criminal justice in general—shifted toward new directions in the United States.[16] Beginning in the 1980s, the machinery of mass probation was coupled with a machinery of mass incarceration, unseen in other Western countries. That trend could be explained, in part, by the continuing de facto segregation applied by criminal justice while other institutions tried to get rid of it following the civil rights movement's advances. It was as if, reduced to "waste management," prisons remained the last institutional bastions where the American race problem was dealt with so harshly, behind the safety of high walls.[17] Without ignoring certain resistances and deeply entrenched practices, as shown in studies of courts that were far less dynamic than those in the capital cities of France and Massachusetts, we will examine the modernity of juvenile justice systems at the forefront of the prevention and treatment of delinquency, which foretold profound social changes.[18] To that end, we shall use different time scales in order to explore the deep movements and currents that agitate the surface of events and individual lives.

To understand the fundamental process behind the history of juvenile courts, it is useful to look back to Alexis de Tocqueville's *Democracy in America*. In this seminal work, written after a journey to assess prison reform in the United States, democracy is treated not only as a political configuration but also as a "social state" that stands in opposition to the aristocratic state. Democratization partly accounts for the invention of juvenile justice, its popularity, and the directions it took from the start of the nineteenth century. In the 1950s, the process of democratization accelerated in the United States as well as in France, which had been until then a noted laggard. In 1955, a journalist for *Time* magazine made a number of intriguing observations about the younger generation in French society. But he missed the changes under way when he claimed with some exaggeration that "class boundaries in France are often as rigid as Hindu caste lines" and that the youthful population "is locked at birth into firmly built cellblocks."[19] In the two countries, mass culture, consumer society, and modern family (dis)organization were increasingly denounced by politicians as well as by intellectuals and child protection professionals as sources of juvenile delinquency, which had apparently gone up again after a period of postwar calm.[20] Studies on these issues began to grow in number. A specialized research center was opened by the Ministry of Justice in Vaucresson, a suburb of Paris.[21] In the United States, the Senate initiated a long-term survey with the creation of the Subcommittee to Investigate Juvenile Delinquency in 1953.[22]

The political and economic climate was marked by a relative redistribution of wealth after World War II. Postwar prosperity also encouraged a certain homogenization of society, which was accompanied by the development of the welfare state—one of its components being juvenile justice. In the mid-twentieth century, in this context of "democratization," authority was facing a crisis of which contemporary observers were acutely aware and that was reflected in the rise of a new form of delinquency. Juvenile delinquents typically came from the working class. However, middle-class and even upper-class youths began to be brought before the court for bizarre and disturbing behaviors, as they sought a sense of direction in life but refused to follow traditional paths. This is echoed by films like the famous *Rebel Without a Cause*, which was released in the United States in 1955, or the very Parisian *Les Tricheurs* (The Cheaters), which was released in France in 1958. Indeed, French juvenile records mention "existentialist delinquents" and American records refer to "beatniks." Although such teenagers were only a small minority, they symbolized a change in mentalities, announcing the Swinging Sixties.

Authority can be defined in opposition to both the use of force and the reliance on persuasion.[23] In face of the rapid changes that occurred after World War II, a general weakening of authority encouraged the practice of probation, which aimed at gently convincing individuals to actively participate in their self-improvement. Upon closer view, we shall see how probation and related measures came to be at the heart of a new, adjustable, and flexible machinery. Social control operates less and less by means of direct domination and violence, and more and more by fostering mutual understanding and dialogue. We shall then take a long-term perspective, looking at the change from disciplinary societies, conceptualized through the idea and architecture of the Panopticon prison, to modern-day societies that have tended to be organized around probationary systems and "free floating control."[24]

Juvenile Justice and the Tocquevillian Process of Democratization

As we showed in an earlier study, the United States and France followed the same rationale of humanist and exploratory juvenile justice although certain differences appeared over time, as the United States began earlier and went further than France in breaking with the criminal system.[25] Working-class urban youths constituted the bulk of the minors referred to juvenile justice. The latter was created to deal with poor children who lived in cities grown formidably large by an influx of a formerly rural population or, in the United States, large numbers of foreign immigrants. It was no longer possible to rely on community self-surveillance, which had prevailed in traditional village-based societies, where everyone knew everyone else.[26] Since the beginning of the nineteenth century, a more educational approach was being progressively employed to monitor the conduct of young offenders, in spite of some resistance and an occasional step backward. Techniques and expertise drawn from social, psychological, and medical sciences would gradually yield a better knowledge of these juveniles to normalize them, according to Michel Foucault's formulation. But the workings of power-knowledge so brilliantly dismantled in *Discipline and Punish* should not obscure the importance of the subjects' sentiments and motivations, which also account for the success of juvenile justice.

The development of photography, and then of cinema, bore witness to a renewed sense of connection between people. Physical gestures expressing attention, benevolence, and trust (the judge's hand on a child's shoulder, for example) became recurrent symbols of a feeling of altruism that came to be associated with juvenile courts on both sides of the Atlantic.[27] As Alexis de Tocqueville observed, in aristocratic centuries, "the general notion of *fellow* [*semblable* in French] is obscure" whereas in democracies the movement for equality of conditions encouraged "sympathy" and "compassion" between human beings.[28] The juvenile courts were part of this overall rise and then consolidation of the democratic movement, where "great services are scarcely accorded" but "good offices are rendered constantly" because, while the links between men are weakened, the circle of fellows widens.[29] The gestures of the social actors involved, together with the court's organization, expressed this more acute democratic feeling, which no longer allowed the poor and their offspring to be classified as a separate group, or at least not with the same ease as before.

If we look back to the 1830s, when Tocqueville conducted his study in the United States, we find ourselves in the Jacksonian Era, which saw the rise of the "common man." At that very time, America was witnessing the gradual birth of juvenile justice, notably in the development of the first reformatories. These school-prisons would be reoriented toward a "family format," on which experiments in Europe, such as Mettray in France, had put the focus.[30] This sequence of events did not come together by pure chance. The inexorable rise of democracy eventually broke down the aristocratic vision equating "laboring classes" with "dangerous classes" and blurred the lines between delinquent children and children in need of protection, to the point that the juvenile courts that emerged at the turn of the nineteenth and twentieth centuries seemed to be turning into "coercive casework agencies."[31]

A number of other factors certainly helped lead to the ultimate worldwide prevalence of juvenile courts. In the context of capitalist development and exploitation, urbanization and industrialization prompted the search for innovative solutions to the threat of social chaos. Theories on institutional diffusion, processes of emulation, and penological reasons also explain the global diffusion of juvenile courts.[32] But the process of democratization, as described by Tocqueville, may well be the funda-

SUPERVISING FREEDOM | 107

mental key to the history of juvenile justice and juvenile probation—insofar as the effects of democratization would be felt more intensely among the young offenders, with the scientific, pedagogical, and social "discovery" of adolescence (around 1890–1900), this period of life no longer being seen as a solely upper-class phenomenon.[33]

But what about totalitarian or authoritarian regimes, such as those in Francoist Spain or in the People's Republic of China, which accommodated, or sometimes even encouraged, specialized courts for minors based on educational means and probation?[34] And didn't the Vichy regime in France promote reforms in juvenile justice, which would be taken up after the Liberation by the highly "humanist" 1945 law?[35] Explanatory factors can be identified: the relative autonomy of the child protection field from the political field, and the remarkable flexibility of the model of the juvenile court, not to mention the influence of the international trends and the force of habit. They may appear more relevant than a Tocquevillian perspective. It should be borne in mind, however, that democracy is an "ambivalent" concept in Tocqueville's work, covering two principal meanings: a political regime defined as government by the people and a "social state" characterized by the rejection of inherited hierarchies and an irrepressible movement toward the equalization of conditions.[36] From the latter perspective, it carries the potential risk of developing into a mass society composed of isolated and atomized individuals, who are inclined to follow the guidance of providential men, and where freedom tends to be destroyed by the urge for equality.[37] In *Brave New World*, Aldous Huxley illustrates one of the possible outcomes of such a movement. In the foreword to the 1946 edition, Huxley states: "A really efficient totalitarian state would be one in which the all-powerful executive of political bosses and their army of managers control a population of slaves who do not have to be coerced, because they love their servitude."[38] It should come as no surprise, then, that juvenile courts, with their gentle violence supported by new sciences and techniques, and their use of persuasion rather than coercion, have been adopted by regimes as politically diverse as liberal democracies and as popular democracies and other oppressive regimes born in the twentieth century. All were compelled by the march of history to break, in whole or in part, with the old aristocratic tradition. The democratic revolution gives rise to freedom, but it also produces servitude.[39] The juvenile justice system in the twentieth century, with its heavy reliance on probation, must be seen as an outgrowth of new forms of control. It was born out of modern society's ambiguities, manifested in the struggle between freedom and equality, servitude and emancipation, as its practices make it clear.

Juvenile Delinquents on Either Side of the Atlantic

On the basis of the figures produced by the BJC[40] and statistics compiled at a later date for a division of the Seine Juvenile Court,[41] let us try to determine the main characteristics of the delinquency cases handled in the mid-twentieth century by juvenile justice.[42]

In Boston, as in the Seine *département*, more than half the complaints—around 55 to 60 percent—concerned theft and property offenses. The other main category, accounting for roughly a fifth to a quarter of complaints, was a catchall classification, ranging from prostitution to behavior considered to be immoral or dangerous to social or family harmony, with girls under closer surveillance in this area than boys.[43] Although legal definitions vary, making exact comparisons difficult, the systems had approximately the same main structures of juvenile crime. It is as if, after the initial experimentation phases, and in relation to social, cultural, and economic changes, the practices of juvenile courts in large cities drew closer.

The age of majority was set at seventeen in Massachusetts and eighteen in France. In accordance with law or tradition, no proceedings would be brought against an offender under the age of seven. For the most part, the defendants were adolescents: between 80 and 90 percent ranged in age from fourteen to seventeen for the Seine *département*, and thirteen to sixteen for Boston, with each institution seemingly adapting to the applicable age limits of majority. In terms of gender, for the Seine, the proportion of girls to boys was quite stable over time, with roughly one girl for every four or five boys; in Boston, the proportion was more balanced (40 percent girls). This high percentage (compared with the results usually available) was not found in the rest of Massachusetts and, according to the BJC, was due to the presence of department stores in the area served by the court, proving "to some girls a source of strong temptation to shoplifting."[44]

Certain classifications, such as race, differed.[45] But, in the two environments, and in accordance with the usual data, most juvenile delinquents clearly belonged to the working class. This overrepresentation can be linked to social segregation on the basis of self-reported delinquency surveys.[46] Interestingly, at about the same time, in the 1950s, both juvenile justice systems were faced with a new type of delinquency that affected the middle and upper classes. It was an atypical form of delinquent behavior but highly significant and a source of much anguish, because it challenged ordinary social divisions and order. To cite two telling examples involving middle-class offenders, let us look at the case of fourteen-year-old Ellen, who appeared before the BJC in 1957 on charges of stubbornness, and that of Henri, a seventeen-year-old high school student, who was brought before the Seine Juvenile Court in 1950 for vagrancy.[47]

Henri's offenses consisted in hanging out with the bohemian student population, going to bed and getting up late, philosophizing, writing poems, and refusing "to work eight hours a day."[48] After being sent to an observation center, he incited concern among the personnel who found his case to be a prime example of "maladjustment . . . brought on by socialization within the special milieu of the Latin Quarter and Saint-Germain-des-Prés,"[49] comparable to other similarly "poisoned"[50] adolescents. Hence, Professor Georges Heuyer, a well-recognized specialist in child neuropsychiatry, was called on to draw up a medicolegal report that revealed, above all, the psychiatrist's perplexity and difficulty in dealing with the young man's insolence and flagrant rebelliousness. When Henri was asked if he practiced homosexuality, which was supposed to be widespread in the "peculiar underworld" of Saint-Germain-des-Prés, he replied that he liked women: "Even if I were homosexual, what would that have to do with anything?" The professor then segued into a discussion on literature with "that poet" only to learn, to his surprise, that Henri only knew a few plays by Jean Racine and Pierre Corneille, boasting "I belong to only one school: mine." The report concluded by expressing "the utmost reservations about this boy's future mental health."[51] Other statements in the case file pointed to his links with the literary and political avant-garde, which was more Lettrist and Situationist than really existentialist, and, in any event, in opposition to "bourgeois" values.[52] Henri was granted probation thanks to his parents, who were from a respectable background and were seen as trustworthy.

Ellen could be considered his female counterpart, transposed into the context of an East Coast city, with an added touch of mystical qualities. Her thick BJC file reveals the transformation of a "demure . . . Beacon Hill girl" into an easy girl, sporting "exaggerated" makeup, who "wore her hair like a femme fatale," with "huge baubles dangl[ing] from her exposed ears." She underwent a final metamorphosis after running away several times and stumbling into the folk underground world in the neighboring college town of Cambridge, where she crossed paths with beatniks, becoming a member of Allen Ginsberg's circle.[53] Later, at twenty-eight, she was found by the police begging in a Pakistani bazaar, while preparing to head off for the Himalayas "to see her guru." Her mother had confided that, just before running away and after being placed on probation, Ellen had torn up almost every picture of herself she could find, "as if she wanted to destroy every connection with her past."[54]

As an intellectual debate raged in the 1950s around the issue of mass culture and mass society, Hannah Arendt published an article on "the crisis in education," linking the problem to the crisis of authority.[55] In Arendt's view, the past was no longer respected, and the growing challenges to political authority in a democratic environment had contributed to undermining educational authority. In a world "that is neither structured by authority nor held together by tradition,"[56] where individuals increasingly found themselves in "the gap between past and future,"[57] even well-off youngsters were turning against their parents; and more and more youths, like Ellen and Henri, were denying, denigrating, or simply ignoring their inheritance.[58] Disciplinary structures, modeled after Jeremy Bentham's carefully thought-out Panopticon design, were beginning to crack. They were no longer in line with the zeitgeist and less and less in sync with both the democratic system and the production model—the steep vertical hierarchies of Taylorism were declining, as society transitioned toward a service-oriented economy. That is why the very simple technique of probation, updated and modernized in the middle of the nineteenth century by an obscure Boston boot-maker, John Augustus, would prove increasingly popular.[59] By giving priority to the probationary system, which facilitates exchanges and dialogue, instead of using the Panopticon machine to "see without being seen,"[60] the juvenile court embarked on a vast experiment in the exercise of soft control, an experiment that would gradually overtake the entire judiciary system and eventually extend beyond it.

Probation and Extension of Control

In 1950–51, juvenile courts were primarily probation oriented, especially in Boston where the presiding justice was a former probation officer.[61] More than 60 percent of the youths found to be wayward or delinquent by the BJC were put on probation.[62] In Paris, probation accounted for nearly one-half of the measures taken to deal with juvenile delinquents.[63] In both cities, the social workers' recommendations had a crucial bearing on the judge's final decision,[64] leading to a relative disconnection between the judgment and the offense, as the police investigation was given only secondary consideration. This line of thinking and acting kept with the original intent of the founders of the juvenile court from the Progressive Era, who felt that an assessment of the individual and his environment should be given priority over the actual facts of the delinquent act.

Placement in various institutions and the harsh reality of confinement should not be ignored, but they were generally reserved for only the gravest cases, such as that of a seventeen-year-old Parisian male prostitute who appeared before the Seine Juvenile Court in 1946.[65] Having transgressed the law, gender norms, and moral standards through his sexuality and by offering his body for sale, he was incarcerated in a psychiatric facility after he justified his behavior by a simple and somewhat provocative explanation: "I needed cash for the movies." Article 64 of the old Napoleonic Penal Code on the state of madness was applied without hesitation.[66] Placements were also used as forms of short-term punishment because of growing doubts as to the rehabilitative value of confinement over the long term. In this regard, Massachusetts was ahead of France. Lengths of stay were much longer at the French institutions for juvenile delinquents, since the belief in their educational effectiveness persisted longer and was accompanied by a policy to provide a complete training program over several years.[67]

Moreover, the institutions evolved, if not in terms of their practices at least in terms of the image they sought to project of themselves. Once again, the United States made the greatest strides. French institutions, like most institutions for juvenile delinquents in Europe,[68] often still constructed a disciplinary image replete with bare-torsoed youths walking outside in drill team style, taking part in educational programs largely inherited from the nineteenth century, under the influence of the medical-hygienist power, and even of military and economic forces.[69] The goal was to transform boys into productive, socially adjusted men.[70] In Westborough, Massachusetts, the Lyman Training School[71] sought to convey another image, touting the beneficial aspects of play and pleasure.[72]

Logically, the American National Probation Association took this rhetoric even further. The probation officer was no different from a volunteer with the Big Brother and Big Sister program, with whom he occasionally cooperated in an effort to reintegrate youths into the community. There was the same complicity and the same attitudes behind creating a "friendly and useful relationship" with the teenager.[73] From a legal standpoint, Massachusetts probation officers enjoyed the powers of police officers, but it was understood that the exercise of such powers could doom the educational undertaking to failure.[74] His French counterpart did not have the same scope of powers and would long remain a volunteer,[75] selected "according to the needs of each case" so as to be perfectly "suited" to the needs of the juvenile (which, unsurprisingly, would raise recruitment problems).[76] Not only was the probation officer progressively transformed into a full-on social worker without firearm or uniform, but also increasingly the juvenile police officer came to resemble him.[77] Those changes were a part of blurring the traditional boundaries between the ideological and repressive functions of the state apparatuses.[78] The soft authority approach by police forces, including recreational programs and so on, was more limited in France than in North America, where it took on different forms in different places and times.[79] In the mid-twentieth century, the "Montreal Miracle" of youth policing, analyzed by Tamara Myers (see chapter 4), had no equivalent in Boston whose police had no juvenile squad and only a few policewomen specially trained.[80] However, the Boston Junior Police Corps appeared to have been active until the beginning of the 1940s (in 1942, 21,000 boys, between ten and sixteen, were enrolled as members of the Corps) and, in the 1960s, a Juvenile Aid Section would be created in the Boston Police Department.[81]

Numerous studies and official reports, issued by international and national organizations, showed how juvenile courts served as laboratories for the development of probation whose "full importance" and "expanding power" were "taken note of" by the participants of the twelfth International Penal and Penitentiary Congress in 1950.[82] The genealogy of probation has yet to be traced because research has focused predominately on prisons.[83] This is so despite the fact that all official statistical indicators compiled over decades show the same tendency, which was initiated by juvenile courts, to place probation and community supervision at the core of judicial decisions.[84] However, we can perhaps propose a defining moment of the new misconduct management system, the objective of which is less a matter of having the individual return to a completely normal life, but, rather, of managing abnormalities, in their different ways, with a relative degree of tolerance ("I hope that she will find herself," as Ellen's probation officer concluded with resignation in a letter to the girl's mother).[85] That defining moment might be found in an "unorthodox" English survey conducted in 1942, where delinquent boys were asked the question: Do you like your probation officer?[86] This closed the circle of control and broke the circle of discipline. Both circles had previously overlapped; the "affectional discipline" used in the Victorian Era shows that love had for quite some time figured in the specialists' reflections and intentions (dating back to Mettray, at least).[87] Undoubtedly, the various discourses and practices coexisted before one eventually overtook the other. Love was no longer just talked about, it was now expected. Never before had the system seemed so fruitful. The child saver (or his avatars) was not content to say to juvenile delinquents "I am going to improve you" or "I am going to cure you," instead of "I am going to punish you."[88] He now told them "I love you" and asked for their love in return. It was boundless love, since probation extended into prevention policies and parole or after-care programs.

In Massachusetts, juvenile delinquents were committed to the Youth Service Board; and this public agency, created in 1948, used parole extensively in determining the course of treatment.[89] Numerous initiatives and projects developed in different fields in order to observe and control juveniles even before they committed any offenses.[90] In France, for instance, in 1946, a group of experts from the École de psychologie et de pédagogie (School of Psychology and Pedagogy) in Lyon proposed the "screening" of all maladjusted children. This "early and comprehensive" screening would "take place in the family, in the street, at school, in educational centers, youth organizations, vacation camps, and apprenticeship workshops."[91] If necessary, informal probation could also be used to ensure smooth transitions. The practice had been especially prevalent in the United States since the creation of juvenile courts;[92] and the district attorney for Suffolk County (where Boston is located) continued to rely on such a procedure in the 1950s,[93] as frequently did the juvenile judge who, in turn, could enter a continuance without a finding (thereby allowing the delinquent to be placed on a kind of informal probation). Probation has taken on a variety of forms throughout a variety of institutions. In the world of education, for example, students undergo continual assessments, which replace the final examination.[94] In short, nobody knows if he is truly *in* or *out*.

Power is exerted with less violence but in a more continual and far-reaching manner. Undoubtedly, juvenile courts follow a "diversionary rationale,"[95] which has spared many youths from incarceration, but they also have avoided incarceration for youths who would never have been subjected to it but found themselves placed on probation. Aside from the social stigma attached to probation, can it be considered a "trivial sanction"?[96] In France, follow-ups were somewhat modest because of the limited professionalization among probation officers, who were essentially volunteers. Juvenile follow-ups seemed to be organized more scrupulously in the United States, at least in Boston, as evidenced by the BJC probation files. For example, Ellen had to submit weekly reports, and reporting frequency was reduced only if her behavior was satisfactory. Her academic performance was monitored and her letters could be intercepted and read. The young girl and, indirectly, her relationships were placed under supervision through a network of social, medical, and educational services and associations (Guidance Center, YWCA, Big Sisters). She was required to undergo evaluations on a regular basis, ranging from vocational testing to a gynecological checkup after she admitted to being sexually active.

Conclusion

After the era of public torture and execution, came, with the Enlightenment and the democratic revolution initiated in the eighteenth century, the period of disciplinary societies' prisons, followed by the days of "supervised freedom." The probationary system, which characterizes the societies of control, developed in the twentieth century in conjunction with the crisis that beset the traditional enclosed environments (family, school, and so forth). Although more research remains to be done,[97] these claims are supported by the present study, which suggests that the historical shifts that we continue to experience can be best observed while looking at juvenile justice, where a dramatic ideology of education and protection is coupled with repression. While comparative history has long been advocated, it has not been extensively practiced.[98] The comparison of cities in different, but interconnected, countries, with a multiscale local and national approach, is a good starting point for finding the "deep structure" in juvenile justice and through it for understanding the new mechanisms of social control.[99] The postwar period is most pertinent for analysis, as probation was becoming the "workhorse" of modern justice systems and, amid international delinquency panics, acute questions concerning authority were being raised.[100]

In a short postscript that he wrote in 1990, a few years before his death, Gilles Deleuze compared the disciplinary society to a mole, while viewing societies of control (which he helped conceptualize) as snakes, arguing that "the man of control is undulatory, in orbit, in a continuous network."[101] In calling for the development of research into the new regimes of domination, Deleuze urged us not to be distracted by the seeming progress of our time, and gave us this final warning: "The coils of a serpent are even more complex than the burrows of a molehill."[102]

NOTES
1 The Citizenship Training Group, Inc., Research Department, compiler and ed., *Boston Juvenile Court: Annual Report, 1951*, title page.
2 See Louis Althusser, "Idéologie et appareils idéologiques d'État (Notes pour une recherche)" [Ideology and ideological state apparatuses (Notes towards an investigation)], April 1970 text printed in *Positions* (Paris, 1982), 79–137.
3 Unless otherwise specified, the term "American" will be used in relation to the United States of America.

4 Édouard Julhiet, "Les tribunaux pour enfants aux États-Unis," in *Les tribunaux spéciaux pour enfants* (Paris, 1906), 10, 20–23; accessed August 29, 2013, www. archive.org. Unless otherwise indicated, all translations from French-language primary sources are the author's. Édouard Julhiet meant "prison" in the strongest sense of the term. Reform schools or other kinds of disciplinary facilities with a view to "reforming" youths in fact remained possible solutions, even if the "decision" made "the most often" and "which constituted the main reason behind the existence of juvenile courts" was probation.

5 The official term used in the 1912 law was *tribunal pour enfants et adolescents* (literally, court for children and adolescents.) The 1945 law relating to juvenile delinquency simply retained the expression *tribunal pour enfants* (court for children) as if to insist upon the protective side of this special court "for" minors, who were considered as "children" in comparison with adults. Although the expression *tribunal des enfants*—children's court—was sometimes used, it was not in the law.

6 The February 2, 1945 Ordonnance relative à l'enfance déliquante (a law relating to juvenile delinquency) is still in force in France today, although it has been amended several times since.

7 Hélène Campinchi, "L'ordonnance du 2 février 1945 relative à l'enfance délinquante," *Revue de l'Éducation Surveillée*, no. 1 (March–April 1946), 14.

8 Jean Chazal, "Vers un néohumanisme judiciaire," chapter 2 in *Études de criminologie juvenile* (Paris: Presses universitaires de France, 1952), 6, 50.

9 Several authors have demonstrated this. For example, David S. Tanenhaus, *Juvenile Justice in the Making* (New York: Oxford University Press, 2004).

10 In 1923, the *Juvenile-Court Standards* were published. They were reprinted and distributed by the Children's Bureau, a federal body, until 1954 when new standards were released. (United States, Children's Bureau, prepared in cooperation with National Probation and Parole Association [and] National Council of Juvenile Court Judges, *Standards for Specialized Courts Dealing with Children* [Washington, DC, 1954]).

11 Regarding the intensification of the transatlantic exchanges in social policies and ideas during the "Progressive Age," see Daniel T. Rogers, *Atlantic Crossings: Social Politics in a Progressive Age* (Cambridge: Harvard University Press, 1998).

12 This was the third American juvenile court, according to Richard Klayman in "The Boston Juvenile Court and the Progressive Challenge of Child-Saving, 1906–1986," *Historical Journal of Massachusetts* 16, no. 2 (Summer 1988): 205. However, this seems to be an error on the part of the author because, in 1906, the juvenile courts of Chicago, Philadelphia, Denver, and others already existed. Édouard Julhiet noted that "five and a half years after the creation of the first juvenile court," that is, in 1905, twenty-four American states had already "adopted this new judicial machinery." Julhiet, "Les tribunaux pour enfants aux États-Unis," 8.

13 For the concept of the "disciplines," see Michel Foucault, *Surveiller et punir: Naissance de la prison* [Discipline and punish: The birth of the prison] (Paris: Gallimard, 1975). For a description of this movement and a general comparison

between the juvenile courts of Paris and Boston, see Guillaume Périssol, "'The Quality of Mercy Is Not Strain'd': Ideological and Repressive Modes of Juvenile Justice—A Comparison between Paris and Boston in the Mid-Twentieth Century," *Journal of Social History* 48, no. 2 (Winter 2014): 289–312, accessed August 31, 2015, doi:10.1093/jsh/shu082, www.jsh.oxfordjournals.org.

14 Steven L. Schlossman, *Transforming Juvenile Justice: Reform Ideals and Institutional Realities, 1825–1920* (DeKalb: Northern Illinois University Press, 2005). Originally published as *Love and the American Delinquent* (Chicago: University of Chicago Press, 1977).

15 In France, on the period of the twentieth century, let us mention a few studies or special journal numbers: Marie-Sylvie Dupont-Bouchat and Éric Pierre, eds., *Enfance et justice au XIXe siècle: Essais d'histoire comparée de la protection de l'enfance, 1820–1914, France, Belgique, Pays-Bas, Canada* (Paris: Presses universitaires de France, 2001); David Niget, *La naissance du tribunal pour enfants: Une comparaison France-Québec (1912–1945)* (Rennes: Presses universitaires de Rennes, 2009); no. 5 (2003) of the *Revue d'histoire de l'enfance "irrégulière": Pratiques éducatives et systèmes judiciaires*. In America, the work produced has been relatively substantial but has tended to focus on the United States during the Progressive Era. Anthony M. Platt's 1969 book on "child savers" has given rise to much literature around the social control arguments he put forward. A good historiographical overview around and beyond Platt's book can be found in the fortieth anniversary edition published in 2009: Miroslava Chávez-García, "In Retrospect: Anthony M. Platt's *The Child Savers: The Invention of Delinquency*," in *The Child Savers: The Invention of Delinquency*, by Anthony M. Platt (New Brunswick, NJ: Rutgers University Press, 2009), xi–xxxvi. The juvenile courts have, in fact, been instrumental in allowing researchers in the United States to understand and assess the so-called progressivism of the turn of the nineteenth and twentieth centuries.

16 The expression "more humane method" is drawn from the explanatory statement for the 1912 law establishing juvenile courts in France: Loi sur les tribunaux pour enfants et adolescents et sur la liberté surveillée (July 22, 1912).

17 African Americans suffer the highest rates of imprisonment compared to other ethnic groups in the United States. However, the history of mass incarceration should not be reduced to a single defining problem. It helps to shed light on several key facets of the social, political, and economic history of America. See Heather Ann Thompson, "Why Mass Incarceration Matters: Rethinking Crisis, Decline, and Transformation in Postwar American History," *Journal of American History* 97, no. 3 (December 2010): 703–734.

18 David Niget's study of the juvenile court for the medium-sized French city of Angers showed that the local system was long challenged by a lack of resources and cumbersome institutions (Niget, *La naissance du tribunal pour enfants*). In the United States, Steven L. Schlossman was one of the first researchers to underscore the need to study the practices of smaller juvenile courts that received less media

attention than those in large cities like Chicago and New York, so as to avoid the pitfalls of "child savers" discourses. See the introduction to *Transforming Juvenile Justice*, xi–xxviii.

19 Stanley Karnow, "France: The Younger Generation," *Time* (May 30, 1955), accessed June 17, 2013, www.content.time.com. Karnow overlooked the fact that there was a trend in that era toward the lengthening of the period of schooling and the democratization of studies, as discussed by Antoine Prost in *L'enseignement s'est-il démocratisé? Les élèves des lycées et collèges de l'agglomération d'Orléans de 1945 à 1980* (Paris: Presses universitaires de France, 1986).

20 See James Gilbert, *A Cycle of Outrage: America's Reaction to the Juvenile Delinquent in the 1950s* (New York: Oxford University Press, 1986); Sarah Fishman, *La bataille de l'enfance: Délinquance juvénile et justice des mineurs en France pendant la Seconde Guerre mondiale* (Rennes: Presses universitaires de Rennes, 2008).

21 Jean-Jacques Yvorel, "Au carrefour de la construction des savoirs sur la délinquance juvénile: Le centre de recherche et de formation de Vaucresson (1951–1980)," *Savoirs, politiques et pratiques de l'exécution des peines en France au XXe siècle* (March 25–26, 2014), accessed August 26, 2015, www.criminocorpus.revues.org.

22 See Gilbert, *A Cycle of Outrage*.

23 I am referring here to the definition proposed by Hannah Arendt in "Qu'est-ce que l'autorité?" [What is authority?], in *La crise de la culture* [Between past and future] (Paris: Gallimard, 1995), 123.

24 On the Panoptican, see Foucault, *Surveiller et punir*. For "free floating control," see Gilles Deleuze, "Post-scriptum sur les sociétés de contrôle" [Postscript on the societies of control], May 1990 text in *Pourparlers, 1972–1990* (Paris: Editions de Minuit, 2005), 241.

25 Périssol, "'The Quality of Mercy Is Not Strain'd.'"

26 See the work of Jean-Claude Farcy, notably his *Meurtre au bocage: L'affaire Poirier (1871–1874)* (Chartres: Société archéologique d'Eure-et-Loir, 2012).

27 For example, we can look to the use made of images by Denver's juvenile judge Ben Lindsey, such as the picture where he is photographed with a small girl on his knee. Some of these photographs are available on the Library of Congress website, including an eloquent image in which the famous mustached judge faces a child whose dog is placed on the desk and points to them with a finger that symbolizes the severity of a good father, as well as perhaps a certain complicity in the staging of the scene: www.loc.gov (accessed September 10, 2013). Similarly, in France, one of the posters for the 1955 film *Chiens perdus sans collier* (literally, lost dogs without collars) shows the character of Judge Lamy, played by a gruff and kindhearted Jean Gabin, with his hand placed on a juvenile's shoulder. The poster is available at www.cinemapalaceequeurdrevillelesannees50.blogspot.fr (accessed August 26, 2013).

28 Alexis de Tocqueville, *Democracy in America: Historical-Critical Edition of De la démocratie en Amérique*, ed. Eduardo Nolla, trans. James T. Schleifer (Indianapolis: Liberty Fund, 2010), vol. 3, 883. Tocqueville underlined the fact that the

harsh treatment of the black population, excluded from citizenship and reduced to slavery in the United States, confirmed his theory that, rather than civilization, it was the democratic principle of equality that made mores milder, as each citizen then feared the same misfortunes, leading individuals to aid one another in the interest of all, and to feel "sympathy" toward their "fellows."

29 Tocqueville, *Democracy in America*, vol. 4, 1006.

30 See the introduction (pages xix and following) and part 1 of Schlossman, *Transforming Juvenile Justice*, for the author's rebuttal of Anthony M. Platt's theory, as set out in *The Child Savers*, suggesting that juvenile delinquency had been "invented" during the Progressive Era.

31 Louis Chevalier, *Classes laborieuses et classes dangereuses à Paris pendant la première moitié du XIX siècle* [Laboring classes and dangerous classes in Paris during the first half of the nineteenth century] (Paris: Plon, 1958). For "coercive casework agencies," see Thomas J. Bernard and Megan C. Kurlychek, *The Cycle of Juvenile Justice*, 2nd ed. (New York: Oxford University Press, 2010), 80.

32 See Franklin E. Zimring and Máximo Langer, "The Search for a Deep Structure in Global Juvenile Justice," chapter 10 in *Juvenile Justice in Global Perspectives* (New York: New York University Press, 2015), 383–411.

33 See Agnès Thiercé, *Histoire de l'adolescence, 1850–1914* (Paris: Belin, 1999). The chronology in America closely matches the periodization established for France by Thiercé. So, if we take the example of research in psychology, the influential work by Granville Stanley Hall led to the publication in 1904 of his monumental study titled *Adolescence: Its Psychology and Its Relations to Physiology, Anthropology, Sociology, Sex, Crime, Religion and Education.*

34 On Nazi Germany, for example, see Frieder Dünkel, "Juvenile Justice in Germany: Between Welfare and Justice," in *International Handbook of Juvenile Justice*, ed. Josine Junger-Tas and Scott H. Decker (Dordrecht, Netherlands: Springer, 2006), 225–262. For Spain, see the work of Amélie Nuq, e.g., "Des *jurisdictions d'exception* pour 'protéger' et 'redresser' la jeunesse? Les tribunaux pour mineurs sous la dictature franquiste (1939–1975)," *Tracés*, no. 20 (2011), accessed August 31, 2015, www.traces.revues.org. On China, see Weijian Gao, "The Development and Prospect of Juvenile Justice in the People's Republic of China," chapter 3 in *Juvenile Justice in Global Perspectives*, 121–144.

35 See Fishman, *La bataille de l'enfance.*

36 Jean-Claude Lamberti, *Tocqueville et les deux démocraties* (Paris: Presses universitaires de France, 1983), 14, 28.

37 Since Tocqueville, several major thinkers have turned their attention to the risks inherent in democracy. For the twentieth century, which witnessed the rise of new kinds of repressive regimes under the name of fascism or communism, the works of José Ortega y Gasset, Karl Mannheim, and Hannah Arendt are noteworthy.

38 Aldous Huxley, foreword to the 1946 edition of *Brave New World*, cited in Raychel Haugrud Reiff, *Aldous Huxley: Brave New World* (Tarrytown, NY: Benchmark Books, 2009), 65.

39 On the different ways of reading Tocqueville in France, which emphasized the positive or negative aspects of democracy, see Serge Audier, *Tocqueville retrouvé: Genèse et enjeux du renouveau tocquevillien français* (Paris: Vrin Année, 2004).

40 The Citizenship Training Group, Inc., Research Department, compiler and ed., *Boston Juvenile Court: Annual Report, 1951*.

41 Juan Mérat, "Les enfants devant le juge, 1945–1958: Les stratégies normatives au sein d'un cabinet du Tribunal pour enfants de la Seine" (master's thesis, Université Paris VIII, 2001).

42 In absolute terms, there were 567 juvenile delinquency complaints in Boston in 1951, involving 486 minors, as well as 14 neglected child complaints involving 47 minors, and over 50 complaints against adults for neglecting children or contributing to the delinquency or waywardness of children. This corresponded roughly to the equivalent of the caseload of two of the six divisions of the Seine Juvenile Court, according to my counting of the files of the Seine Juvenile Court for 1950. The BJC report includes in the 567 cases of delinquency the cases of 27 stubborn children that could be compared to French cases of *correction paternelle* (paternal punishment, a provision by which the person responsible for a minor could request the placement of the latter until he/she reached the age of twenty-one; such cases did not count as "delinquency" in the French meaning of the word) or perhaps more to cases of *vagabondage* (vagrancy, in a very large sense), which was decriminalized in 1935 but was still considered in practice as a form of delinquency or predelinquency (hence, my rationale for classifying it as juvenile delinquency); plus 5 cases of wayward children, who were not legally delinquents but were considered as such for the purposes of the procedures actually followed by the court.

43 In the Seine jurisdiction, the catchall was entitled "vagrancy," whether actual or simply a pretext on which to intercede, and corresponded to the sum of the American categories of "runaways" and "stubborn children," to which we have added the five complaints about "wayward children" and the twelve cases of "truancy."

44 *Boston Juvenile Court: Annual Report, 1951*, 17.

45 The process of classifying relates to forms of knowledge and ordered visions and divisions of the social world. Racial classifications worked quite differently in France and in the United States. In the French case files, any mention of race was prohibited as the nation-state focuses only on the distinction between citizens and noncitizens, leading to official myopia on this question (this did not, however, prevent certain officials involved from occasionally making remarks with racial or racist undertones). The American files, on the other hand, could and did use racial or ethnic categories.

46 These surveys began being conducted in the United States in the 1950s, and would commence later in France. See Josine Junger-Tas and Ineke Haen Marshall, "The Self-Report Methodology in Crime Research," in vol. 25 (May 1999) of *Crime and Justice: An Annual Review of Research*, ed. Michael Tonry, 291–367.

47 I have respected the anonymity of the individuals involved in accordance with the instructions of each institution (e.g., names have been changed). The quotes involving Ellen and Henri have been taken from their case files in Boston (Massachusetts Supreme Judicial Court Archives, BJC Oversamples, Box 2, Probation File 5049) and in Paris (Archives of Paris, 1418 W 67, Case File no. 11831).

48 Hearing before the juvenile judge, May 8, 1950.

49 Report from the Observation Center of Savigny-sur-Orge, June 27, 1950.

50 The word ("*intoxiquée*," literally intoxicated) was used to describe a young girl arrested the same year as Henri. She claimed to be an "existentialist" and was found "wandering" in the Latin Quarter after running away from home (Archives of Paris, 1418 W 17, Case File no. 7648).

51 Medicolegal report by Professor Georges Heuyer, June 28, 1950.

52 Information on these movements can be found in English in Greil Marcus, *Lipstick Traces: A Secret History of the Twentieth Century*, 20th anniversary ed. (Cambridge: Harvard University Press, 2009), in particular the chapter titled "The Assault on Notre-Dame."

53 For a discussion of the "folk years" in Cambridge, see Eric von Schmidt and Jim Rooney, *Baby, Let Me Follow You Down: The Illustrated Story of the Cambridge Folk Years* (Garden City, NY: Doubleday, 1979).

54 All quotes are taken from documents contained in Ellen's probation file. They reflect the general content of this captivating file, which cannot be further detailed here.

55 For mass culture and society, see "The Intellectuals and Mass Culture," chapter 7 in Gilbert, *A Cycle of Outrage*, 109–126.

56 Hannah Arendt, "La crise de l'éducation" [The crisis in education], in *La crise de la culture*, 250.

57 See the preface to *La crise de la culture*, 11–27.

58 The scale of the phenomenon and its evolution in the context of the "crisis of authority" distinguish it from bohemians and rebel youths in the nineteenth century. See Pierre Bourdieu, "L'invention de la vie d'artiste," *Actes de la recherche en sciences sociales* 1, no. 2 (March 1975): 67–93.

59 See John Augustus, *A Report of the Labors of John Augustus for the Last Ten Years, in Aid of the Unfortunate* (Boston: Wright & Hasty, Printers, 1852).

60 See "Discipline," part 3 in Foucault, *Surveiller et punir*, 135–229.

61 Peter C. Holloran, *Boston's Wayward Children: Social Services for Homeless Children, 1830–1930* (Rutherford, NJ: Fairleigh Dickinson University Press, 1989), 245.

62 *Boston Juvenile Court: Annual Report, 1951*, 21. The categories of "probation" and "probation and suspended sentence" were added together for this calculation.

63 France, Ministère de la Justice, Direction de l'Éducation surveillée, *Rapport annuel à M. le Garde des Sceaux* (Melun, 1951), 24. Juvenile delinquency is to be understood, here, in the strictest sense of the term, and does not include vagrancy cases.

64 For the Seine Juvenile Court, there is both a qualitative and quantitative analysis of this point in Guillaume Périssol, "La mauvaise herbe? Regards sur la délin-

quance juvénile dans le département de la Seine" (master's thesis, Université de Paris–Sorbonne, 1999), 86–92.

65 On the severity of confinement, see, for example, the very painful path taken by a "stubborn child" born in 1948, through the Massachusetts institutions, in this autobiographical work: Mark Devlin, *Stubborn Child* (New York: Atheneum, 1985).

66 The story of this young prostitute is analyzed in Guillaume Périssol, "Des couloirs du métro à l'hôpital psychiatrique: La trajectoire d'un jeune prostitué parisien en 1946," *Revue d'histoire de l'enfance "irrégulière"*, no. 10 (October 2008): 97–115, accessed September 1, 2015, www.rhei.revues.org.

67 For Massachusetts, see Stuart A. White and G. Tom Eisele, "A Survey of the Massachusetts Youth Service Board" (third-year law paper, Harvard Law School, May 1, 1950); the annual reports of the Youth Service Board (some of which can be found in the Harvard Library). For France, see the annual reports of the Direction de l'Éducation surveillée (Ministry of Justice), available online at www.criminocorpus.org/fr, and Anne Thomazeau's studies on the institution for delinquent girls at Brécourt: "La formation professionnelle des mineures placées en internat de rééducation de la Libération aux années 1960," in *Genre et éducation: Former, se former, être formée au féminin*, ed. Bernard Bodinier et al. (Mont-Saint-Aignan: Publications de l'Université de Rouen et du Havre, 2009), 399–414.

68 If we are to believe the message conveyed in most of the illustrations used in Thorsten Sellin, ed., *Actes du douzième Congrès penal et pénitentiaire international, La Haye, 14–19 août 1950* (Berne: Commission internationale pénale et pénitentiaire, 1951), vol. 1–2.

69 See "L'éducation du corps," chapter 9 in Maurice Crubellier, *L'enfance et la jeunesse dans la société française, 1800–1950* (Paris: Armand Colin, 1979), 187–206. See also Pierre Arnaud, ed., *Les athlètes de la République: Gymnastique, sport et idéologie républicaine, 1870–1914* (Toulouse: Bibliothèque historique Privat, 1987).

70 In this regard, institutions for juvenile delinquents were not very different from other educational establishments or youth organizations (let us recall that programs were not required to be fully coeducational in French schools until 1975). See Alain Corbin, Jean-Jacques Courtine, Georges Vigarello, eds., *Histoire de la virilité* (Paris: Le Seuil, 2012). On the treatment of girls in the juvenile justice system, see the studies undertaken by Anne Thomazeau (cited above) and by Véronique Blanchard (see the website www.enfantsenjustice.fr, which also contains numerous images).

71 Lyman was one of the euphemistically designated "training schools," disciplinary facilities described as "open" institutions, identified in quotation marks in the text in Massachusetts, Division of Youth Service, *Service to Youth: "The Story of the Youth Service Board"* (March 1, 1955), 10–13. In Massachusetts, there were two "schools" for boys and one for girls.

72 Lyman School for Boys, *100 Years of Progress in the Making of Men* (Westborough, MA: 1947?).

73 Julhiet, "Les tribunaux pour enfants aux États-Unis," 62.

74 For the authority of probation officers, see Massachusetts, Acts of 1949, Chapter 783.

75 The French probation officer is supervised by a professional known as the *délégué permanent à la liberté surveillée*, a kind of chief probation officer for the juvenile court. A special issue of the journal *Rééducation* (last quarter 1952) presented an overview of their duties and of the French ideals of probation: *La liberté surveillée, rapport présenté à Monsieur le Directeur de l'Éducation Surveillée par M. H. Michard*. Other useful information on the differences between probation services in juvenile courts in France and in the United States can be found in Périssol, "'The Quality of Mercy Is Not Strain'd,'" 293–295.

76 Special issue of *Rééducation: La liberté surveillée*, 17.

77 The social worker image was evident throughout the ten-minute film *Boy in Court* (Willard Pictures, 1940), which was sponsored by the American National Probation Association (David H. Lion, director; Edward C. Kienle, producer; and Robert T. Furman Jr., writer), accessed May 26, 2012, www.archive.org. The ideals laid down by this film were not shared everywhere in the country. But Massachusetts had played a pioneering role in the field of probation (in 1891, the state law was revised to prohibit police officers from being appointed probation officers). And we did not find any references to Massachusetts juvenile probation officers carrying weapons or being authorized to do so. In 2001, after the get-tough movement of the 1980s and 1990s, some juvenile probation officers could carry firearms on duty in eleven states (but not Massachusetts), according to the Adult and Juvenile Probation and Parole National Firearms Survey. The survey, which was carried out by the American Probation and Parole Association, is cited in Patrick Griffin and Patricia Torbet, eds., *Desktop Guide to Good Juvenile Probation Practice* (2002), 104, accessed January 18, 2016, www.ncjj.org.

78 On the distinction between the "repressive state apparatus" and "ideological state apparatuses," see Althusser, "Idéologie et appareils idéologiques d'État."

79 For France, see Mathias Gardet, "La police des mineurs à l'heure de la prevention (1935–1966): Une mission oubliée?," *Revue d'histoire de l'enfance "irrégulière"*, no. 12 (2010): 111–137, accessed January 18, 2016, www.rhei.revues.org.

80 Testimony of Thomas Sullivan, Commissioner of Police, Boston, Mass., in United States, Congress, Juvenile Delinquency (Boston, Mass.): Hearings Before the Subcommittee to Investigate Juvenile Delinquency of the Committee on the Judiciary, United States Senate, 83rd Cong., 2nd Sess., pursuant to S. Res. 89, Investigation of Juvenile Delinquency in the United States, January 28, 29, and 30, 1954 (Washington, DC, 1954), 260, 265–266, accessed March 14, 2012, www.archive.org.

81 On Junior Police Corps, see Martin Alan Greenberg, "A Short History of Junior Police," *Police Chief* 75, no. 4 (April 2008), accessed January 13, 2016, www.policechiefmagazine.org. Statistics from Massachusetts, Police Commissioner for the City of Boston, *Thirty-Seventh Annual Report of the Police Commissioner for the City of Boston for the Year Ending November 30, 1942* (Boston, 1943), 12, accessed January 20, 2016, www.archive.org.

82 See the statement by Marc Ancel in *Actes du douzième Congrès penal et péniten-tiaire international*, vol. 1, 538–551. Of interest also are the replies to the question of "the applicability of juvenile treatment to adults" and conclusion number four (vol. 1, 412).

83 In a special issue (vol. 102, no. 1, June 2015) of the *Journal of American History*, the term "probation" appears only five times out of more than 160 pages devoted to "Historians and the Carceral State," showing that potential links between mass incarceration and mass probation in the United States garnered scant attention. For a sociological perspective on the subject, see Michelle S. Phelps's work, e.g., "Mass Probation: Toward a More Robust Theory of State Variation in Punishment," MPC Working Paper no. 2014-4 (July 4, 2014), accessed July 26, 2015, www.ssrn. com.

84 Without going beyond the remit of this chapter, let us give some useful references. For the problems in the analysis of judicial statistics in France, see Philippe Robert, Bruno Aubusson de Cavarlay, Marie-Lys Pottier, and Pierre Tournier, *Les comptes du crime: Les délinquances en France et leurs mesures* (Paris: L'Harmattan, 1994). On juvenile delinquency in France, see Maurice Levade, *La délinquance des jeunes en France, 1825–1968* (Paris: Éditions Cujas, 1972); Laurent Mucchi-elli, "L'évolution de la délinquance juvénile en France (1980–2000)," *Sociétés Contemporaines*, no. 53 (2004) : 101–134; no. 133 (February 2015) of *Infostat Justice: Une justice pénale des mineurs adaptée à une délinquance particulière*, by T. Mainaud. In the United States, the Office of Juvenile Justice and Delinquency Prevention provides data for the last decades (www.ojjdp.gov). On criminal justice in general, official websites are essential information resources. For France: www.justice. gouv.fr. See also (for earlier periods) the *Comptes Généraux de la Justice* (available in the digital library of the Bibliothèque nationale de France: www.gallica. bnf.fr). For the United States: www.bjs.gov (in particular, *Historical Corrections Statistics in the United States, 1850–1984* [December 1986], accessed September 1, 2015, www.bjs.gov). The report on this website allows the reader to imagine what the prevalence of probation in the American population could be: Thomas P. Bon-czar, *Prevalence of Imprisonment in the U.S. Population, 1974–2001* (August 2003), accessed September 1, 2015, www.bjs.gov. And for Europe, see www.andromeda. rutgers.edu (with links to the SPACE data of the Council of Europe).

85 Letter from the probation officer to Ellen's mother, January 25, 1965.

86 John Vardy, *Their Side of the Story* (Newton-le-Willows, Lancashire, 1942), 5, 36.

87 See "Domesticating the House of Refuge: The Family Reform School in Victorian America," chapter 3 in Schlossman, *Transforming Juvenile Justice*, 33–54; and M. Demetz, *Notice sur la colonie agricole de Mettray* (Tours, 1865).

88 See the interview with Michel Foucault in Radioscopie, March 10, 1975, available at www.ina.fr.

89 See White and Eisele, *A Survey of the Massachusetts Youth Service Board*, and the annual reports of the Youth Service Board. In France, see this order published in the *Journal officiel* [Legal Gazette] (May 29, 1952): Arrêté du 26 mai 1952 modifiant

l'arrêté du 25 octobre 1915 portant règlement provisoire des Institutions Publiques d'Éducation Surveillée [Order of 26 May 1952 modifying the Order of 25 October 1915 concerning provisional regulation of Public Institutions for Juvenile Delinquents].

90 See, as an example of the continued importance of this trend, Expertise Collective Inserm, ed., *Trouble des conduites chez l'enfant et l'adolescent* (Paris: Les éditions Inserm, 2005), accessed January 25, 2016, www.ladocumentationfrancaise.fr/. This 2005 report of the French Institut national de la santé et de la recherche médicale (National Institute of Health and Medical Research) raised an important controversy in France over conduct disorder in children and adolescents, in particular its screening and its treatment; see Le collectif "Pasdeodeconduite," *Pas de o de conduite pour les enfants de 3 ans!* (Ramonville Saint-Agne, 2006).

91 J. Dechaume et al., *L'enfance irrégulière: Psychologie clinique* (Paris: Presses universitaires de France, 1946), 255.

92 See the introduction and chapter 8, "The Operational Meaning of Noninstitutional Treatment," in Schlossman, *Transforming Juvenile Justice*, 142–156. Although limits were set (notably regarding the role of the police), reference was still made to "informal adjustment" in the 1954 *Standards for Specialized Courts Dealing with Children*, 37, 43–45.

93 Statement of Garrett H. Byrne, District Attorney, Suffolk County, Mass., in United States, Congress, Juvenile Delinquency (Boston, Mass.): Hearings Before the Subcommittee to Investigate Juvenile Delinquency, 33.

94 For other examples, see Deleuze, "Post-scriptum sur les sociétés de contrôle."

95 See Franklin Zimring, "The Common Thread: Diversion in the Jurisprudence of Juvenile Courts," in *A Century of Juvenile Justice*, ed. Margaret K. Rosenheim, Franklin E. Zimring, David S. Tanenhaus, and Bernardine Dohrn (Chicago: University of Chicago Press, 2002), 142–157.

96 See Michelle S. Phelps's sociological analysis (Phelps, "Mass Probation").

97 See Foucault, *Surveiller et punir*. The recent publication of the lectures delivered by Foucault in 1971–1972 at the Collège de France helps understand the genesis and preparation of *Discipline and Punish* (published in France in 1975): Michel Foucault, *Théories et institutions pénales: Cours au Collège de France, 1971–1972* (Paris: EHESS/Gallimard/Seuil 2015). See also Deleuze, "Post-scriptum sur les sociétés de contrôle."

98 In *Becoming Delinquent: British and European Youth, 1650–1950* (Aldershot: Ashgate, 2002), editors Pamela Cox and Heather Shore urged that more comparative studies should be carried out on the phenomenon of juvenile delinquency. About a decade later, a conference was held in Berlin that aimed to explore the construction of juvenile delinquency in a global context. Nevertheless, most of the contributions were not explicitly comparative. The conference resulted in the publication of a special issue of the journal *Social Justice* (December 2012) and a collective volume, *Juvenile Delinquency and the Limits of Western Influence 1850–2000*, published in 2014 by Palgrave Macmillan.

99 For comparisons of interconnected countries, see Marc Bloch, "Pour une histoire comparée des sociétés européennes," *Revue de Synthèse Historique*, no. 46 (1928): 15–50. For deep structure, see Zimring and Langer, "The Search for a Deep Structure in Global Juvenile Justice."

100 The workhorse expression is borrowed from Patricia McFall Torbet, "Juvenile Probation: The Workhorse of the Juvenile Justice System," *Juvenile Justice Bulletin* (March 1996), accessed January 24, 2016, www.ncjrs.gov.

101 Deleuze, "Post-scriptum sur les sociétés de contrôle," 244.

102 Deleuze, "Post-scriptum sur les sociétés de contrôle," 247.

6

"Unclaimed Forlorn Monsters"

Perceptions of Youth Crime and the Limits of Juvenile Justice Reform in Turkey, 1979–2005

NAZAN ÇIÇEK

This chapter delves into the ways in which juvenile delinquency was perceived and regulated in the Turkish Republic, a non-Western country with professed aspirations to become "modern" along Western lines. It opens with a brief account of the Republican founding elites, beginning in the 1920s, deploying the modern concept of protected childhood as part of their nation and nation-state building strategies. It contextualizes the treatment of juvenile delinquency by sketching out the meaning and value attributed by society and by policymakers to the concepts of the child and childhood as well as the normative qualities of proper childhood in the early Republican era. Against this backdrop the chapter expounds on the possible reasons that induced Turkish decision-makers to exclude "criminal" children from the category of "children in need of protection" and to deny the former the right of state protection and support. It then summarizes the perception and treatment of juvenile delinquency in Turkey before 1979 and the reasons that prompted the Turkish government to introduce specialized courts for juveniles through the Law on the Establishment, Duties and Trial Procedures of the Juvenile Courts of 1979 (hereafter the Law of 1979). It also lays out the debates and circumstances that resulted in the enactment of the Child Protection Law of 2005, which not only replaced the Law of 1979 but also claimed to correct its deficiencies. The conclusion examines and critiques the latest body of regulations with respect to juvenile delinquency in Turkey.

The Republic's efforts to reform its juvenile justice system on the basis of a Western model are incomplete. The extent to which this new institution generated a perceptive change of mindset toward juvenile delinquency in Turkish society by the end of the twentieth century can be measured through media coverage of a sensational criminal case in 1998–99. That coverage reflected an unenthusiastic reception for juvenile courts following the brutal attack, rape, and murder of a young kindergarten teacher in Istanbul by four children whose ages ranged from 13 to 17. This analysis demonstrates that although the Republic's claim to be "modern" and "civilized" was at stake in its attempts to reform its juvenile justice system on the basis of the Western model, in practice it insisted on handling the juvenile delinquency *allaturca*. In fact, the Turkish Republic mostly failed to strongly commit to the legal model it constructed without much grassroots support in the first place.

The Turkish Republic as a Newborn Child: Innocent, Hardworking, and Law Abiding

The Turkish Republic emerged from the remnants of the Ottoman Empire in 1923 as its founding elites set out to construct a nation-state largely modeled on Western lines. The eventful and indisputably traumatic years of the dissolution of the Ottoman Empire throughout the nineteenth century ended in its ultimate defeat in the First World War, followed by the military invasion of the Turkish heartland, Anatolia, by the Allied powers. The Treaty of Sèvres (10 August 1920) sealed the end of the Ottoman Empire and sparked the Turkish resistance movement that lasted until the commanders of the resistance movement, the Turkish nationalists, announced the foundation of the Turkish Republic in October 1923. This founding military and politico-bureaucratic elite, or the Kemalists as they came widely to be known, were people mostly with cultural capital in Pierre Bourdieu's terms: their cognitive map was largely shaped by a Western style education acquired in the Ottoman military, medical, or public administration schools that were structured on the Western model together with their contact with Europe in various ways. Although they felt some level of bitterness toward the Western world because of the role imperialistically driven Western policies played in the gradual decline of the Ottoman Empire and the invasion of Anatolia, the Kemalists nevertheless believed that the key to power and prosperity for a state and society would be to grasp Western knowledge, norms, values, institutions, and technologies, to embrace Western civilization holistically.

The process of Europeanization/Westernization for the Kemalists included an eager rejection of the Ottoman heritage with its all Eastern and Islamic associations and a thorough embrace of the secular Western *habitus*. While the new Turkish nation was being "imagined" and "invented," children were placed at the center of nation and nation-state building strategies. They acquired a politically potent image that regarded them as the hope and future of the new regime, nation, and society. For the founding elites, in other words, the child allegorically stood for the Turkish Republic as well as the Turkish nation. This allegory was constituted both visually and discursively in many texts representative of the zeitgeist of the early Republic.[1]

The official rhetoric portrayed children as the most valuable assets of the Republic. They deserved the best of everything that the society could provide them.[2] The level of children's well-being and happiness was regarded as a yardstick to measure society's advancement on the road to civilization. Accordingly, the concept of the child was reconstructed and furnished with a powerful symbolic value.[3] This, however, was a double-edged sword. The politically fashioned image of the child as the very personification of the new regime and society dramatically limited actual Turkish children's margin of enjoying the luxury of being simply children and acting childishly. Their successful development represented and spoke for the success of the Turkish Republic. Their irreplaceable value for the nation ironically imposed many responsibilities and duties on children in order to prove that they were worthy of the new regime's hopes for them. The most important of all duties called on children to internalize the norms and values of the newly built society and become law-abiding citizens. Implicitly, the same official rhetoric also avowed that in conducting its child policies the Turkish state was emulating the Western world, which had been regarded as the highest form of "civilization" and the sole point of reference for Turkish modernization. Yet the indisputable belatedness of the Turkish state to establish children's courts, which were part and parcel of the modern notion of childhood, reveals that the Turkish understanding and conceptualization of the child and childhood differed remarkably from the modern Western notion of childhood.

Turkish Republican officials applied a selective interpretation of the sentimental Victorian conceptualization of childhood, which lay the groundwork for the child-centered society of the twentieth century. Although "childhood innocence" as an essential component of modern childhood enjoyed an undeniable discursive power in the cognitive map of the Turkish intelligentsia, owing largely to the politically constructed image of the Turkish child, "innocence" could not allude to complete oblivion with respect to the realities of the adult world.[4] Instead, Turkish children, as embodiments of the hopes and future of the new regime, were expected to be precocious, a situation that would ineluctably erode their "childhood innocence" in a romanticized Victorian sense.

Accordingly, from the very beginning of the Republican era, juvenile delinquents had been overtly excluded from the definition of the "child in need of protection" in Turkey.[5] As the Law for Children Who Need Protection of 1949 proved, the Turkish state preferred to act as *parens patriae* only for a strictly defined group of children whose physical, spiritual, and moral development was thought to be in danger, whose parents were unknown, and, most important of all, who had not yet committed a crime.[6] With the alterations made to the Law in 1957, the definition of "children in need of protection" was expanded to include children neglected by their parents and judged to be in danger of becoming prostitutes, beggars, drug addicts, alcoholics, or tramps.[7] But officials resisted elevating juvenile offenders to the level of law abiding yet poor, orphaned, or abandoned youngsters. As a result, legal proceedings regarding these two different groups of children remained separate far later than they did in most Western societies. Until the introduction of the Child Protection Law of 2005, Turkish lawmakers and officials carefully avoided mixing "criminal children" with other "problem" children who were believed to have maintained their "innocence." Although never expressed explicitly, the mentality governing this attitude obliquely assumed that, by committing a crime, juvenile delinquents forfeited their claim to childhood and entered the terrain of adulthood. Thus ostracized from the legal protections of childhood, juvenile delinquents were no longer entitled to the state's paternal affection, protection, and support. The ethos that rigidly regulated the Turkish attitude toward crime was punitive rather than rehabilitative, affording few if any exceptions for peculiar conditions such as "the essential otherness of the young."[8] Turkish society sought repression and expulsion of its criminals regardless of their age.

Thus, "innocence" for Turkish children connoted a complete absence of criminality. The exclusionary dynamics that Chris Jenks identified in the preservation of the category of childhood in the case of children who commit acts of violence were, and in fact still are, at play in Turkey's handling of juvenile delinquents.[9] Juvenile delinquents were excluded from the category of children and relegated to another category. They were cast as criminals and represented through images of evil, immorality, or pathology. As the Turkish state and society saw it, they had crossed a line that caused them to be permanently expatriated from the cosmos of childhood and they had only themselves to blame. In short, juvenile delinquents ran afoul of the idealized image of the "true" Turkish child who in fact was received as an adult in the making with many responsibilities toward the nation and society.

As early as 1927, four years after the founding of the Republic, the idea of establishing children's courts was entertained and voiced by some members of the Turkish intelligentsia, although it remained an unrealized idea for decades.[10] From 1945 onward there were a couple of ephemeral attempts in the Parliament to debate the necessity of a specialized body of legislation for juveniles. Yet amid myriad pressing matters regarding children ranging from malnutrition, epidemic disease, illiteracy, orphanage, and abandonment, juvenile delinquents did not elicit much attention from the public and the state. Until children's courts were introduced in 1979, Turkey tried and "punished" young offenders through adult criminal courts and had them serve their sentences in children's quarters in adult prisons, a situation that remains largely unchanged today because of an inadequate number of reformatories for juvenile delinquents. Although the Turkish Penal Code of 1926 contained special provisions for juveniles, such as reducing of sentences in appropriate cases, there was not a separate body of laws and regulations exclusively designed for juvenile delinquents. They were caught up in the same criminal justice system as adults. The decades-long outcry of a small group of Turkish intelligentsia consisting mainly of jurists, law practitioners, social workers, and child psychiatrists finally culminated in the establishment of children's courts in 1979 with the Law on the Establishment, Duties and Trial Procedures of the Juvenile Courts of

1979.[11] Yet the new law largely failed to please the champions of juvenile courts. They criticized the law, explaining that it was a mere window dressing lacking any substantial notion of rehabilitation, education, or correction. All of this, according to its critics, signified the lawmakers' failure to grasp the proper meaning of modern childhood as well as the logic behind juvenile courts. Unless children were perceived and treated as a sui generis group essentially different from adults with special needs and inherent vulnerabilities, the critics argued, children's courts would merely reproduce the prevailing criminal justice system for adults, albeit on a smaller scale and in a seemingly different attire.

As the law's critics aptly argued, the introduction of children's courts in 1979 did not point to a radical change in attitudes toward juvenile delinquents in the Turkish Republic. The process that led to the introduction of children's courts was not induced and informed by a redefinition of childhood, or by a transformation in Turkey's politics of crime and punishment. Instead, the courts had been established because Turkish decision-makers and policymakers thought they could no longer avoid it.[12] The courts appeared to be imperative for the reconstruction of Turkey's image as a modern and civilized country, which had been severely undercut by decades of coup d'états, ongoing political instability, and economic crises. The absence of separate children's courts created bad publicity for Turkey in the Western world. With the twenty-first century fast approaching, Turkey's maintenance of a criminal justice system that still lacked juvenile courts contributed to an image of Turkey as a third world country and caused shame for its modernizing, Western-oriented elites. As one government spokesman at the time remarked, the Turkish Parliament would complete one more task in the Republic's endeavour to catch up with the modern world by passing the Law of 1979. Two and a half decades later, state authorities voiced a similar justification as they set about reforming the Turkish juvenile justice system to meet the demands of the European Union. As the director-general of prisons and detention centers of the Ministry of Justice explained in a symposium on juvenile delinquency in 2002, "The country has decided to undergo a radical transformation and reconstruction in all areas, including the juvenile justice system, so that it can take its much deserved place in modern world."[13]

Although the Law was enacted in 1979, it took the Republic nine years to establish its first juvenile court, an undeniable indicator of the country's lack of commitment to improve the juvenile justice system along Western or, as the policymakers saw it, "modern," lines. The Law called for juvenile courts to be established in every province or district with a population of 100,000 or more, yet by 2004 there were only 10 juvenile courts in seven provinces. After the enactment of the Law of Child Protection in 2005, 19 "juvenile courts for serious offences" were established. The number of children's courts reached 73 by 2012.[14]

While a small group of children's rights advocates constantly complained about the defects and "backwardness" of the juvenile justice system that had been constructed by the Law of 1979, their voices fell on deaf ears and were largely ignored by the public. For instance, children's advocates were concerned that adolescent children over 15 had not been included within the jurisdiction of the juvenile courts.[15] As remarked by some participants in a symposium held in Ankara in 1983, this was in open conflict with the Turkish Penal Code as well as the Civil Code that provided that every citizen reached adult status at the age of 18.[16] Esin Onur, an academic and the editor of the symposium proceedings, reminded attendees that the original version of the Law of 1979 as drafted by the Ministry of Justice initially had included children under 18, but this was changed during the debates in the Turkish Grand National Assembly on the grounds that children in Turkey go through an early maturation process owing to geographical and social causes. Onur then asserted that there had been no scientific findings that could justify this reasoning. "On the contrary," she argued,

> all scientific work points out that adolescence is a sui generis life period in which children experience a great deal of psychological turmoil and display self-contradictory behaviours. During this period the child acquires the quality of abstract thinking but lacks the knowledge and life experience that are necessary to act like an adult, hence is always prone to make mistakes. It is also a universal characteristic of adolescence to prompt the child to protest and disobey the rules and norms imposed upon by the parents and the society.[17]

Onur was convinced that "the Law of 1979 had the misfortune to be debated and enacted at a time while political violence and chaos were at their peak in Turkey."[18] She was referring to the period preceding the coup d'état of 1980 whereby thousands of young people, mostly high school and university students, were engaged in legal or illegal and sometimes extremist political movements, involved in politically motivated bank robberies, kidnapping, armed street fights, and the like, and clashed with one another as well as with the state security forces almost on a daily basis. According to Onur's reasoning, the Turkish Parliament must have held a very negative opinion of adolescents at the time that led them to see them not as children but as potentially violent young adults fit to be tried by adult criminal courts. Regarding and treating them as children, the Parliament probably thought, would only embolden them and exacerbate the situation. Out of such concerns, Parliament amended the draft law to exclude adolescents from the protections offered by the new children's courts.

In 2002, the issue of adolescents was raised again in another national symposium on juvenile delinquency. Ahmet Nezih Kök, an academic and forensic science expert, pointed out that by leaving adolescents outside the jurisdiction of juvenile courts, the Law of 1979 contradicted the UN Convention on the Rights of the Child of 1989, which, as an international document ratified by the Turkish Parliament, was supposed to be completely binding and in harmony with national laws.[19] This concern was repeated by other participants, especially jurists, such as Judge Refik Dizdaroğlu from the Supreme Court of Appeals and lawyer Nesrin Hatipoğlu, who exhorted the government to resolve the problem without delay.[20] Many participants from both symposia also objected to the Turkish state's insistence on trying children who were accused of taking part in "terrorist" activities in specialized criminal courts instead of in children's courts.[21]

None of this signified the opening of a new era for juvenile delinquency in the Turkish Republic. In fact, the introduction of children's courts into the Turkish justice system and demands for juvenile delinquents were viewed as "luxurious" by the rest of society. This is exemplified in the Serpil case discussed below. My analysis demonstrates that even though all the perpetrators were under the age of 18, the Republican authorities were reluctant to make use of the children's courts and could easily evade using them although all the perpetrators involved were under the age of 18. Far from being hailed as children, these youths' capability of committing a particular crime, be it rape, abduction, theft, or murder, almost automatically verified their nonchild/adult status. The perception was that had they been children they would not have been able to cause harm on purpose. Accordingly, the Law ruled that past the age of 11 every Turkish citizen had criminal liability, and after age 15 every offender would be tried as an adult. Ironically, however, no one could vote, sign a contract, or own a driver's license until age 18. The Serpil case is also representative in that the reason it is still remembered by the public after so many years has less to do with the age of the perpetrators than the "lenient" punishment they received in return for their atrocities.

Four "Children" and a Shocking Murder: How to Tell the Evil Little Man from the Innocent Child?

On October 5, 1998, all mainstream newspapers in İstanbul published a bone-chilling news item about a 40-year-old mother and her 20-year-old daughter Serpil, a kindergarten teacher, who had been abducted in front of their apartment building in a lower class neighborhood as they were leaving for a visit to their relatives who also lived on the same street. The assailants were four unidentified males who drove up in a white car and blocked the couple's way. It was around 10 o'clock in the evening. Their target was the young woman, but when the mother fought back they forced both of them into the car and left. The police were notified and in a few hours the mother was found in a nearby wooded area. She had been brutally raped, knifed 28 times, and left bleeding to death. There was no sign of the young kindergarten teacher. Police also found the getaway car abandoned in another neighborhood and established that it had been stolen hours before the crime.[22] The mother was in the intensive care unit, fighting for her life, and was unable to give evidence. The relatives who had witnessed the incident informed the police that the girl did not have a boyfriend and that the assailants were total strangers.[23] Before long the police identified the perpetrators and through their confession discovered the victim's body in a large wooded area outside İstanbul. She had been raped multiple times, ferociously tortured, stabbed 91 times, and her body mutilated beyond recognition. Her attackers were four children between 13 and 17 years old. Though the children's identity could not be disclosed because of their age, they were immediately characterized as something other than children by the mainstream media. *Hürriyet*, the most widely circulated center-right Turkish daily, opted to use the word *genç* (youth) instead of *çocuk* (child) in referring to the perpetrators and frequently employed the word *canavar* (monster) in the narration. *Zaman*, a widely circulated right-wing newspaper, labeled them "unclaimed and forlorn monsters." Yet the overall treatment of the incident by the media was to place it under the rubric of the atrocities caused by children who were living in the streets, committing or falling prey to all sorts of crimes and mostly being ignored by the authorities. These street children were typically referred to as *tinerci çocuklar* (thinner-addicted/glue-sniffing children).

The accused children—S. D. (13), İ. A. (16), İ. Ç. (16) and S. K. (17)—were not unknown to İstanbul police. They lived in a ghetto of İstanbul, came from lower middle class, underprivileged, and dysfunctional families where they had been ill-treated. One of them, S.K., for example, was missing an ear because his older brother had cut it off as a punishment for taking his car without permission. They were primary school dropouts. They had been previously involved in several relatively less serious crimes ranging from grand theft auto to smash and grab and begging. Two of them had already served time in prison, one for two and a half months and the other for sixteen months, for theft.[24] All of them were suffering from substance abuse, mostly using thinner and glue as they were cheap, and easily and legally available.

Hürriyet did not feel obliged to conceal its discomfort from the very beginning that the attackers would receive lenient sentences for such a vicious crime thanks to their young age. The regretful tone that dominated *Hürriyet*'s coverage of the incident implied that the existing laws would prevent justice being served and would fail to mollify or appease the public conscience. It repeatedly reminded readers that one of the accused, S. D., would be "tried" by a children's court because he was younger than 15. The others, being older than 15, would be "tried" by adult criminal courts but their sentences nevertheless would be significantly reduced. *Hürriyet* explained that it was possible that Serpil's attackers would be sentenced to death but due to their young age they would never be executed.[25] It quoted an unnamed source, a seasoned police detective, who asserted that he was shocked and revolted by the confessions of the accused and that he had no doubt in his mind that these juveniles would become worse and commit more serious crimes after they served their prison sentences:

> Before the Bakırköy Prison for Women and Children was opened, these juveniles used to be sent to Bayrampaşa Prison where inmates more often than not felt it incumbent upon themselves to execute rapists. Nowadays we place juveniles convicted of rape and such serious crimes in the children's section of the Bakırköy Prison for Women and Children in order to protect their lives. Yet the prison always fails to rehabilitate them. In this particular case, these juveniles will become the bullyboys in their ward and dominate and control the other juvenile convicts who committed less serious crimes.[26]

According to *Hürriyet*, this atrocity appalled everyone in Turkey. Parents of children who attended Miss Serpil's kindergarten protested that the accused juveniles were not humans and should be punished by death. Similarly, *Zaman* emphasized that one of the accused juveniles, S. K., had gotten out of jail merely days before he committed this new crime. He had been released from prison without receiving any rehabilitative treatment and wasted no time returning to his old habits. The correspondent reminded readers that according to the Code of Criminal Procedures the upper limit for children younger than 15 was seven years in prison regardless of their crime. He then added that juvenile delinquents were not given severe penalties, and regretted that in the Serpil case three of the accused would serve only one-third of their sentences and one of them would get only seven years because he was 13.[27] Many mainstream media columnists agreed that these "pervert youngsters" deserved to be executed while only a couple of them suggested that these children themselves could be victims of the horrific conditions surrounding their lives as well as of the social apathy toward them.[28]

When the accused children were taken to the crime scene for reenactment a large crowd attempted to lynch them. A group of about 70 enraged people clashed with the police demanding that the "monsters" should be handed to them. At some point the police lost control of the crowd, which then severely beat the accused children. All newspapers reported the lynching attempt without censure, thus hinting that this mob violence was normative under the circumstances.[29] On the same day another widely circulated newspaper, the center-left Turkish daily *Milliyet*, published an exclusive interview with the accused children conducted by a well-known journalist and novelist Duygu Asena, who had become the so-called mascot of popular feminism in Turkey back in the 1980s. Throughout the interview, and despite the legal ban, Asena not only disclosed the first names of children but also included their photos. She started her narrative by describing them as "quiet, embarrassed, remorseful and confused kids." Yet she quickly emphasized that this was only a misleading façade. Alluding to the lynch attempt, she asked the children: "You do deserve this, don't you?" The children replied that they do. Then she continued asking what they would do if, because of their ages, they did not get the proper punishment they deserve, that is, the death sentence or life sentence. The children declared that "they would kill each other since they did not deserve to be alive." S. D. (13) insisted that "he would hang himself." Asena concluded that if you did not know what they had done, watching these people helplessly cry might invoke pity. "On the outside," she said, "they look so innocent."[30]

As the investigation expanded, the police arrested two more children, S. Ö. (16) and H.E. (17), who allegedly helped the quartet sell the stolen jewelry from the victims during the attack. After seven hours of police interrogation, all children were taken to the court.[31] They were not "tried" by a children's court because the age limit set by the Law of 1979 provided that juvenile offenders older than 15 would be prosecuted as adults. Even the 13 year old was not tried by a children's court because he had acted as an accomplice with the older ones. These children were not even tried in an ordinary adult's court. Their case was heard in an extraordinary court known as the State Security Court (Devlet Güvenlik Mahkemesi) that had been established in May 1984, four years after the coup d'état of 1980, to try cases involving organized crime or crimes against the security of the state. Constructed under the security and prohibitive mentality of the coup d'etat, and reflecting the praetorianist and militarist parameters of the time in Turkish public life, until 1999 the panels in these courts included, alongside two civilian judges, a military judge who was a member of the armed forces. The presence of military judges in the panels was a bone of contention that led the European Court of Human Rights to rule in several cases that the fair trial principles itemized in Article 6 of the European Convention for the Protection of Human Rights and Fundamental Freedoms had been violated. As part of Turkey's negotiation process with the EU the State Security Courts were formally abolished in 2004. But in 1998 they were having their heyday with no discernible possibility of change either in their structure or in their public legitimacy. The prosecutor decided that the attack on Serpil and her mother was an organized crime involving six young offenders. Because organized crime purportedly posed a threat to the security of the Turkish state, the children in question were tried in State Security Court No. 2 in İstanbul.

Close relatives of Serpil gathered in front of the court and talked to the press. Her uncle worried that because of their age the accused would not get the necessary punishment they deserved. "In the United States," he claimed,

> courts mete out proper punishment even if the criminal is 13 years of age. Some people prate about so-called human rights and state of law. [The] human rights argument cannot apply here because these are not humans. Those who can be involved in such savagery, torture and murder cannot be regarded as children just because their age is so young.[32]

While Serpil's relatives were demanding the death penalty for her attackers, *Hürriyet* published another article emphasizing that crime rates among young people were increasing in all European countries and the United States of America, and that Turkish youth appeared relatively crime-free compared to their Western counterparts. Citing some statistical data from unnamed sources and referring to the assessment of a report by the Economic and Social Research Council in the *Sunday Times*, *Hürriyet* gave many examples displaying how dangerous and uncontrollable European youth had become. The president of the General Directorate of Criminal Records and Statistics, Mustafa Taranyücel, was also quoted in the same article saying that the Serpil case had caused such a media sensation because this kind of crime committed by children was a rarity in Turkey. He asserted that this particular case was creating the misleading impression that the crime rate among Turkish children was on the rise. The apparent increase in the crime rate was in direct proportion to the general population growth. The article suggested possible solutions to the problem of criminal children. Many people, including public figures such as the secretary of state, argued that children guilty of very serious crimes should be lynched. But surely this could not be a real solution. Turning to the experts, the article quoted a medical doctor, Elvan Balım, chief physician at the Center for Children's Education and Medical Treatment in the capital city of Ankara, who disapproved of the police-led witch hunt to collect and chastise the children living in the streets after the Miss Serpil incident. She emphasized that law enforcement could be only a part of the solution but could not erase the problem on their own. Both Dr. Balım and psychologist Emre Konuk, who was also consulted for the article, stated that the public appeared shocked and appalled when such horrible incidents occurred, without any insight into why they occurred. They explained the need to consider multidimensional causes mostly engendered by the country's transformation from a traditional agricultural society to an urban industrial one. Children of underprivileged families living in the ghettos of big cities were extremely vulnerable in the face of violence and crime. Both experts pointed out that the real culprits were loosening family ties and weakened social controls in big cities owing largely to migration and poverty.[33]

When Serpil's mother was discharged from the hospital, she told her story to *Hürriyet*. She regretted that desolate and mostly harmless children living in the streets were stigmatized on account of the incident. She claimed that her attackers did not live in the streets; they had families, some of which were not even poor. "Even if they had been poor," she said, "poverty could not have been an excuse for crime. We are poor too but we never hurt anyone or get involved in any crime." She then begged the authorities to execute her daughter's murderers.

> If I had been assured that they would stay behind bars for the rest of their lives I would not demand they are hanged, but this is Turkey, there is always a general pardon or some kind of reduction in the sentence. I fear they will be released in no time and then I will have to take the matter into my own hands.[34]

Six thousand people attended a memorial service held in a shopping mall in Serpil's neighborhood. Also in attendance were representatives of government agencies and all prominent political parties, who listened to a miniconcert given by popular singers. The mayor promised better-lit streets and public gardens cleared of glue sniffers and drunkards. Secretary of State Hasan Gemici, who was responsible for the Social Work Services, addressed the press about the crime. Describing the accused children as "drug abusing and psychopathic habitual criminals," he reminded families of their responsibilities toward their children. In the last analysis, he concluded, families, society, and the state shared in the guilt for Serpil's ordeal.[35]

When the trial began, *Hürriyet* updated the story and revised the nature of its coverage. Within the space of three months, *Hürriyet* had distanced the case from the street children narrative, which seemed to have prompted reactions from some sociologists and nongovernmental organizations who stressed the responsibility of the public toward these unclaimed children and who evoked considerable sympathy for them. *Hürriyet* insisted that these "monsters" were urban outlaws living with their families. They should not benefit from the emerging public sympathy toward the tragedy of thinner-addicted street children.[36] Despite their young age they had *chosen* a lifestyle that involved sexual assault, rape, murder, and robbery, all with the tacit consent of their indifferent parents. They had planned to attack Serpil and killed her in a demonic ritual. The account also mentioned that the prosecutor of the State Security Court was asking for the death penalty but explained that because of the ages of the accused they could not be executed and would serve a life sentence instead. "This murder," *Hürriyet* opined, "is a grave disgrace in the history of İstanbul which has recently become a dangerous jungle. . . . Our sole hope is that the Turkish justice system will deliver a verdict that might give solace to Serpil's loved ones as well as everyone who still retains their humanity." A statement from famous lawyer Ergin Cinmen questioned why these children were being tried by a State Security Court. He called the situation "a freak of the Turkish judicial system" and believed that the police were also in favor of this measure because, unlike cases heard in civilian courts, State Security Court cases allowed the police to conduct the investigation in strict confidence, leaving the lawyers of the accused outside the procedure and lengthening the custody period.[37]

Once they were in court, the accused children confessed to the crimes of abduction, rape, and murder. The hearings were held in closed sessions over several months. As expected, the prosecutor asked for the death sentence.[38] The lawyer for Serpil's mother demanded that the families of the criminal children who evidently failed to raise them properly should also be punished by the court and serve time in prison.[39] In the end, all four children were sentenced to life in prison. According to the Turkish Penal Code, the upper limit for a life sentence was 36 years. Because the convicts were under the age of 18, their sentence was halved and reduced to 18 years. They were placed in the children's quarters of Bakırköy Prison in İstanbul. After serving seven years they were all released in 2005 when the Turkish National Assembly passed a new Penal Code that contained some provisions in favor of convicts who had been tried according to the previous penal code. As a heated debate on the new penal code emerged in the media, Serpil's case was reprised by those who were critical of the criminal execution system in particular and the instability of the Turkish judicial system in general.

Hürriyet published many items reminding the public that "monsters" would soon be set free.[40] The Internet edition of *Hürriyet* includes readers' comments protesting the release of the murderers. Without exception, all commentators claimed that these people should not have been treated as children because they were perfectly aware of what they were doing. Many comments asserted that if they had been in the United States, they would have been executed or would never see daylight again. Two columnists in the *Hürriyet* severely censured the "injustice" caused by this "judicial scandal." Bekir Coşkun, an extremely popular and influential columnist, wrote that the "justice system was better functioning even in African tribes than it was in Turkey" and invited the law practitioners "to raise their voice and reclaim the honor of their profession."[41] Another columnist, Oktay Ekşi, saw the situation as the epitome of the commonplace deception, fraud, and intrigue dominating Turkish social life. He claimed that the "Turkish state proved that it was in favor of this corrupted unjust life by freeing the murderers of Miss Serpil."[42]

In the days prior to the enactment of the new Penal Code, *Zaman*, in a piece titled "They Will Be Released Soon Because They were Children When They Committed the Crime," informed readers that Serpil's murderers would be out of prison thanks to the new law. It also quoted a lawyer, Ali Başarır, saying that criminals whose crime caused such righteous public indignation should remain in prison until they die.[43]

When the new Code came into effect in late December 2005, a columnist, Mehmet Kamış, wrote in *Zaman* that in Serpil's case, the Turkish judiciary had punished the innocent deceased instead of her murderers. He lamented that "so-called human rights activists both in Turkey and in Europe were always indifferent to the injustice that fell upon the victims of such ferocious crimes. . . . What is more important than the right to life?," he asked. He added:

> Those who raise hell when there is a violation of freedom of speech invariably remain silent about these murders. Murderers are released from prison in a couple of years and nobody not even the EU cares about this. When there is much talk about the rights of the convicts, it is also time to talk about the rights of the innocent victims.[44]

As the above analysis of the media coverage of Serpil's case illustrates, children who committed vicious crimes such as rape and murder did not evoke any genuine sympathy from the Turkish public at the turn of the century. Even the law practitioners stood aloof, refraining from any suggestion that age might form an important consideration. They did not envision the accused juveniles as children who might be less capable of grasping the gravity of their criminal conduct or more prone to irrevocable mistakes. On the contrary, a large group of opinion leaders—politicians, lawyers, and newspaper columnists—complained about laws that regarded people under the age of 18 as minors who could not be executed and whose sentences should be significantly reduced. The public clamor echoed those criticisms, relentlessly decrying the prospect of "these monsters" being lightly punished for their atrocity just because they were regarded as children or underage youth by the law. No significant criticism was voiced as to their being "tried" and put in prison instead of receiving psychological treatment and being placed in a rehabilitative correctional facility. Likewise, no one truly questioned why they were tried by a State Security Court instead of a children's court. The "judicial scandal" emerged, as the Turkish public saw it, when the children were released from prison after seven years and certainly not when they were sentenced to 18 years in prison. Clearly, the mainstream media and their readers did not perceive the murderers of Miss Serpil as children.

As the century drew to a close, the rhetoric surrounding children and crime had changed little from the sort that had dominated the child policies and juvenile justice system of the early Republic in the 1920s. Like that earlier period, most observers continued to maintain that young people surrendered their claim to childhood once they committed a crime. In fact, both the Turkish state and the larger society agreed that juvenile delinquents were individuals with proper agency differing little from that of adults. They similarly threatened public security and order, as well as innocent, law-abiding citizens who required protection from the state. At the turn of the twenty-first century, the national consensus continued to hold that juvenile delinquents should be isolated from the rest of society, and should be harshly punished as a warning to others. Turkish society prioritized punishment for the sake of retribution over rehabilitation and reintegration. When disagreements did arise, as in the Serpil case, it stemmed from anger at punishment that was perceived as too lenient rather than the reverse. Moreover, denunciations of overly lenient sentencing tended to lay blame on external pressure from the EU to "favor" criminals in the name of human rights.

As Chris Jenks argued, the notion of protected childhood was incompatible with the commission by children of violent crime. "[T]hat children are capable of violence, of rape, muggings and even murder is an idea that clearly falls outside traditional formulations of childhood."[45] Referring to the media reaction to the infamous James Bulger incident of 1993 in Great Britain, where a two-year-old boy was tortured and murdered by two 10-year-old boys, Jenks opined that "children who commit such violent acts pose a conundrum for they disassemble the traditional binary opposition between the categories of 'child' and 'adult' . . . whereby innocence is a hallmark of 'the child' and corrupting knowledge that of the 'adult.'"[46] Jenks's assertion is certainly verified in Serpil's case.

In Turkey in the last decade of the twentieth century, however, the expulsion of children from the arena of childhood extended much beyond the realm of violent acts and encompassed all sorts of crimes itemized in the Penal Code. One can argue that children like the Turkish ones who murdered Serpil would fail to evoke any genuine compassion from the public anywhere in the world because of the gruesome nature of their crime; therefore, the complete absence of humanitarian concern toward these children cannot and should not be generalized and taken as a benchmark in grasping and gauging Turkish society's approach to its young law offenders. It may come to mind that the same society and the juvenile justice system it produced might treat children who were accused of less serious crimes, such as property offences, with much leniency and understanding. Yet this does not seem to be the case insofar as Turkish society is concerned. This is evident from another notorious case that occurred around the same time as Serpil's murder and got nationwide media attention.

In 1997 four children, all under the age of 18 and some as young as 12, were accused of breaking into a famous *baklava* shop in Gaziantep, a large city in southeast Turkey, and stealing a few kilograms of *baklava* and pistachios without touching the money that had been left in the shop's safe. Each member of this so-called *baklava* gang received a six to nine years' prison sentence.[47] Their case provoked enormous public clamor not because these were mere children but because the case came to represent the allegedly discriminative character of the justice system in the country. Indeed, around the same time many politicians and public figures accused of organizing and involvement in crime gangs that embezzled enormous public funds were mostly released without any serious charges. And yet those convicted of stealing some *baklava*, probably the nation's favorite traditional dessert, were punished severely. This was the main reason for the public's interest in and indignation at the case.[48]

Here, the protest was not about throwing children into prison for nine years, it was about not throwing corrupt politicians into prison. Again, it was the exact reason why the 1999 case of 16-year-old E. E. B., who, armed with a knife, had stolen two pigeons and been sentenced to 11 years in prison, found itself a place, however small, in the mainstream media. "The relatives of the accused," *Milliyet* reported, "protested that people robbing the State and stealing billions from the public funds can go free while people who steal two pigeons are left to rot away in prison."[49] It is possible to multiply these examples and see that regardless of the magnitude of the crime and despite the concerns of a small group of children's rights activists, juvenile delinquents did not acquire much sympathy from civil society. As the number and efficiency of juvenile courts increased in the 2000s, "the percentage of convicted children [for property offences] peaked in 2006 and increased thirty-fold after one year of practice of the new Penal Code [of 2005] that is characterized by more severe penalties for property crimes."[50]

Along with this expansion in juvenile courts came a systemic reluctance to embrace alternatives to prison for juvenile offenders. FeridunYenisey, a jurist and academic who had taken part in the parliamentary commission that drafted the new Turkish Penal Code in 2001, recalled that he had found it

> very hard to persuade many members of the commission that incarceration should be the last resort for juvenile offenders. Even judges from high courts as well as law practitioners working in the commission believed that lenient measures toward criminal children should never be adopted because these would result in children's being used by adults as tools in crime.[51]

As exemplified by the amendment made to the Penal Code of 2005, in some cases with respect to the property offences, the Turkish legislature acted in a much more liberal and Western-oriented way than the society itself but before long was forced to retreat from that position because of vigorous public protest. In its original version, the new Penal Code allowed mediation for crimes committed by juveniles punishable by a sentence of two years or less. In December 2006, mediation was abandoned after a loud public outcry protesting the leniency for repeat offending by juveniles involved in theft, pickpocketing, and mugging.[52]

In Cooperation with the EU: The New Turkish Penal Code (2005) and the Child Protection Law (2005)

Turkey became an associate member of the European Union in 1999 and entered into an accession partnership in 2003. The "deficiencies" in the Turkish juvenile justice system formed one of the problems that the EU asked the Turkish government to address to prove its commitment to the prospective membership. The EU expected reforms to Turkish juvenile justice that would address "a strong interest in harmonizing laws and institutions with European standards; poor interagency cooperation; a relatively weak civil society; limited government-civil society cooperation; the prevalence of punitive attitudes towards crime and offenders; and the low priority given to adolescents."[53] This EU analysis was considered fair and justified by the critics of the prevailing juvenile justice system since it echoed the objections that a small circle of domestic agents had directed against the Turkish juvenile justice system for decades.

While the draft of the new Penal Code awaited debate in the Turkish National Assembly in the summer of 2004, a group of law practitioners launched a campaign demanding that the harsh provisions related to children who committed serious crimes (Article 31) be removed from the Penal Code. They asked for independent legislation for children that was not constructed by the punitive ethos of the Penal Code. The initiative for the Construction of a Juvenile Justice System (Çocuk Adalet Sistemi Yapılandırma Girişimi: ÇASYAG), representing Turkish Bar Associations in 23 cities, criticized the draft for persistently confining juvenile delinquents in adult prisons. Although the minimum age of criminal liability was raised from 11 to 12, the lawyers believed that it should be raised to 15. ÇASYAG's campaign neither attracted much media attention nor had an impact on the Turkish Parliament. The new Penal Code came into effect in June 2005 and the controversial Article 31 of the draft with respect to the status of juvenile delinquents was kept intact. According to Article 31:

> Children who have not reached the age of twelve years at the time of committing the offence shall have no criminal liability. Criminal prosecution may not be initiated against them; however, protective measures specific to children may be implemented. Those who have not reached the age of 15 years but are older than 12 years at the time of the offence shall have no criminal liability where they are incapable of perceiving the legal significance and consequences of their act or where their faculties of autonomous action are not sufficiently developed. However, protective measures specific to children shall be applied. Where the offender is aware of the legal significance and consequences of the offence and has developed the faculties of autonomous action with respect to the offence in question, they shall be imprisoned for a term of from 12 to 15 years, where the offence is punishable by aggravated life imprisonment, and a term of from 9 to 11 years where the offence is punishable by life imprisonment. Other

penalties shall be decreased by one half and in this case the term of imprisonment for each act shall be not greater than seven years. Those who have not reached the age of 18 but are over 15 at the time of the offence shall be imprisoned for a term of from 18 to 24 years where the offence is punishable by heavy life imprisonment; and a term of from 12 to 15 years where the offence is punishable by life imprisonment. Other penalties shall be decreased by one third and in this case the term of imprisonment for each act shall be not greater than 12 years.[54]

Fewer than two months after the new Penal Code went into effect, another law that reconstructed the status of juvenile delinquents in Turkey also took effect. Turkish lawmakers opted to design the Child Protection Law not as an independent body of rules but as a complement to the Penal Code that, in many aspects, reproduced its punitive logic in a specialized form. The Child Protection Law, the new Penal Code, and the Code of Criminal Procedure, all adopted in 2005, now formed part of the new legal framework vis-à-vis the juvenile justice system. The former was exclusively demanded by the EU

> to bring Turkish law into conformity with the Convention on the Rights of the Child, and to respond to the recommendations made by the Committee on the Rights of the Child, which had expressed "deep concern at the major discrepancies between domestic legislation concerning juvenile justice and the principles and provisions of the Convention."[55]

With the Child Protection Law of 2005 that replaced the Law of 1979, juvenile delinquents were included, for the first time in the history of the Turkish Republic, in the category of "children in need of protection." The term that was employed to describe the juvenile delinquents was no longer "criminal children"—a household phrase dominating the legislative body until then—but became "children who were pushed to crime."[56]

Under the new Penal Code, the minimum age of culpability was raised from 11 to 12, and the age at which juvenile offenders could be prosecuted as adults was raised from 15 to 18. Adolescents, at last, were embraced within the juvenile justice system. In the justification of the draft of the Child Protection Law the government also recognized that some of the offences committed by children were caused by the peculiar

conditions of adolescence.[57] Children between 12 and 15 may be prosecuted and sentenced to imprisonment for a term of 9 to 15 years depending on the quality of the crime if the judge decided that the child
was capable of comprehending the legal significance and consequences
of his crime and if his capacity to control his conduct was not underde-
veloped. This last provision raised objections from some law practitioners and children's rights activists who claimed that in practice judges
would invariably find the child fit for imprisonment unless the child was
mentally retarded.

The Child Protection Law appears to address many issues that were
deliberately ignored by the Law of 1979 because they were controversial. For example, the new Law provided that juveniles detained by law
enforcement agencies (gendarme or police) were to be kept in special
rooms allocated for this purpose, would not be handcuffed, and would
be allowed to receive visits from family members.[58] Accused children
younger than 15 were not to be detained prior to trial unless they were accused of offences punishable by a sentence of five years or more.[59] Prosecutors had discretion not to prosecute if the accused was a first-time
offender and the crime was not a serious one.[60] Sentences of less than
one year must be converted into noncustodial sentences. Alternatives to
detention included fines, enrollment in an educational institution, bans
on activities and freedom of movement, and community service.[61] And
if a judge or prosecutor considered it necessary, an inquiry describing
the individual characteristics and social environment of the accused juveniles would be conducted by social workers. The court could then take
social inquiry reports into account when assessing the juvenile's capacity
to comprehend the legal significance and consequences of his conduct.[62]
Convicted juvenile offenders are placed in correctional facilities for sentenced offenders: children's prisons, if available, or in children's sections
in adult prisons. All facilities for convicted juvenile offenders are open
facilities; families are allowed to pay prearranged visits, while children
may visit their family for a certain period of time during the year. In addition, children are permitted to attend school and participate in other
educational activities during the daytime.

Yet, in reality, most juveniles deprived of liberty are in pretrial facilities, not correctional facilities for sentenced offenders. This practice
subverts the intent of the reforms. The trial process is a long one be-

cause of the insufficient number of juvenile judges. According to the estimates of the Head of the Prison Department, "45 per cent of juveniles arrested prior to trial and placed in pretrial facilities are found not guilty."[63] As a UNICEF Report of 2009 remarks, "this is a serious indicator of the unnecessary use of deprivation of liberty before trial. The use of pre-trial detention to punish, as the Committee on the Rights of the Child has pointed out, violates the presumption of innocence."[64] Additionally, although accused children are no longer brought to the courtroom in handcuffs, the courtrooms they are brought to nevertheless remain the same. Juvenile courtrooms by no means differ from ordinary courtrooms and, as observed by the UNICEF, no special efforts are made to create an atmosphere in which children might feel at ease and comforted.[65]

Generally, UNICEF finds that the Child Protection Law recognizes many of the principles contained in the Convention on the Rights of the Child, yet it also points out that there are significant differences in the way some principles are formulated. In so doing it implies that the Turkish Parliament attempts to find a middle ground and submits to the expectations and demands of the EU by accepting the general framework of international (Western) standards of juvenile justice but also seeks avenues either to make exceptions to the rules or to allow itself some room for maneuver in accordance with the expectations and demands voiced by the general public, security forces, law practitioners, and some domestic agents that are critical of the impositions of the EU. For example, after agreeing to include juvenile delinquents within the category of "children in need of protection" for the first time in 2005, the legislature passed the Law for the Amendments to the Law on Social Services and Child Protection Agency of 2007 through which new institutions exclusively designed for juvenile offenders were established so that they will not be placed in the same residential facilities with other "children in need of protection."[66] Accordingly, UNICEF remarks that

the Child Protection Law alludes to "safeguarding the interest and well-being of juveniles," for example, but does not provide that the best interests of the child must be "a primary consideration" in all actions affecting a child. It provides that a "Penalty of imprisonment and measures that restrict liberty shall be the last resort for juveniles," but does not mention that they shall be for the shortest appropriate period of time. The Law refers to the "participation of the juvenile and his/her family in the process," but equates this with "keeping them informed."[67]

Since the foundation of the Republic civil society in Turkey has never actively sought or demanded any other measures than some sort of imprisonment for its juvenile offenders and the Turkish Parliament and government have been frequently accused by the public of not being adequately deterrent in implementing the justice policy. This gives insights into the punitive cultural codes under which the juvenile justice system was constructed and operated. The assessment of the application of the Law reveals that alternatives to imprisonment were not implemented.[68] Even the internal audit reports of the Turkish Ministry of Justice submitted in 2012 point out that measures like mediation and negotiation and settling should be prioritized over trial and imprisonment when dealing with juvenile delinquents and suggest reforms in the prevailing practice.[69] It is clear that regardless of the legislative regulations that show increasingly more resemblance to the Western examples since the foundation of the Republic, the more punitive "Turkish style" largely remains in place.

Conclusion

As has been the case since the establishment of the Republic, the ideal of becoming European and an indisputable part of the European/Western community informs Turkey's governmental policies affecting children, including juvenile justice. However, this aspiration has not necessarily caused Turkish political culture readily to adopt, embrace, and reproduce those European ideals.

As the public outcry exemplified both in the Serpil case in 1998 and in the amendments made to the Article of Penal Code with respect to the mediation in 2006 indicates, the Turkish public still considers the European understanding of juvenile justice as well as the European measures to deal with juvenile offenders too lenient. By contrast, Turkish perceptions of the American justice system are more positive because they believe that the United States punishes young criminals more harshly.

Legislative measures adopted largely with the motivation of meeting conditions for membership in the EU occasionally tend to remain effec-

tive mainly on paper due largely to resistance from juvenile justice practitioners who think that European measures do not take the peculiar
local dynamics into consideration. Because the Law emerged more from
external EU pressure than organically from Turkish civil society, UNI-
CEF believes that judges and prosecutors tend to apply the new legislation superficially while evincing little genuine interest in the well-being
of the accused juveniles.[70]

All in all, the juvenile justice policies produced in Turkey, as anywhere else, have never been entirely free from the political conflicts and
polarizations as well as economic troubles that dominate the society's
agenda of the time. Changes in the policy vis-à-vis a particular political,
social, and economic problem also lead to alterations or have reflections
in the terrain of juvenile justice. For example, in a political atmosphere
where the State Security Courts and the mentality that generated them
played a domineering role the Turkish Parliament added provisions to
the Anti-Terror Law of 1991 for children aged between 15 and 18 that
called for "trying them in specialised courts for terrorist activities" and,
as was the case with adults convicted for similar activities, their sentence
was doubled. In a different milieu of political values and understanding
that emerged in 2000s, which led to the abolishment of the State Security Courts and the beginning of Turkey's partnership negotiations with
the EU, the Turkish Parliament made amendments to the Anti-Terror
Law in 2010 and abandoned the rule of "doubling the sentence" for children. It also provided that "children who participated in the activities
organized by the terrorist organizations will be tried but will not be regarded and treated as members of the terrorist organizations."[71]

Despite the indisputable gains acquired on the legal plane thanks to
the Child Protection Law of 2005, the question of juvenile delinquency
continues to be in need of strongly voiced concern from civil society. As
in the early decades of the Republic, juvenile delinquents still fail to at-
tract attention or sympathy from the public, which in turn pushes them
to the margins of childhood territory. The society continuously associ-
ates childhood with innocence, and regards criminality and childhood
innocence as mutually exclusive phenomena. The fact that children have
been increasingly exploited by criminal networks does not help either.
Unless there is a significant transformation in society's perception of
and attitude toward juvenile delinquency as well as in the conditions

that push children into crime, the introduction and implementation of some genealogically Western institutions and measures such as children's courts do not seem enough to bring about dramatic changes in juvenile delinquents' lives.

NOTES

1 Yasemin Gencer, "We Are Family: The Child and Modern Nationhood in Early Turkish Republican Cartoons (1923–28)," *Comparative Studies of South Asia, Africa and the Middle East* 32, no. 2 (2012): 294–309, here 295–296.

2 The Kemalists even invented a National Children's Festival that has been celebrated on the 23rd of April every year, the day of the opening of the Turkish Grand National Assembly in 1920. The festival was presented as the ultimate proof of the Kemalist regime's dedication to children and their rights and happiness. With the participation of all schoolchildren as well as children from many countries across the world in parades, folkloric shows, and many other entertaining events, children's day came to represent the identification of the Republic with Turkish children whose destinies were inseparably intertwined.

3 Güven Gürkan Öztan, *Türkiye'de Çocukluğun Politik İnşası* [Political construction of childhood in Turkey] (İstanbul: İstanbul Bilgi Üniversitesi Yayınları, 2011).

4 For the Victorian notion of romanticized childhood and loving innocence, see Anne Scott MacLeod, *American Childhood, Essays on Children's Literature of the Nineteenth and Twentieth Centuries* (Athens: University of Georgia Press, 1994); Peter N. Stearns, *Childhood in World History* (New York: Routledge, 2006); Anthony Fletcher, *Growing Up in England: The Experience of Childhood 1600–1914* (New Haven: Yale University Press, 2008).

5 For a detailed analysis of the Turkish Republican approach toward juvenile delinquency before the establishment of children's courts in 1979, see Nazan Çiçek, "Mapping the Turkish Republican Notion of Childhood and Juvenile Delinquency: The Story of Children's Courts 1940–1990," in *Juvenile Delinquency and the Limits of Western Influence, 1850–2000*, ed. Heather Ellis (Basingstoke, UK: Palgrave Macmillan, 2014), 248–275.

6 5387 Sayılı Korunmaya Muhtaç Çocuklar Hakkında Kanun, Türkiye Büyük Millet Meclisi, 23 Mayıs 1949 [Law for Children Who Need Protection, Turkish Grand National Assembly, 23 May 1949].

7 6972 Sayılı Korunmaya Muhtaç Çocuklar Hakkında Kanun, Türkiye Büyük Millet Meclisi, 15 Mayıs 1957 [Law for Children Who Need Protection, Turkish Grand National Assembly, 15 May 1957].

8 Janet Ainsworth, "Achieving the Promise of Justice for Juveniles: A Call for the Abolition of Juvenile Court," in *Governing Childhood*, ed. Anne McGillivray (Aldershot: Dartmouth, 1997), 87.

9 Chris Jenks, *Childhood* (London: Routledge, 1996), 127–133.

10 See Rıdvan Nafiz, "Mücrim Çocuklar Hakkında" [On criminal children], *Terbiye Dergisi* [*Journal of Education*], no. 3 (1 Mayıs 1927 [1 May 1927]): 211–219, reproduced in Yahya Akyüz, "Çocuk Suçluluğu Konusunda Türk Eğitim Tarihinde İlk Önemli Araştırma" [The first notable research in Turkish educational history on juvenile delinquency], I. *Ulusal Çocukve Suç: Nedenlerve Önleme Çalışmaları Sempozyumu* [First National Symposium on Child and Crime: Reasons and Preventive Measures], Bildiriler [Proceedings], Ankara, 2002, 35–46.

11 2253 Sayılı Çocuk Mahkemelerinin Kuruluşu, Görev ve Yargılama Usulleri Hakkında Kanun, Türkiye Büyük Millet Meclisi, 7 Kasım 1979 [The Law for the Establishment, Duties and Trial Procedures of Children's Courts, 7 November 1979].

12 For an incident that convinced the Turkish decision-makers that introducing juvenile courts would save the Republic a great amount of embarrassment in the international arena, see Çiçek, "Mapping the Turkish Republican Notion of Childhood and Juvenile Delinquency."

13 Ali Suat Ertosun, "Adalet Bakanlığı Cezave Tevkifevleri Genel Müdürü'nün Konuşması" [Speech by the director general of prisons and detention centers, Ministry of Justice], in Emine Akyüz et al., eds., *II. Ulusal Çocukve Suç Sempozyumu, Yargı Öncesive Yargılama Süreci* [II. National Symposium on Child and Delinquency, Pre-trial and Trial Process], 10–13 Nisan [April], Proceedings, with the Contribution of Mission of European Commission in Turkey, Türkiye Çocuklara Yeniden Özgürlük Vakfı, Ankara, 2003, 9–11, here 9. All translations from the Turkish are the author's.

14 Ibrahim Demirtaş, "Aile ve Çocuk Mahkemelerinde İstihdam edilen uzmanların (Psikolog, Pedagog, Sosyal Çalışmacı ve Sosyal Hizmet Uzmanı) verimliliklerinin azami seviyeye çıkarılması konusunda yaşanan sorunların tespiti ve çözüm önerisi geliştirmesiyle alakalı inceleme raporu" [The report on how to maximize the efficiency of professionals (psychologists, pedagogues, social workers) employed in family courts and children's courts: Problems and suggestions], 26 April, 2012, www.icdenetim.adalet.gov.tr.

15 The text of the Law of 1979 did not employ the term "adolescent." It used the word "küçük," meaning "underage," and classified underage people as "the ones younger than 11," "the ones older than 11 but younger than 15." People older than 15 were not included in the Law.

16 See Emine Akyüz, "Çocuk Mahkemeleri Kanununun Çocuğun Güvenliği Açısından Değerlendirilmesi" [An assessment of the Law of Children's Courts in terms of child's safety], in Esin Onur, ed., *Çocuk Suçluluğuve Çocuk Mahkemeleri Sempozyumu* [Symposium on Juvenile Delinquency and the Children's Courts], 22–23 Haziran [June] 1983, Ankara Üniversitesi Basımevi, Ankara, 1983, 101–110, here 103.

17 Esin Onur, "Çocuk Mahkemeleri Yasasının Genel Değerlendirilmesi" [A general assessment of the Law of Children's Courts], in Esin Onur, ed., *Çocuk Suçluluğu ve Çocuk Mahkemeleri Sempozyumu* [Symposium on Juvenile Delinquency and

the Children's Courts], 22–23 Haziran [June] 1983, Ankara Üniversitesi Basımevi, Ankara, 1983, 7–32, here 17–18.

18 Onur, "Çocuk Mahkemeleri," 18.

19 Turkey signed the Convention on 14 September 1990. The Turkish Grand National Assembly ratified the Convention on 9 December 1995 through Law No. 4058. The Convention then came into effect and became part of Turkish legislation on 27 January 1995 through its publication in *Resmi Gazete* (Official Gazette). Ahmet Nezih Kök, "Çocuk Mahkemeleri Mevzuatı ve Adli Tıp" [Legislation on the children's courts and forensics], in Emine Akyüz et al., eds., *II. Ulusal Çocuk ve Suç Sempozyumu, Yargı Öncesi ve Yargılama Süreci* [II. National Symposium on Child and Delinquency, Pretrial and Trial Process], 10–13 Nisan [April], Proceedings, with the Contribution of Mission of European Commission in Turkey, Türkiye Çocuklara Yeniden Özgürlük Vakfı, Ankara, 2003, 91–98, here 93–94.

20 See Refik Dizdaroğlu, "Çocuk Mahkemelerinin Yargılama Sorunları" [Problems with the trial process in children's courts], in Emine Akyüz et al., eds., *II. Ulusal Çocukve Suç Sempozyumu, Yargı Öncesive Yargılama Süreci* [II. National Symposium on Child and Delinquency, Pretrial and Trial Process], 10–13 Nisan [April], Proceedings, with the Contribution of Mission of European Commission in Turkey, Türkiye Çocuklara Yeniden Özgürlük Vakfı, Ankara, 2003, 168–170, here 170; and Nesrin Hatipoğlu, "Avukatların Çocuk Yargılaması Sürecinde Karşılaştıkları Sorunlar" [Predicaments that lawyers face in the process of children's trial], in Emine Akyüz et al., eds., *II. Ulusal Çocuk*, 172–174, here 172.

21 Esin Onur, "Çocuk Mahkemeleri Yasasının," 17; Ahmet Nezih Kök, "Çocuk Mahkemeleri Mevzuatı," 94; Nesrin Hatipoğlu, "Avukatların Çocuk Yargılaması," 172–173; Emine Akyüz, "Uluslararası Standartlara Göre Çocuk Yargılaması" [Trial of children according to international standards], in Emine Akyüz et al., eds., *II. Ulusal Çocuk*, 123–151, here 151.

22 "Magandalar Azdı" [Churls are running rampant], *Hürriyet*, 5 October 1998.

23 "Zorbalardan Birinin Eşgali Belli" [Relatives give description of one of the attackers], *Hürriyet*, 5 October 1998.

24 "Küçük Caniler Cinayet Makinesi" [These little murderers are like a murder machine], *Milliyet*, 10 Ekim 1998. Later, in her exclusive interview with the accused children, journalist Duygu Asena would dismiss these sentences as "next to nothing."

25 Capital punishment with the exception for war crimes was abolished in 2002. See Çeşitli Kanunlarda Değişiklik Yapılmasına İlişkin Kanun [The Law for the Amendments to Some Laws], Türkiye Büyük Mllet Meclisi [Turkish Grand National Assembly], no. 4771, 3 August 2002.

26 "Seri Katil Çıktılar" [They are serial killers], *Hürriyet*, 10 October 1998.

27 M. Fatih Uğur, "Sahipsiz Canavarlar" [Unclaimed and forlorn monsters], *Zaman*, 10 October 1998.

28 Melih Aşık, "Vahşetin Ötesi" [Beyond savagery], *Milliyet*, 10 October 1998, Umur Talu, "İçimizdeki Canavar" [Monsters living inside us], *Milliyet*, 11 October 1998;

Ahmet Sever, "Yok Edelim Demek Sorunu Yok Etmiyor" [Killing these children would not solve our problem], *Milliyet*, 13 October 1998.

29 Servet Dağ, "Vahşete Büyük Öfke" [Great anger at savagery], *Zaman*, 11 October 1998; "Canavarlar Linçten Dondu" [The monsters barely escaped lynching], *Hürriyet*, 11 October 1998; "Tinerciler Linçten Kurtuldu" [Thinner addicts escaped lynching], *Milliyet*, 11 October 1998.

30 Duygu Asena, "Cezayı Hak Ettik" [We deserve to be punished], *Milliyet*, 11 October 1998.

31 "Canileri DGM Tutukladı" [DGM arrests the cutthroats], *Milliyet*, 13 October 1998.

32 "Vahşetin Sorgusu DGM'de Başladı" [Savagery is being interrogated at DGM], *Hürriyet*, 13 October 1998; Abdullah Dirican, Ercan Gün, "Canileri İdam Edin" [Execute the monsters], *Zaman*, 13 October 1998.

33 "Sokak Çığlık Atıyor" [Cry coming from the street], *Hürriyet*, 18 October 1998.

34 "Üçüncü Bıçakta Bayıldım" [I fainted when they stabbed me the third time], *Hürriyet*, 14 October 1998.

35 "Hepimiz Suçluyuz" [We all are guilty], *Zaman*, 10 November 1998.

36 The objections of some nongovernmental organizations and other groups that children living in the streets in large cities of Turkey were mostly the victims of crime rather than perpetrators seem to have been verified by the statistics collected by the Ministry of Justice and published by the Turkish Statistical Institute in 2006. Accordingly, "Eighty-five per cent of juvenile delinquents report that they live with both parents. Only 8 per cent have a history of substance abuse." Turkish Statistical Institute, Prison Statistics 2006, Table 7 and Table 9.

37 "Ümraniye Canileri Hakim Önünde" [Ümraniye monsters are at court], *Hürriyet*, 14 January 1999.

38 "Tinercilere İdam İstemi" [Prosecutors ask for death sentence for the thinner addicts], *Milliyet*, 14 January 1999.

39 "Siz Asmazsanız Ben Asacağım" [If you do not hang them I will], *Hürriyet*, 17 July 1999.

40 Ayşegül Usta, "Öğretmenin Katilleri 15 Gün Sonra Serbest" [Teacher's murderers will be free in 15 days], *Hürriyet*, 10 December 2005; Ayşegül Usta, "Hani 36 yıldı?" [We were told they would serve 36 years], *Hürriyet*, 24 December 2005; "Ümraniye Tecavüzcüsü Serbest Bırakıldı" [Ümraniye rapist is free now], *Hürriyet*, 24 December 2005.

41 Bekir Coşkun, "Çığlık" [Outcry], *Hürriyet*, 27 December 2005.

42 Oktay Ekşi, "Adresi Doğru Yazalım" [Let us see the problem be addressed], *Hürriyet*, 13 January 2006.

43 Büşra Erdal, "Suçu Çocukken İşledikleri İçin Çıkıyorlar" [They will be released soon because they were children when they committed the crime], *Zaman*, 11 December 2005.

44 Mehmet Kamış, "Serpil Öğretmene Hakkını Kim Verecek?" [Who will do justice to Miss Serpil?], *Zaman*, 28 December 2005.

45 Chris Jenks, *Childhood* (New York: Routledge, 1996), 127.

46 Jenks, *Childhood*, 127–128.

47 For an exclusive interview with the so-called baklava gang in prison, see Nedim Şener, "Acı Bir Baklava Öyküsü" [A bitter story of baklava], *Milliyet*, 18 October 1998.

48 As a famous columnist opined in *Milliyet*, "theft, whether it is small or big, is inexcusable under any circumstances. Yet one cannot help but ask what kind of justice this is. On the one side, there are those who steal trillions from the public and become more prestigious with each theft and on the other side there are these children who steal two slices of baklava and get six years in prison. Does our justice system[,] which seems very swift, determined and firm when it comes to baklava stealing people[,] work in the same way vis-a-vis everyone?" Hikmet Bila, "Çocuklar Cezaevinde" [Children in prison], *Milliyet*, 19 October 1998.

49 Bahar Memiş, "Umutları Yargıtay'da" [Their hope rests with the Supreme Court], *Milliyet*, 18 July 1999.

50 Bengü Kurtege, "The Historical Politics of the Juvenile Justice System and the Operation of Law in the Juvenile Court in Istanbul in Regard to Property Crimes," unpublished master's thesis, Boğaziçi University, İstanbul, 2009, 311.

51 Feridun Yenisey, "Türk Ceza Kanununun 2001 Tasarısı ve Çocuk" [The draft of 2001 for the new Turkish penal code and the child], in Emine Akyüz et al., eds., *II. Ulusal Çocukve Suç Sempozyumu, Yargı Öncesive Yargılama Süreci* [II. National Symposium on Child and Delinquency, Pretrial and Trial Process], 10–13 Nisan [April], Proceedings, with the Contribution of Mission of European Commission in Turkey, Türkiye Çocuklara Yeniden Özgürlük Vakfı, Ankara, 2003, 297–307, here 301.

52 See 5560 Sayılı Çeşitli Kanunlarda Değişiklik Yapılmasınaİlişkin Kanun, Türkiye Büyük Millet Meclisi, 6 Aralık 2006 [The Law as to the Amendments to Some Laws, Turkish Grand National Assembly, 6 December 2006].

53 Assessment of Juvenile Justice Reform Achievements in Turkey, UNICEF Regional Office for Central and Eastern Europe/Commonwealth of Independent States, July 2009, 4.

54 5237 Sayılı Türk Ceza Kanunu, Türkiye Büyük Millet Meclisi, 26 Eylül 2004 [Turkish Penal Code, Turkish Grand National Assembly, 26 September 2004], Article 31. For the English translation, see www.tuerkeiforum.net.

55 Assessment of Juvenile Justice Reform Achievements in Turkey, UNICEF Regional Office for Central and Eastern Europe/Commonwealth of Independent States, July 2009, 7.

56 5395 Sayılı Çocuk Koruma Kanunu, Türkiye Büyük Millet Meclisi, 3 Temmuz 2005 [The Child Protection Law, Turkish Grand National Assembly, 3 July 2005], Article 1.

57 Çocukları Koruma Kanunu Tasarısı ve Adalet Komisyonu Raporu [The Draft of the Child Protection Law and the Report of the Parliamentary Commission of Justice], (1/991), Dönem: 22, YasamaYılı: 3, TBMM, Sayı: 963, 10.03.2005.

58 The Law of Child Protection, Articles, 16, 18, and 31, respectively.

59 The Law of Child Protection, Article, 21.

60 Code of Criminal Procedures, Article 171.

61 Penal Code, Article 50.

62 The Law of Child Protection, Article 35.

63 Assessment of Juvenile Justice Reform Achievements in Turkey, UNICEF Regional Office for Central and Eastern Europe/Commonwealth of Independent States, July 2009, 16.

64 Assessment of Juvenile Justice Reform Achievements, 16.

65 Assessment of Juvenile Justice Reform Achievements, 21.

66 See 26430 Sayılı Sosyal Hizmetlerve Çocuk Esirgeme Kurumu Kanununda Değişiklik Yapılması Hakkında Kanun, Türkiye Büyük Millet Meclisi, 1 Şubat 2007 [The Law for the Amendments to the Law on Social Services and Child Protection Agency, Turkish Grand National Assembly, 1 February 2007].

67 The Law of Child Protection, Article 4(1)(a), (c), (1) and (f), respectively, Assessment of Juvenile Justice Reform, 8.

68 Çocuk Koruma Kanunu'nun 4 Yıllık Değerlendirme Toplantısı Raporu [Report of the meeting for the assessment of the application of the Law of Child Protection], Adalet Bakanlığıve UNICEF [Ministry of Justice and UNICEF], Aralık 2009 [December 2009], 18–19.

69 Adalet Bakanlığı [Ministry of Justice], İç Denetim Birimi Başkanlığı [Directorate of Internal Auditing], İnceleme Raporu [Inquiry Report] 26.04.2012, Ankara, 33–34.

70 As cited in the UNICEF Assessment Report of 2009, according to the members of the Child Rights Committee of the Ankara Bar Association, "many judges and prosecutors need to improve their skills in listening to children and treating them as individuals." Assessment of Juvenile Justice Reform Achievements in Turkey, UNICEF Regional Office for Central and Eastern Europe/Commonwealth of Independent States, July 2009, 11.

71 General Comment No. 10, CRC/C/GC 10, para. 37–38, and the UNICEF Assessment report of 2009 finds this measure "discriminatory." Assessment of Juvenile Justice Reform, 19.

Conclusion

Whose Children? A Comparative Anatomy of Moral Panics

WILLIAM S. BUSH AND DAVID S. TANENHAUS

This volume's transnational perspective on the spread and practice of modern juvenile justice during the twentieth century simultaneously emphasizes the agency of local actors in making this history. The case studies provide a ground-level view of the circulation, implementation, and contestation of ideas about juvenile delinquency and crime in a variety of settings across the twentieth century. These histories help to fill in important details about particular places and practices in a global history of youth governance whose broad outlines are coming into clearer focus.

Collectively, these histories also demonstrate the utility of the socio-logical concept of a "moral panic" for understanding social reactions to juvenile deviancy and crime. And, as this chapter contends, there are several policy lessons to be learned from this history of confrontations. But first we need to understand what a moral panic is, and consider why this concept is so potentially useful for understanding concerns about youth, crime, and justice.

In his classic study *Folk Devils and Moral Panics: The Creation of Mods and Rockers*, which was published initially in 1972 and now is in its third edition, Stanley Cohen explained:

> Societies appear to be subject, every now and then, to periods of moral panics. A condition, episode, person or group or persons emerges to become defined as a threat to societal values and interests; its nature is presented in a stylized and stereotypical fashion by the mass media; the moral barricades are manned by editors, bishops, politicians and other right-thinking people; socially accredited experts pronounce their diag-

noses and solutions; ways of coping are evolved or (more often) resorted to; the condition then disappears, submerges or deteriorates and becomes more visible. Sometimes the object of the panic is quite novel and at other times it is something which has been in existence long enough, but suddenly appears in the limelight. Sometimes the panic passes over and is forgotten, except in folklore and collective memory; at other times it has more serious and long-lasting repercussions and might produce such changes as those in legal and social policy or even in the way the society conceives itself.[1]

As Cohen later explained, he and his colleague Jock Young, who was the first scholar to use the term in print,[2] probably picked up the concept from their reading of Marshall McLuhan's *Understanding Media* (1964).[3] Cohen and Young were interested in the role that the media and other moral arbiters played in amplifying and spreading fear about deviancy. These fears led, as Cohen's research demonstrated, to societal overreactions such as the aggressive policing and prosecuting of "expressive fringe delinquency."[4]

Cohen used his findings about the English reactions to youth subcultures in the 1960s to develop a theoretical model to analyze the structure and stages of a moral panic. Since then, Erich Goode and Nachman Ben-Yehuda have refined his model to emphasize the five crucial elements in moral panics from concerns over witchcraft during the Renaissance to modern feminist antipornography crusades.[5] These elements include their *volatile* nature: "they erupt fairly suddenly (although they may lie dormant or latent for long periods of time, and may reappear from time to time) and, nearly as suddenly, subside." In addition, moral panics must include heightened *concern* about a how a certain group is acting, *hostility* to that group, and widespread agreement or *consensus* that the threat from the group is real. Finally, and more controversially, Goode and Ben-Yehuda stress that *disproportion*, or the idea that the public response is "in excess of what is appropriate if concern were directly proportional to the objective harm," is an essential element of the theory. Because measuring risk and reactions is a tricky business, critics of the concept of a moral panic question this core assumption about judging the beliefs of others, especially those whom scholars may not understand or respect.

By the turn of the twenty-first century, the concept of a moral panic had become a staple of academic literature and a part of the transatlantic public discourse about social reactions.[6] As David Garland has noted, "The claim that a social reaction is, in fact, merely a moral panic, has become a familiar move in any public conversation about social problems or societal risks."[7] He added, "If Cohen hadn't introduced the term in 1972, it would have been necessary for someone else to invent it."[8] Similarly, Kenneth Thompson contends that the concept is so critical because the phenomenon it describes is a standard and recurring feature in modern societies in which "the rapidity of social change and growing social pluralism create increasing potential for value conflicts and lifestyle clashes between diverse social groups, which turn to moral enterprise to defend or assert their values against those of other groups."[9]

Yet Garland properly cautions that scholars and others should use the concept of a moral panic to do more than just "expose" and "debunk" seemingly irrational social overreactions. Instead, the concept should be used as a diagnostic tool to analyze *symbolic meaning, social relations,* and *historical temporality.*[10] To do so, investigators need to ask probing questions about the social construction and constructors of the "folk devil," and why these events happened when they did. And, as Corrie Decker's chapter about colonial Zanzibar reminds us, sometimes the panic that did not happen, like the hound that did not bark, is the real story.

Scholars, as Chas Critcher admonishes, must exercise caution in applying overly rigid analytical models. In a survey of the scholarly literature on moral panics, Critcher observes that "[m]oral panic analysis is better understood as an ideal type: a means of beginning an analysis, not the entire analysis in itself."[11] "Threats to children or from youth," he points outs, "have become pervasive themes in moral panics."[12] Indeed, historians have shown how generations of youth have stood at the forefront of the "value conflicts and lifestyle clashes" highlighted in the scholarly literature on moral panics. Nearly every significant policy response to juvenile delinquency (real or perceived) has stemmed to some extent from moral concerns: sheltering children from immoral influences; protecting children and adolescents from their "dangerous peers"; or protecting a given society from corrupted or violent delinquents.

Each of these ostensibly moral concerns has emerged from sweeping social, cultural, economic, and political changes.

In perhaps the best-documented example, the nineteenth-century United States, the industrial city became a symbol for moral disorder for a range of worried social reformers, as numerous historians have noted.[13] Holding up the moral order of the eighteenth-century village as their model, American reformers urgently developed private and public responses to the interrelated "urban" problems of crime and poverty.

Nowhere was this more the case than where children and youth were concerned. For example, Charles Loring Brace, founder of the Children's Aid Society, warned in 1854 of the "unconscious society" of street children in New York City, who might engage in "collective action" in youth gangs or political mobs.[14] His solution was to remove those children from the city entirely and place them with rural families on the American frontier. Meanwhile, Brace's contemporaries experimented with asylums, orphanages, Sunday schools, didactic literature, and settlement houses, each of which met with mixed results and ultimately did little to quell recurring anxieties about youth in a rapidly modernizing society.

Two competing approaches to youth took hold. The first viewed children as vulnerable and in need of protection, what the legal historian Michael Grossberg has dubbed "sheltered childhood." The second perspective, emerging with greater force in the twentieth century, has feared children and especially adolescents as dangerous, incipient criminals.[15]

By the turn of the twentieth century, "child savers" invented public policies, laws, and institutions to address increasingly complex problems even as they continued to imagine them in largely moral terms. Progressive Era juvenile justice incorporated both approaches and created the framework for the modern dual system in which either a juvenile court or criminal court can process the case of an adolescent lawbreaker.

The establishment and spread across the globe of a dual system to process the cases of adolescents meant that anxiety about juvenile delinquency and crime could either strengthen or weaken public support for the juvenile court. As we explained in the introduction, "youth specific" concerns about "our kids" theoretically supported the idea of a juvenile court, but "crime specific" concerns about "other people's kids" could undermine its legitimacy.

As outlined in the introduction, our two-by-two model can be used to identify four types of moral panics:

Table 1

1. Youth Specific and Endogenous	2. Youth Specific and Exogenous
3. Crime Specific and Endogenous	4. Crime Specific and Exogenous

"Youth specific and endogenous" moral panics should be rare occurrences because people are unlikely to consider their own children to be "folk devils." Yet dominant social groups have typically worried more about their children rather than about other people's children, so endogenous juvenile delinquency or deviancy can trigger moral panics directed at either the social conditions or bad actors deemed responsible for corrupting "our youth."[16] Such panics can also blur the line between "endogenous" and "exogenous." The postwar panic about mods and rockers in England, which inspired Stanley Cohen's study of "folk devils," shows how mutable such classifications can be. Our kids, if we're not careful, may start acting like theirs.

In the United States after World War II, a panic arose over the influence of comic books on American children. Dubbed "the marijuana of the nursery," comic books were accused of encouraging otherwise healthy children to become juvenile delinquents. In response, private individuals and groups mounted censorship campaigns that led many municipal and state governments to restrict or ban the sale of comic books. In 1954–55, a widely publicized investigation in the United States Senate pressured the comic book industry to adopt a strict censorship code that prohibited such things as negative portrayals of adult and religious authorities, sexual images, and graphic violence. This panic spread outside the United States; the national governments of Canada, Great Britain, and France all adopted laws restricting the importation of American comic books.[17]

Meanwhile, the exportation of American music, film, and fashion aimed at teenagers promulgated anxieties in numerous countries about the decline of traditional authority and national identity. While some countries such as West Germany suggested that juvenile delinquency was a reflection of "American civilization," governments from Great Britain to Brazil took steps toward censorship amid public outcries.[18] These histories followed the model for moral panics outlined by Cohen, Garland, and Thompson, in which a concern erupted suddenly through the national media, producing a governmental response. However, in his recent study of a "Soviet moral panic" during the Nikita Khrushchev regime of the late 1950s and early 1960s, historian Gleb Tsipursky describes how the national government identified and popularized a youth crisis around working-class hooliganism and the growing appeal of "Western" popular culture. Unlike examples from Western societies, the Soviet story illustrates a "leadership-induced moral panic" driven by government officials and spread through government-controlled media.[19]

The administration of juvenile justice itself can be influenced by moral panics. The case studies in this volume about Mexico City, Montreal, Paris, and Boston all addressed moral panics, even if they were somewhat muted, which led to expanded policing of "at-risk" children and youth. This included using forms of "soft power," such as police prevention programs and juvenile probation, to monitor and control youth. In such instances, law enforcement and juvenile justice widened their nets in response to moral panics. Although the state expanded its power to define, classify, and control youth, this policing remained "youth specific." Thus, the consideration of youth ultimately mattered more than classifying troublesome teenagers as either our kids or theirs.

The creation of the Chicago Juvenile Court at the turn of the twentieth century is perhaps the classic example of institution-building in response to a "youth specific and exogenous" moral panic. In this instance, women reformers from notable "American" families, such as Jane Addams and Julia Lathrop, led the crusade to establish a "youth specific" entity to treat and control first- and second-generation immigrant youth from southern and eastern Europe. The juvenile court, in effect, tried to make these foreign children "endogenous." This example demonstrates that a moral panic about "other people's children," if led by reformers committed to bridging the divide between social classes, can produce positive "youth specific" and beneficial reforms. In this case, the creation of the juvenile court diverted children from being either harmed or destroyed by the criminal justice system.

David Niget's chapter described how European "child savers" drew on this American history to establish international norms about child welfare and juvenile justice. Much of this history lacked the intensity of a moral panic, and instead should be classified as a social movement. Yet the reformers did champion "youth specific" policies for other people's kids. After World War I, European and especially Belgian child welfare workers, animated by a desire for a "moral reconstruction" of Europe, advocated child protective reforms. At its 1921 congress, the International Association for Child Welfare called for the "moral preservation of childhood," a movement that culminated in the adoption in 1924 of the Declaration of the Rights of the Child by the League of Nations. The broadly worded declaration called for rights to education, a separate justice system, adequate health care, and other very broad provisions couched largely in moral terms. Building on these milestones, a movement of children's and juvenile court judges, embodied in the International Association of Children's Judges, circulated scientific ideas about child welfare alongside the broad moral concerns articulated previously. The post–World War II emergence of human rights provided a new paradigm for a growing transnational consensus, articulated by the IACJ (later the International Association of Youth Magistrates), that "child welfare aimed to epitomize democratic values." Moreover, these judges propounded legal and scientific arguments for children's rights in civil and criminal cases, which formed an important basis for the 1959 Declaration of the Rights of the Child. These foundational ideas still inform international norms in the twenty-first century.

The important role played by juvenile court judges in shaping this emerging global consensus on child welfare and children's rights thus expands the borders of these judges' influence, heretofore thought to be largely local, regional, or national in scope. This study also illustrates how the deployment of law and science gradually began to provide a framework for responses to youth deviance, including moral panics of varying intensities. And, as we saw in Shari Orisich's chapter, social workers in Mexico City used these scientific ideas to structure their home visits and reporting on "at-risk" youth.

Moral panics about exogenous children, as the creation of the Chicago Juvenile Court suggests, often emerge from anxieties within the majority population of a given society about "outsiders," such as recent immigrants or stigmatized minority groups. The late twentieth-century influx of Latin American and Caribbean-origin youth into Spain, for example, has prompted harsh media portrayals of their alleged danger-ousness. "Racialized" in the Spanish media, these youth must navigate a system of schools, child welfare services, and juvenile justice agencies under a cloud of suspicion.[20]

Moral panics can affect resource allotment in systems that often in-volve a mixture of social welfare and crime control. Elizabeth Hinton, for example, has shown how crime specific concerns in the 1960s led U.S. policymakers to replace social workers with law enforcement per-sonnel to run programs for "at-risk" youth in highly segregated urban areas.[21] This reassignment of the police was reminiscent of the Montreal Miracle, but also foreshadowed the increasingly militarized policing of minority communities during the final decades of the twentieth century, and thus suggests the value of studying juvenile justice for a better un-derstanding of the complicated relationship between law enforcement and communities of color in the United States.

Moral panics about crime have had lasting structural effects on how highly segregated urban areas in the United States are policed. As James Forman Jr. has shown, in Washington, DC, residents of "the city's poor-est neighborhoods, especially young people," face aggressive policing on a daily basis.[22] This includes officers "swearing and yelling, making belittling remarks, issuing illegitimate orders, conducting random and unwarranted searches." As he explains, "this treatment became part of the social contract, a tax paid in exchange for the right to move in public space."[23] Sadly, "Police mistreatment, that is, became part of growing up."[24] Sociologists, most notably Victor Rios, have documented the im-pact of this policing on the lives of Black and Latino adolescents.[25]

There is, however, a critical difference between a "youth specific" and "crime specific" moral panic. The former may expand the reach of the juvenile justice system for either benevolent or repressive motives, but the latter may destroy it. For example, in the United States, a panic over so-called super-predators reached its zenith in the 1990s amid racial-ized concerns about violent juvenile crime. The resulting imposition of harsher punishments for juvenile offenders disproportionately affected African American and Latino youth. Each of the cases we discuss below was distinct in the conditions that gave rise to a moral panic and the ex-tent to which it was motivated by a desire for protecting youth who were included in society, or for punishing "outsiders" who often belonged to minority populations.

One of the "super-predator" era's first episodes was the Central Park Jogger case, which took place in New York City between 1989 and 1990. Five African American and Latino teenagers from Harlem were charged with assaulting and raping a white woman, a twenty-eight-year-old investment banker. She remained in a coma for twelve days and barely survived the attack. The case quickly became "one of the most widely publicized crimes of the 1980s," as the *New York Times* later recounted.[26] Within days, the police announced at a press conference that they had arrested five boys, all between the ages of 14 and 16, who had been part of a larger youth gang that allegedly had been out "wilding," randomly assaulting joggers and bicyclists in the park that evening. In violation of existing protocols, the police also released the boys' names, prior to announcing any formal charges.[27]

The ensuing media frenzy portrayed the boys as "savage, wild animals."[28] Tabloids ran headlines such as "Wolf Pack's Prey" and "Park Marauders Call It 'WILDING' . . . and It's Street Slang for Going Berserk." One month after the boys' arrest, businessman Donald J. Trump took out a full-page advertisement in four of the city's newspapers, including the *New York Times* and the *New York Daily News*, which called on the Empire State to reestablish the death penalty for the "roving bands of wild criminals who roam our neighborhoods." Lamenting the "complete breakdown of life as we knew it," the advertisement offers one of the clearest expressions of the "crime specific and exogenous" thinking that characterized the era.[29] Trump declared:

> Mayor Koch has stated that hate and rancor should be removed from our hearts. I do not think so. I want to hate these muggers and murderers. They should be forced to suffer and, when they kill, they should be executed for their crimes. . . . Yes, Mayor Koch, I want to hate these murderers and I always will. I am not looking to psychoanalyze or understand them, I am looking to punish them. . . . I recently watched a newscast trying to explain the "anger in these young men." I no longer want to understand their anger. I want them to understand our anger. I want them to be afraid.[30]

The police and prosecutors coerced the Central Park Five, as the boys became known, into giving false confessions. These confessions served as the main evidence during their trials in adult criminal court in August and December 1990. Despite the lack of eyewitness testimony or DNA evidence tying them to the crime, the boys were convicted and served between five and thirteen years in prison. Criminologist John J. DiIulio later cited the Central Park jogger case as evidence for the emergence of a generation of "super-predators" who were uniquely violent.[31]

Ashley Nellis, a senior research analyst with the Sentencing Project, examined how terms such as "super-predator" became a part of national and state legislation during the 1990s. She found that "Florida became ground zero for the political rhetoric around the surge in violent juvenile crime."[32] Congressman Bill McCullom, who represented the state's 11th District, became a leading national advocate of "the super-predator myth and pushed for federal legislation that would greatly stiffen penalties for juvenile offenders."[33] In his position as the chair of the House Subcommittee on Crime in the U.S. House of Representatives Committee on the Judiciary, he introduced legislation to create "an Armed Violent Juvenile Predator Apprehension program" and "strategies for removing armed violent youth predators from the streets."[34] Although the youth crime rate had been dropping since 1993, McCullom argued, "Today's drop in crime is only the calm before the coming storm" and that Americans needed to brace themselves "for the coming generation of 'super-predators.'"[35]

Moreover, as Nellis has shown, instead of reporting on the drop in youth crime rates, "Media stories not only exaggerated the amount of crime during this decade but also joined in mischaracterization of its perpetrators as animals."[36] She added, "Media-reinforced messages that youth of color commit the most crime had substantial and long-lasting consequences for people of color."[37] Such portrayals of American youth of color as "exogenous" and "criminal," much like the Central Park Five had been cast, became a part of mainstream American culture during the 1990s.

By century's end, however, social scientists had convincingly refuted the "super-predator" theory. In 2001, the Office of the Surgeon General issued its first report on youth violence in the United States, which examined the unprecedented epidemic of lethal youth violence between 1983 and 1993.[38] The report sought to discredit "false notions and misconceptions about youth violence" because "such myths were intrinsically dangerous."[39] Among these ten myths was DiIulio's assertion that "[a] new violent breed of young superpredators threatens the United States." The epidemic of youth violence, according to the Surgeon General, did not result from "a basic change in the offending rates and viciousness of young offenders. Rather, it resulted primarily from a relatively sudden change in the social environment." This change included the crack epidemic and "the introduction of guns into violent exchanges among youth," which led to homicides. "The violence epidemic was, in essence, the result of a change in the presence and type of weapon used, which increased the lethality of violence incidents."[40]

The evidence supporting this environmental explanation included a similar increase "across all age groups" in the homicide rate. If there had been a change in the moral character of youth, then there should have been a progression of viciousness in "each succeeding age group" during the epidemic. If "a new breed of superpredators" were roaming the streets, then the rates of "burglaries, auto thefts, and larcenies" should have also increased, but they did not. Similarly, there was not an increase in homicides caused by knives and other types of weapons. There was also a decline in "family members killed by youths," which challenged the idea of "a new breed of frequent, vicious, and remorseless killers."[41]

As it turned out, the Central Park Five, whose case DiIulio had cited to support the "super-predator" thesis, were, in fact, innocent. In 2002, a serial rapist already imprisoned for other crimes came forward and confessed to having assaulted the Central Park jogger in April 1989. DNA evidence subsequently validated his confession. The boys, who had maintained their innocence consistently over the years, suddenly found their convictions vacated. In June 2014, the Central Park Five, by then approaching middle age, won a $40 million settlement from the city of New York for their wrongful conviction and imprisonment.[42]

Poor and working-class white teenagers also found themselves swept up by the moral panic over "super-predators" in the United States during the 1990s. In 1994, three white teenage boys in West Memphis, Arkansas, were convicted of the gruesome torture and murder of three young children primarily on the basis of the teens' supposed adherence to a Satanic cult. There was no direct evidence connecting them to the crime. While police and prosecutors coerced confessions from the boys, religious and political leaders portrayed them as "evil people."[43] According to the definitive account of the case, the media presented "ministers as experts" due to the alleged Satanism of the accused boys.[44] Against this backdrop of public outrage, the judge in the case dismissed defense arguments that the boys lacked the "mental maturity" to be tried in criminal court, citing the "serious, grievous, heinous" nature of the crime.[45] Convicted in adult court, the alleged ringleader, seventeen-year-old Damien Echols, was sentenced to die, while his two codefendants were sentenced to life in prison.

Over the next two decades, a growing campaign sought to overturn their convictions. The West Memphis Three, as the boys became known, were the subject of three widely viewed documentary films, numerous books and articles, celebrity events that raised funds for legal appeals, and websites devoted to proving their innocence.[46] Finally, in July 2007, DNA previously collected from the crime scene was tested; none of the DNA matched the three boys, now men in their thirties, who had been convicted of the murders. However, some DNA did match that of the stepfather of one of the victims.[47] In addition, some witnesses changed their testimony, and the jury foreman in the original trial admitted to misconduct. The case was appealed to the Arkansas Supreme Court, which in 2010 ordered the lower court to consider whether the new evidence exonerated the West Memphis Three. Before this review could occur, however, the defendants entered into an Alford plea deal, by which they verbally asserted their innocence while pleading guilty; this allowed them to be released from prison immediately.[48]

Reflecting on the case, the head of the Chicago Innocence Project, David Protess, decried the "predictable cycle" of "media hysteria" about a horrific crime that fueled wrongful convictions.[49] Indeed, the judge in the West Memphis Three case echoed officials in the Central Park Jogger case in his focus on the crime's severity rather than the defendants' juvenile status. Where racial and ethnic identities made the Central Park Five targets for a crime-specific moral panic about exogenous youth, class and cultural identities (real or imagined) produced a strikingly similar result for the West Memphis Three. In both cases, juveniles were convicted amid an atmosphere of intense public anger, only to have their convictions overturned after having spent many years in prison.

In other states, the rush to punish "other people's children" during the 1990s proved more lethal. Perhaps most notable was Texas, which led the nation in the use of the juvenile death penalty before the U.S. Supreme Court abolished it in *Roper v. Simmons* (2005). In the summer of 2002, the state executed three African American men for crimes they had committed at the age of seventeen. One of them, Napoleon Beazley, presented a case that offers important insights into the "super-predator" panic of the 1990s.[50]

Unlike the accused perpetrators in the Central Park Five or West Memphis Three cases, Beazley never disputed his guilt. In October 1994, Beazley shot and killed a man in his garage during a carjacking in the midsized city of Tyler, Texas. A few weeks later, police arrested Beazley, who had just graduated from high school in the nearby town of Grapeland. Described by the county district attorney as "a predatory hunt-down . . . in a totally random manner," the crime appeared reminiscent of other high-profile episodes of juvenile violence in the news. Beazley's arraignment and trial the following spring took place amid heightened public anger. After Beazley's conviction for capital murder, it took an all-white jury barely two hours to return a death sentence.

But the case took a surprising turn during the appeals process, in large part because Beazley did not fit the stereotypical profile. He had been the president of his senior class, an honor student, a star athlete, and a popular figure, well liked by most "respectable" whites in his small town. This made the news of Beazley's arrest especially shocking to his friends, teachers, and practically every other observer who had ever met him. It turned out that Beazley had been leading a double life, dabbling in drugs and crime surreptitiously to impress some of the tougher kids in "the Quarters," the historically black section of Grapeland. Beazley's tragic story led an array of prominent individuals to advocate for clemency. In addition to "his high school principal, football coach, teachers, friends, and fellow church members," advocates included the tough-on-crime district judge who had presided over his trial; the county district attorney who lived in Grapeland; and nearly half of the members of the Texas State Board of Pardons and Paroles.

Although the case attracted national and international media, Texas governor Rick Perry refused to heed pleas to commute Beazley's sentence to life in prison without possibility of parole. On June 7, 2002, the state of Texas executed Napoleon Beazley by lethal injection.

These three cases illustrate not only the dimensions and destructive results of the "super-predator" panic, but also the rapidity with which a panic can rise and fall. In the Central Park case, a crime-focused panic over "exogenous" children propelled a rush to judgment and the wrongful conviction of five black and Latino youths. The revelation of their innocence has contributed to an ongoing debate in the United States about racial profiling and police brutality toward youth of color, punctuated by the Black Lives Matter movement. The West Memphis Three case has illustrated similar concerns about wrongful convictions arising from crime-specific moral panics, and adds class and culture to the potential categories of difference that can induce government officials and their publics to put aside protections for juveniles. Like that episode, Napoleon Beazley's case occurred during the peak of the national panic over "super-predators" in the early 1990s. And yet, despite his horrific crime and the social pressures of the time, Beazley's plight moved numerous individuals to push back against the dehumanizing narrative of the crime-focused panic. Those who knew Beazley refused to see him as someone else's child, as "exogenous" to the community. However, their objections failed in the face of the punitive policies enacted during the moral panic.

In retrospect, two features of the moral panic in the United States about youth violence in the late twentieth century stand out. First, government at all levels, from municipalities to the U.S. Congress, promulgated laws to combat youth violence during this "crime specific and exogenous" panic. The 1990s, for example, witnessed city after city establishing curfews for youth, state after state making it easier to prosecute and punish children as adults, and the federal government funding prison expansion at record rates. Second, many of those manning the "moral barricades" used rhetoric that went far beyond describing other people's children as simply exogenous. They denied the humanity of other people's children and disregarded baseline international norms about how minors should be treated. European nations, by contrast, largely resisted similar punitive impulses partly due to "the strong framework of international and European human rights standards that apply to [them], courtesy of the 1989 U.N. Convention on the Rights of the Child" and other international agreements.[51]

Nevertheless, European nations did experience moral panics during this era. One of the most notorious cases, the murder of two-year-old James Bulger by two ten-year-old boys in February 1993, fueled an unusually punitive policy response in England that put that nation in conflict with the European Court of Human Rights. The case differed in important respects from those described above. Not only were the two murderers, Jon Venables and Robert Thompson, clearly guilty of the crime, they also stood as the youngest convicted murderers in British history.[52] The crime itself was especially horrifying; Venables and Thompson had lured Bulger away from his mother at a Liverpool shopping center, inflicted forty-two separate injuries upon him, and finally left him to die on a railroad track. The boys were tried publicly, in adult court, amid a climate of public outrage; while hundreds of protesters gathered outside the court proceedings, the families of Venables and Thompson had been relocated with new identities due to numerous death threats. After a seventeen-day trial, the boys were convicted, sentenced to the maximum length of imprisonment allowable for juveniles (eight years), and their names were released to the public for the first time.[53]

Public outrage ran high; newspapers described Venables and Thompson as "evil, brutal, and cunning," "little bastards," and "freaks of nature." Some government officials echoed these sentiments, with Prime Minister John Major asserting that "society needs to condemn a little more and understand a little less."[54] After being presented with a petition signed by 280,000 people calling for a longer sentence, Home Secretary Michael Howard announced that the boys would be held for a minimum of fifteen years. Howard's extension was overturned on appeal. In 1999, the European Court of Human Rights ruled that the public trial of children in adult court, and Howard's attempt to extend their sentences, had violated Article 6 of the European Convention on Human Rights.[55] The boys were released in June 2001, given new identities, and protected from media scrutiny.

Writing a few years after the trial, journalist Blake Morrison lamented the moral panic surrounding the Bulger case. Citing several other cases in which children committed a terrible crime, Morrison argued that Venables and Thompson were children like many others who "did something horrendous" but "in a childish, first-time daze" that should inspire mercy and compassion rather than retribution and blood-lust. "Only a culture without hope cannot forgive," argued Morrison, "a culture that doesn't believe in progress or redemption."[56] Twenty years after Bulger's murder, England continues to maintain one of the lowest minimum ages of criminal responsibility (ten years old) in the developed world, despite pressure from leading child advocacy organizations and the U.N. Committee on the Rights of the Child.[57]

Meanwhile, the moral panic in the United States did subside due to a combination of historical factors that included the precipitous drop in the juvenile crime rate and the eventual realization by the public and its representatives that juvenile crime was not as threatening as it had seemed during the height of the moral panic. Others posit that post-9-11 fears about Islamic terrorism replaced "youth crime" as the nation's primary fear in the early twenty-first century. And then the Great Recession forced cash-strapped states to look for more effective and cheaper alternatives to costly punitive approaches that had led to mass incarceration as a penal strategy.[58]

Yet we should not forget this recent history. "The tough on crime era," Ashley Nellis cautions, "shows how little is required to dismantle positive reforms given the right political climate and level of public panic."[59] Because the history of juvenile justice in the United States and elsewhere has often been cyclical, policy experts such as law professor Elizabeth Scott are now studying ways to prevent the next moral panic about youth crime from triggering another round of "Get Tough" legislation that ultimately does more harm than good. These proposals for forestalling future panics include encouraging legislators to adopt "pre-commitment strategies" during periods of relative calm. These include restricting the authority of prosecutors, who are elected officials in the United States and particularly susceptible to sudden changes in the political climate, to make the critical decisions about which juveniles should be prosecuted in adult court. In addition, Scott encourages legislators to borrow approaches from other areas of law, such as environmental regulation, that include more outside assessment of policy impacts by experts before adopting new laws.[60]

Historical awareness, and appreciation of human rights, can also help. Children's advocates in this country and abroad must be ready to counter arguments that cast adolescents as "exogenous" during periods when crime-specific fears are on the rise. As history has shown, "youth specific and endogenous" moral panics are less dangerous than crime specific panics about other people's kids. Even more dangerous are media or official characterizations of teenagers as "wild animals," "predators," or "monsters." Bryan Stevenson, who has litigated cases of those condemned to die, including children, reminds us, *Each of us is more than the worst thing we've ever done.*[61] We have exemplars of Stevenson's maxim in an emerging generation of advocates for more humane juvenile justice policies, many of whom were imprisoned during the "get tough" era of the 1990s. Dwayne Betts, sentenced as an adult at the age of sixteen for a carjacking, describes in his memoir *A Question of Freedom* the terrible price he paid for his crime. He was incarcerated for nine years that included being caged in a supermax prison in Virginia. "Each prison has a cast of men who were once juveniles among men," he noted, but very few were "given the space to redeem themselves."[62] Stevenson and Betts present us with a simple yet radical thesis: we are, first and foremost, all human beings.

Youth advocates should champion this moral proposition about our shared humanity because the very idea of a juvenile court at its core is to treat other people's children as children. The best ones treat them as our own.

NOTES

1 Stanley Cohen, *Folk Devils and Moral Panics: The Creation of the Mods and Rockers*, 3rd ed. (London: Routledge Classics, 2002), 1.

2 Jock Young, "The Role of the Police as Amplifiers of Deviancy," in *Images of Deviance*, ed. Stanley Cohen (Harmondsworth, UK: Penguin, 1971), 27–61.

3 Cohen, *Folk Devils*, 249, fn. 1.

4 Cohen used the introduction to the second edition of his book to analyze the literature about delinquency and subcultures. See Cohen, *Folks Devils and Moral Panics: The Creation of the Mods and Rockers*, 2nd ed. (New York: St. Martin's Press, 1980), i–xxxiv.

5 Erich Goode and Nachman Ben-Yehuda, *Moral Panics: The Social Construction of Deviance*, 2nd ed. (Malden, MA: Wiley-Blackwell, 2009).

6 Kenneth Thompson, *Moral Panics* (London: Routledge, 1998). For an overview of scholarship on moral panics, see Chas Critcher, "Moral Panic Analysis: Past, Present, and Future," *Sociology Compass* 2–4 (2008): 1127–1144.

7 David Garland, "On the Concept of Moral Panic," *Crime Media Culture* 4 (2008): 9.

8 Ibid.

9 Thompson, *Moral Panics*, 11.

10 Ibid., 21. Italics in original

11 Critchei, "Moral Panic Analysis," 1138.

12 Ibid., 1136.

13 This scholarship includes Paul S. Boyer, *Urban Masses and Moral Order in America, 1820–1920* (Cambridge: Harvard University Press, 1978), and Michael Willrich, *City of Courts: Socializing Justice in Progressive Era Chicago* (Cambridge: Cambridge University Press, 2003).

14 Boyer, *Urban Masses*, 96–97.

15 Michael Grossberg, *A Judgment for Solomon: The d'Hauteville Case and Legal Experience in Antebellum America* (Cambridge: Cambridge University Press, 1996); see also Steven J. Mintz, *Huck's Raft: A History of American Childhood* (Cambridge: Harvard University Press, 2004); on the late twentieth century, see Darnell F. Hawkins and Kimberly Kempf-Leonard, eds., *Our Children, Their Children: Confronting Racial and Ethnic Differences in American Juvenile Justice* (Chicago: University of Chicago Press, 2005); and William S. Bush, *Who Gets a Childhood? Race and Juvenile Justice in Twentieth-Century Texas* (Athens: University of Georgia Press, 2010).

16 Matthew D. Lassiter; "Impossible Criminals: The Suburban Imperatives of America's War on Drugs," *Journal of American History* 102, no. 1 (2015): 126–140, doi:10.1093/jahist/jav243; Max Felker-Kantor, "'Kid Thugs Are Spreading Terror through the Streets': Youth, Crime, and the Expansion of the Juvenile Justice System in Los Angeles, 1973–1980," *Journal of Urban History* (2016): doi:0096144215623260.

17 David Hadju, *The Ten-Cent Plague: The Great Comic Book Scare and How It Changed America* (New York: Farrar, Straus and Giroux, 2008); Bradford W. Wright, *Comic Book Nation: The Transformation of Youth Culture in America* (Baltimore: Johns Hopkins University Press, 2001), 86–179; Martin Barker, *A Haunt of Fears: The Strange History of the British Horror Comics Campaign* (Jackson: University Press of Mississippi, 1992).

18 Uta G. Poiger, *Jazz, Rock, and Rebels: Cold War Politics and American Culture in a Divided Germany* (Berkeley: University of California Press, 2000); Daniel Biltereyst, "American Juvenile Delinquency Movies and the European Censors: The Cross-Cultural Reception and Censorship of *The Wild One, Blackboard Jungle*, and *Rebel Without a Cause*," 9–26, and Alexandra Seibel, "The Imported Rebellion: Criminal Guys and Consumerist Girls in Postwar Germany and Austria," 27–36, both in *Youth Culture in Global Cinema*, ed. Timothy Shary and Alexandra Siebel (Austin: University of Texas Press, 2007); Adam Golub, "A Transnational Tale of Teenage Terror: *The Blackboard Jungle* in Global Perspective," *Journal of Transnational Studies* 6, no. 1 (2015): 1–10.

19 Gleb Tsipursky, "A Soviet Moral Panic? Youth, Delinquency, and the State, 1953–1961," in *Juvenile Delinquency and the Limits of Western Influence, 1850–2000*, ed. Heather Ellis (New York: Palgrave Macmillan, 2014), 173–198, at 189.

20 Miroslava Chávez-García, "Latina/o Youth Gangs in Spain in Global Perspective," in Ellis, ed., *Juvenile Delinquency and the Limits of Western Influence*, 93–118.

21 Elizabeth Hinton, *From the War on Poverty to the War on Crime: The Making of Mass Incarceration in America* (Cambridge: Harvard University Press, 2016).

22 James Forman Jr., *Locking Up Our Own: Crime and Punishment in Black America* (New York: Farrar, Straus and Giroux, 2017), 171.

23 Ibid.

24 Ibid.

25 Victor M. Rios, *Punished: Policing the Lives of Black and Latino Boys* (New York: New York University Press, 2011).

26 "'Smart, Driven' Woman Overcomes Reluctance," *New York Times*, July 17, 1990.

27 This summary draws largely on Sarah Burns, *The Central Park Five: A Chronicle of a City Wilding* (New York: Alfred Knopf, 2011), 28–66; and Natalie Byfield, *Savage Portrayals: Race, Media, and the Central Park Jogger Story* (Philadelphia: Temple University Press, 2014), esp. 129–152.

28 Burns, *The Central Park Five*, ix.

29 Amy Davidson, "Donald Trump and the Central Park Five," *New Yorker*, June 23, 2014; Oliver Laughland, "Donald Trump and the Central Park Five: The Racially Charged Rise of a Demagogue," *Guardian*, February 17, 2016.

30 Advertisement reproduced in the *Guardian*, see note 23.

31 Cited in Byfield, *Savage Portrayals*, 183–184.

32 Ashley Nellis, *A Return to Justice: Rethinking Our Approach to Juveniles in the System* (Lanham, MD: Rowman and Littlefield, 2016), 43.

33 Ibid.

34 Ibid.

35 Nellis, *A Return to Justice*, 43.

36 Ibid., 44.

37 Ibid.

38 Office of the Surgeon General, National Center for Injury Prevention and Control, National Institute of Mental Health, Center for Mental Health Services, *Youth Violence: A Report of the Surgeon General* (Rockville, MD: Office of the Surgeon General, 2001). Accessed June 23, 2017, www.ncbi.nlm.nih.gov.

39 Ibid.

40 Ibid.

41 Ibid.

42 "5 Exonerated in Central Park Jogger Case Agree to Settle Suit for $40 Million," *New York Times*, June 19, 2014.

43 Mara Leveritt, *Devil's Knot: The True Story of the West Memphis Three* (New York: Atria Books, 2002), 117–118.

44 Ibid., 100–101.

45 Ibid., 131–132.

46 In addition to Leveritt, *Devil's Knot*, see Joe Berlinger and Bruce Sinofsky, directors, *Paradise Lost: The Child Murders at Robin Hood Hills* (1996); *Paradise Lost*

2: Revelations (2000); and *Paradise Lost 3: Purgatory* (2011). A useful summary is given in Nathaniel Rich, "The Nightmare of the West Memphis Three," *New York Review of Books*, April 4, 2013.

47 "New Evidence in West Memphis Murders," *Arkansas Times*, July 19, 2007.

48 "Deal Frees 'West Memphis Three' in Arkansas," *New York Times*, August 19, 2011.

49 "Media Coverage of Wrongful Convictions Shows Distinct Pattern," *Arkansas Times*, August 31, 2011.

50 This discussion draws on Bush, *Who Gets a Childhood*, 203–204, and Pamela Coloff, "Does Napoleon Beazley Deserve to Die?," *Texas Monthly*, April 2002.

51 Frieder Dünkel, "Juvenile Justice and Crime Policy in Europe," in *Juvenile Justice in Global Perspective*, ed. Franklin E. Zimring, Máximo Langer, and David S. Tanenhaus (New York: New York University Press, 2015), 51.

52 This case shared similarities with an English case from 1968, which involved the prosecution of eleven-year-old Mary Bell, who had strangled two young boys. See, e.g., Gitta Sereny, *Cries Unheard: Why Children Kill; The Story of Mary Bell* (New York: Henry Holt and Company, 1999). Bell was sentenced to life in prison but was later released in 1980. Since then, she has become a mother and, more recently, a grandmother. See, e.g., Michael Seamark and Paul Sims, "Child Killer Mary Bell Becomes a Grandmother at 51: But All I Have Left Is Grief, Says Victim's Mother," *Daily Mail*, January 9, 2009; accessed June 26, 2017, www.dailymail. co.uk.

53 Summary draws on Blake Morrison, *As If: A Crime, a Trial, a Question of Childhood* (New York: Picador, 1997); see also "James Bulger Murder: Timeline," *Telegraph*, March 3, 2010.

54 "Tainted by the James Bulger Legacy," *Guardian*, March 2, 2010.

55 *Case of T. v. the United Kingdom* (Application no. 24724/94), Judgment Strasbourg, December 16, 1999; see also "James Bulger's Killers Did Not Get a Fair Trial," *Guardian*, December 16, 1999; "The Judgment in Full," *BBC News*, December 16, 1999.

56 Morrison, *As If*, 205–206.

57 "Were James Bulger's Killers Too Young to Stand Trial?," *Guardian*, February 5, 2013.

58 Elizabeth S. Scott, "*Miller v. Alabama* and the (Past and) Future of Juvenile Crime Regulation," 31 *Law and Inequality* (2012–2013): 542.

59 Nellis, *A Return to Justice*, 125.

60 Scott, "*Miller v. Alabama*," 552–558.

61 Bryan Stevenson, *Just Mercy: A Story of Justice and Redemption* (New York: Spiegel and Grau, 2014), 17 (italics in original).

62 Dwayne Betts, *A Question of Freedom: Learning, Survival, and Coming of Age in Prison* (New York: Penguin, 2010), 232, 237.

ACKNOWLEDGMENTS

Our inspiration for this volume came from scholarly encounters at academic conferences, particularly the annual meetings of the (U.S.) Social Science History Association, the European Social Science History Association, and the Society for the History of Children and Youth. These meetings nurtured a growing dialogue among individuals from various parts of the world who have made the study of youth and governance a major part of their life's work. We hope that this volume spotlights and advances that important dialogue. In a similar spirit, numerous scholars assisted us at various stages of this project. Cian McMahon introduced us to the historiography of transnationalism, Máximo Langer helped us to think comparatively, Mary Wammack superbly edited several chapter drafts, and Michael S. Green offered valuable readings of the introduction and conclusion. Sergeant of the book police Frank Zimring provided indispensable conceptual suggestions at every critical juncture and ensured that *Ages of Anxiety* found a good home in the Youth, Crime, and Justice series.

Texas A&M University–San Antonio provided important support for this project from its inception. In particular, Provost Michael O'Brien and Arts and Sciences Dean M. K. Bala extended necessary resources and librarian Emily Bliss-Zaks procured essential materials. Dean Daniel W. Hamilton of the William S. Boyd School of Law, University of Nevada, Las Vegas, supported this project through several summer research grants. In addition, Boyd law librarians Matthew Wright, Jennifer Gross, and Emma Babler secured the numerous interdisciplinary studies about moral panics that we used to frame our conclusion.

We thank our editors at New York University Press, Ilene Kalish, Caelyn Cobb, and Maryam Arain, who guided this project through a rigorous review process. Special thanks to the four external reviewers whose detailed and thoughtful feedback helped us transform *Ages of Anxiety* into a more coherent and compelling volume. Finally, our spouses (Mary and Ginger) and our children (Alex, Ollie, and Isaac) motivated us to complete this project.

ABOUT THE CONTRIBUTORS

William S. Bush is Associate Professor of History at Texas A&M University–San Antonio. His research focuses on the intersections of race, childhood, and juvenile justice in U.S. history. In 2010, his book-length study *Who Gets a Childhood? Race and Juvenile Justice in Twentieth Century Texas* was published by the University of Georgia Press. His most recent book, *Circuit Riders for Mental Health*, was published in 2016 by Texas A&M University Press.

Nazan Çiçek is Associate Professor of Political Science at Ankara University. She completed her PhD in history at the School of Oriental and African Studies, University of London, in 2006. She is the author of *The Young Ottomans: Turkish Critics of the Eastern Question in the Late Nineteenth Century* (I.B. Tauris, 2010). She won a postdoctoral fellowship provided by the British Academy and Economic and Social Research Council in 2008–2009 for her project "How 'Childish' Were Ottoman/Turkish Children? Childhood as a Social Construction in the 19th-Century Ottoman Empire and the Early Republican Era." Her main area of interest covers the social, cultural, and political history of the Ottoman Empire and the Turkish Republic; she is interested in the parameters of the transformation of the value systems as well as identity formation strategies in the Ottoman and Turkish Republican Muslim societies. She has recently completed a project that delves into the construction of gender regimes in the early decades of the Republic with a special emphasis on the conception of childhood and adolescence.

Corrie Decker is Associate Professor of History at the University of California, Davis. Decker researches the history of development, education, gender, sexuality, and childhood in twentieth-century East Africa. She is the author of *Mobilizing Zanzibari Women: The Struggle for Respectability and Self-Reliance in Colonial East Africa* (Palgrave Macmillan,

2014). Her work has appeared in *Past & Present*, the *Journal of Women's History*, *Africa Today*, and the *International Journal of African Historical Studies*, as well as in edited volumes. Currently, she is writing a book on the history of childhood and adolescence in East Africa during the British colonial era.

Tamara Myers is Associate Professor of History at Lehigh University in Pennsylvania. A specialist in youth, gender, policing, and history, she is the author of *Caught: Montreal's Modern Girls and the Law* (Toronto, 2006), co-editor of *Bringing Children and Youth into Canadian History: The Difference Kids Make* (Oxford, 2017), and her work has appeared in the *Journal of the History of Childhood and Youth*, *Diplomatic History*, the *Journal of the History of Sexuality*, and the *Journal of the Canadian Historical Association*. She is currently working on two research projects involving the history of children and youth: the Miles for Millions walkathons (about youth activism and global consciousness), and policing kids in the 20th-century city. She is a long-term member of the research collective, the Montreal History Group–Groupe d'histoire de Montreal.

David Niget is Assistant Professor of History at the University of Angers, Temos–CNRS. He has a PhD from the Université du Québec à Montréal, Canada, and was a postdoctoral fellow at the University of Louvain, Belgium. His primary research topic is juvenile delinquency and youth culture, expertise and child guidance, moral panics and risk. He is currently a member of a multidisciplinary research program on childhood and youth called "EnJeu[x], Enfance et jeunesse," in which he coordinates research on children's rights and citizenship. He is a member of the editorial board of the *Revue d'histoire de l'enfance irrégulière*. He is also an executive member of the Society for the History of Children and Youth.

Shari Orisich is Assistant Professor of History at Coastal Carolina University. Her research has examined the relationship between crime, class, and youth in postrevolutionary Mexico City. She has presented her research on the topics of Mexican penal institutions, the professionalization of social work, and representations of juvenile crime in popular media. She is currently working on a project that explores the transformation of social science in Latin America during the Cold War era through the lens of criminology. She holds a PhD in History from the University of Maryland, College Park.

Guillaume Périssol is a researcher at the French Ministry of Justice (École nationale de protection judiciaire de la jeunesse). He served as chief librarian at the Historical Library of the City of Paris before obtaining a grant in 2011 from the Région Île-de-France to prepare a doctoral thesis in history at the Paris-Sorbonne University. In 2012, he was an Arthur Sachs Scholar at Harvard University's Department of History. His work is on the history of juvenile delinquency in the mid-twentieth century, specifically comparing how France and the United States approached this issue.

David S. Tanenhaus is Professor of History and James E. Rogers Professor of History and Law at the William S. Boyd School of Law, University of Nevada, Las Vegas. He studies one of the fundamental and recurring problems in the history of law and society—how to treat the young. His books include *Juvenile Justice in the Making* (2004) and *The Constitutional Rights of Children: In re Gault and Juvenile Justice* (2011, 2017). He is co-editor, with Franklin Zimring, of the book series *Youth, Crime, and Justice* for New York University Press.

INDEX

adolescence, 42, 43, 107; in Europe, 18, 29; juvenile court and, 18; Onur on, 133; in Turkey, 148–49; in U.S., 18

Africa: colonial, 59–60; indigenous peoples in, 6; Kenya, 59, 67; South Africa, 59. *See also* Zanzibar Islands

American model. *See* Chicago model

American National Probation Association, 112

Arendt, Hannah, 110

Asena, Duygu, 138

association of magistrates, 27

at-risk youth, 164, 166; Mexico City and, 39–40, 43, 46, 49–50

Augustus, John, 110

authoritarian regimes, 107

authority: modernization of, 40–41, 53–54; probation and, 105; soft authority, 82, 112

baklava case, Turkey, 145, 157n48

Balım, Elvan, 140

Beazley, Napoleon, 171; exogenous children and, 172

Belgium: child guidance clinic in, 29; child savers in, 16; IACJ in, 15, 16, 24; Maus and, 26; medicalizing juvenile delinquency in, 15; postpenal approach in, 15; reform movement and, 26; transnationalism and, 15; Wets in, 23–24. *See also* International Association of Child Welfare

Bell, Mary, 178n52

Ben-Yehuda, Nachman, 160

Betts, Dwayne, 175

BJC. *See* Boston Juvenile Court

Black Lives Matter movement, 172

Bolshevism, 21

Boston, Massachusetts, 7; Boston Junior Police Corps in, 112; Boston Marathon bombing in, 3; prevention policy in, 113

Boston Juvenile Court (BJC), 101, 102, 120n42; categories of cases in, 108; class in, 109; example case in, 110, 114; girls in, 108; lengths of stay and, 111; probation in, 111, 114, 123n77

Boston Marathon bombing, 3

boyology, 82

Brace, Charles Loring, 162

brain science, 3

Brave New World (Huxley), 107

British Empire. *See* Africa; Zanzibar Islands

Bulger, James, 144, 173–74

Burgess, Ernest, 46, 47

Canada, 19. *See also* Montreal Miracle

Carton de Wiart, Henri, 22, 24, 27

Carton de Wiart, Juliette, 17

caseworkers, Mexican, 40, 48; UNAM study by, 42, 45, 52. See also *estudio social*

Central Park Five, 167–68, 170, 171; innocence of, 169

Central Park Jogger case: Central Park Five in, 167–68, 169, 170, 171; Trump on, 167

Century of the Child, 58

rape: Central Park Jogger case and, 167–71; Mexico juvenile court and, 50. *See also* Serpil case, Turkey

reform school: in Kenya, 67; Massachusetts and first, 102; Zanzibar Islands and, 65–68, 71, 73

risk. *See* at-risk youth

Rivière, Albert, 18

Rollet, Henri, 19, 22, 23, 26

Roper v. Simmons (2005), 3, 171

rough justice methods, 87–88

Saavedra, Alfredo M., 57n32; *Manual de Trabajo Social* by, 46, 48

Save the Children International Union (SCIU): IACW compared to, 21, 22–23; IACW merging with, 27; after World War I, 15–16, 21. *See also* International Union for Child Welfare

science, 40

SCIU. *See* Save the Children International Union

Scott, Elizabeth, 174

Seine Juvenile Court, 120n42, 120n43; categories of cases in, 108; class in, 109; girls in, 108; lengths of stay and, 111; probation in, 109, 111

Serpil case, Turkey, 133–34, 151; accused children in, 136, 137; Child Protection Law (2005) and, 142–43; crimes in, 135; hearing for, 141–42; Law of 1979 in, 138; lynching attempt in, 137; media on, 7, 8, 128, 135–37, 139, 140–43; memorial service in, 140–41; State Security Court for, 138–39, 141, 143; street children narrative in, 140–41

Shakespeare, William, 101

Shaw, Clifford, 87

sheltered childhood, 162

social history, 3–4, 57n32; anxiety and, 4

social science, 41

social studies. See *estudio social*

social work, in Mexico City, 41; caseworkers and, 40, 42, 45, 48, 52; *estudio social* and, 5, 40, 47–53; Juárez and, 50; Mexican juvenile court and, 45–46; positivist thought and, 45–46; Saavedra and, 46, 48; transnationalism and, 43–44, 45; Young, P., on, 46–47, 49

Social Work Manual (Manual de Trabajo Social) (Saavedra), 46

soft authority, 82, 112

soft power, 7, 164. *See also* prevention policy; probation

Solís Quiroga, Roberto, 42

South Africa, 59

Stevenson, Bryan, 175

"super-predators," 8, 166; Beazley as, 171–72; Central Park Jogger case and, 167–71; McCullom on, 168; media and, 168; West Memphis Three as, 169–70, 172; white teenage, 169–70

supervised freedom. See *libertad vigilada*; *liberté surveillée*

Supreme Court, U.S., 3, 171

Switzerland, 19

Thompson, Kenneth, 161

Tocqueville, Alexis de, 7; democracy for, 106, 107; *Democracy in America* by, 103–4, 118n28

totalitarian ideologies, 28

totalitarian regimes, 107

transnationalism, 33, 159; Belgium and, 15; cultural lens of, 1; IACJ and, 32; juvenile court and, 2, 15; in *Juvenile Delinquency and the Limits of Western Influence, 1850–2000*, 2; in literature, 2; Mexico City and, 40, 43–44, 45, 54; social work and, 43–44, 45

transnationalization of child welfare: Chicago model and, 17; child savers and, 18; congress and, 16; judges and, 17–18, 19–20

Trump, Donald J., 167